Culloden and the Last Clansman

By the same author:

The Making of the Crofting Community
Skye: The Island
For the People's Cause: From the Writings of John Murdoch
The Claim of Crofting
Scottish Highlanders: A People and their Place
A Dance Called America: The Scottish Highlands, the United States and Canada
On the Other Side of Sorrow: Nature and People in the Scottish Highlands
Glencoe and the Indians
Last of the Free: A History of the Highlands and Islands of Scotland

Culloden and the Last Clansman

JAMES HUNTER

MAINSTREAM
PUBLISHING

EDINBURGH AND LONDON

First published in Great Britain in 2001 by
MAINSTREAM PUBLISHING COMPANY (EDINBURGH) LTD
7 Albany Street
Edinburgh EH1 3UG

ISBN 9781845965426

A catalogue record for this book is available from the British Library

Typeset in ACaslon and Manson
Printed and bound in Great Britain by
CPI Cox & Wyman, Reading, RG1 8EX

For Duror

contents

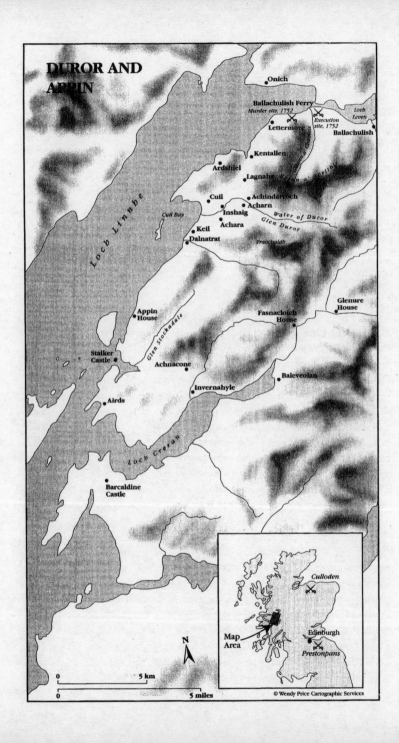

Chapter One

James was as fairly murdered as though the duke had
got a fowling-piece and stalked him.
Robert Louis Stevenson, *Catriona*

In Inveraray, capital of the Highland county of Argyll, at a little after eleven o'clock on the morning of Monday, 25 September 1752, sentence on James Stewart was pronounced by the Scottish High Court's dempster. Nothing is known of this functionary but it's possible, despite that, to guess the way he spoke. From time immemorial in Scotland, the 'dooms', or judgements handed down by trial judges, had been proclaimed publicly by doomsters, or dempsters. Such dempsters must have cultivated forceful voices. It's likely, therefore, that what the High Court's dempster had to say in Inverary was said in tones that carried clearly. His words would definitely have reached all the many folk thronging the church where, due to the lack of a large enough courtroom in Inveraray, the High Court had been sitting since the previous Thursday. Those same words may also have been audible to other folk who'd gathered outside the church's door to learn the outcome of one of the longest and most contentious trials Scotland had ever staged.

In one of the ledger-like volumes kept by them for this purpose, the High Court's clerks were meanwhile penning – with their customary care – the words enunciated by the court's dempster. Some 250 years after they were inscribed there, those words can still be read in the High Court's records. The passing of two-and-a-half centuries has done little to mitigate their harshness.

James Stewart, the dempster told his listeners, was guilty of having been implicated – though as accessory rather than perpetrator – in the murder of Colin Campbell of Glenure. Campbell, when shot four months earlier, had been attending to his business as factor, or manager, on the Ardshiel estate – which the British government, in the wake of the Jacobite rebellion of 1745–46, had seized by way of punishing its owner, Charles Stewart, for his leading role in that failed uprising. James Stewart was Charles' half-brother. And during the several years since Charles (who'd long-since fled abroad) had set foot in Duror (the North Argyll locality which included Ardshiel), James – as he freely conceded – had been doing his best to ensure that his half-brother's confiscated lands were administered in a manner which kept open the possibility of Charles (or, failing this, Charles' wife and children) continuing to get some kind of income (however nominal) from the lands in question.

Prior to its judges turning things over to their dempster, the High Court had heard that James Stewart's interventions in the management of the Ardshiel estate were such as to have guaranteed bad blood between James and Colin Campbell – with the former opposing, even seeking to sabotage, the latter's plans. And for all that James had taken no active part – as was universally acknowledged – in Campbell's assassination, people in Argyll (James included) were not greatly surprised when, shortly after Colin Campbell's murder on 14 May 1752, in the Wood of Lettermore, not far from James Stewart's Duror home, James was arrested on suspicion of having colluded in the factor's killing. Nor was anyone in Argyll (James again included) surprised by the verdict reached in Inveraray on 25 September. The murder of Colin Campbell, after all, was a deeply political act. Both in Edinburgh and in London, politicians were united in their insistence that someone must pay a heavy price for it. And given the failure of the authorities to apprehend the man alleged by those same authorities to have fired on Campbell in the Wood of Lettermore, James Stewart – jailed in connection with the Lettermore crime and known to have been at loggerheads with the dead factor – was the obvious candidate to pay this price. There was thus a certain inevitability about James Stewart's fate.

That fate had become all the more inescapable as a result of James' trial having been presided over by a man with his own axe – indeed a whole set of axes – to grind in the matter of Colin Campbell's death. Archibald Campbell, Duke of Argyll, was Scotland's Lord Justice General,[1] and he was entitled both to adjudicate on High Court cases and, when so adjudicating, to take precedence over such other judges – Lords Elchies and Kilkerran on this occasion – as might be present. But Duke Archibald's decision to involve himself more than was usual in the case of James Stewart, or so it was widely suspected at the time, had less to do with his judicial position than with his other roles. The duke was both the British government's leading representative in Scotland and the chief of Clan Campbell. In each of these capacities, the murdered factor having been an official of the government he served and a member of the clan he headed, Duke Archibald had a personal interest in avenging Colin Campbell's death. Something of this would be revealed in the aftermath of what the High Court's dempster had to say. For the moment, however, the Duke of Argyll – like the rest of the dempster's Inveraray audience – sat silently while James Stewart's sentence was spelled out.

James, the dempster declared, would be held in Inveraray's prison until Thursday, 5 October, when he would be taken north to Fort William – today a substantial urban centre, in 1752 a heavily garrisoned military strongpoint. At Fort William, the dempster went on, James would be kept in army custody until Tuesday, 7 November. Then, under armed guard, he would make one final journey, by way of Onich, to North Ballachulish – where the fiord-like Loch Leven joins the wider waters of Loch Linnhe and where, until it was replaced by a twentieth-century bridge, there was, for several hundred years, a well-used ferry. James, the dempster continued, would be 'transported over [this] ferry of Ballachulish' and 'delivered . . . to the sheriff-depute of Argyllshire or his substitutes, to be carried to a gibbet to be erected by the said sheriff on a conspicuous eminence upon the south side of, and near to, the said ferry'. This eminence is known as Cnap a' Chaolais.[2] It's within a mile of the place where Colin Campbell died. And because of its proximity to the ever-busy Ballachulish Ferry, Cnap a' Chaolais, in 1752, was as public a site as could possibly have been chosen for a gallows.[3]

At Cnap a' Chaolais, the High Court's dempster announced, James Stewart, 'upon Wednesday, the eighth day of November next [and] betwixt the hours of twelve at noon and two afternoon [would] be hanged by the neck until he be dead'. Thereafter, as a dire warning to other wrongdoers, actual or potential, the hanged man's corpse was to be sheathed in chains and suspended high above the approaches to Ballachulish Ferry for an unspecified period of time – a period which, in the event, would last for several years.[4]

A letter written by one of his lawyers on the day he was sentenced reports that James Stewart heard out the High Court's dempster with 'the greatest resolution and appearance of innocence'. James, his lawyer commented, then 'addressed himself' to the Duke of Argyll in these words: 'I do declare, in the presence of Almighty God, that I had no previous knowledge of the murder of Colin Campbell of Glenure.'[5]

Those statements and others to the same effect – not least James' defiant declaration that prosecution witnesses had told 'untruths' in the course of their evidence – were received, or so James' lawyer wrote, with 'great surprise' by Duke Archibald. Angrily, the duke responded to the condemned man's comments by making a speech of his own. No notes of this speech were made during its delivery, though some months later the Duke of Argyll's remarks – with a view to their inclusion in a semi-official account of James Stewart's trial – were reconstructed from the recollections of those of his hearers who were in agreement with the duke's sentiments. By James' sympathisers this published rendering of Duke Archibald's comments was thought less brutally direct than what the duke had actually said by way of winding up James' trial. The 'speech spoke', one such sympathiser insisted, 'was much more acute [i.e., cutting] and bitter than the speech printed'. Maybe so. But even if the published speech is a watered-down version of the words he used on 25 September 1752, the Duke of Argyll's observations, in their surviving form, remain extraordinarily revealing.[6]

Archibald Campbell, it must be emphasised, was one of the more eminent Scots – some would say the most eminent Scot – of his day. Administratively supreme to the north of the border, he also carried great weight in London. Nor were Duke Archibald's interests confined to affairs of state. He was a lover and collector of books, he studied science and engineering, he was a gardener, a forester and an agricultural improver. He strove to promote the economic expansion both of Scotland and of the United Kingdom – a country which, during the Anglo-Scottish union negotiations of 1706 and 1707, he'd helped create. In Archibald Campbell, Duke of Argyll, then, qualities may be discerned which, by later commentators as well as by Duke Archibald's contemporaries, were thought enlightened and progressive. Those qualities, it might be said, were what gave shape and direction to the policies with which Archibald Campbell had identified himself politically – policies, as his admirers might have added, that were helping to turn the United Kingdom of Scotland and England into one of the eighteenth century world's great powers.

And yet, when he spoke to James Stewart at the end of his trial, the Duke of Argyll showed himself to be other than a supremely self-assured symbol of a nation carrying all before it. As his words reveal, Archibald Campbell harboured profound anxieties – anxieties which centred, that September morning in 1752, on the prisoner whose life the duke and his fellow judges had, minutes before, declared forfeit. Something of this is evident in the duke's exploration of the nature of the crime which had brought James Stewart before him. For all its 'uncivilised' nature, the killing of Colin Campbell – a killing which the duke labelled 'heinous', 'horrid', 'base' and 'infamous' – was not, Duke Archibald suggested, a piece of casual and unconsidered violence. On the contrary, the duke contended, Colin Campbell's murder had the most deep-seated causes. Those causes – 'the true original source', as the duke put it, of the offence for which James Stewart had been sentenced – were to be discovered, the duke said, in 'that obstinate and almost incurable disaffection' which had resulted in numerous Highland clans, including the one to which James belonged, more than once resorting to arms in the hope of overthrowing Britain's ruling regime.[7]

This regime owed its existence to what the Duke of Argyll, still addressing James Stewart, called 'the happy revolution' of 1688. As the duke's hearers (none more so than James) were well aware, that particular upheaval inaugurated a political and constitutional order which Duke Archibald and the bulk of his Campbell kin had been determinedly propping up – to their considerable benefit – ever since. So close, indeed, was the duke's identification with post-1688 arrangements that, had the United Kingdom of 1752 been searched for someone thought to be archetypically representative of these arrangements, the search would probably have ended with Archibald Campbell. This, since Duke Archibald regarded Colin Campbell's murder as amounting to an assault on the 1688 settlement, accounts for a good deal of the strong feeling which he displayed in the course of his comments to James Stewart. Accounting for much of the rest of his aggravation is the fact that if the United Kingdom had also been ransacked for a set of folk more rooted than any other in their opposition to everything accomplished in 1688 and subsequently, then the search may have ended with James, with Charles, James' half-brother, and with their Stewart relatives. Those were people for whom battling with the British state, and with this state's Campbell servants, had long been a way of life.[8]

In James Stewart, then, the duke saw no straightforward criminal. He saw, instead, an enemy – an enemy against whom Duke Archibald considered himself to be waging a war which his side might yet lose. This war, if intermittently, had already gone on for the best part of a century. And in the assassination of Colin Campbell of Glenure, the Duke of Argyll glimpsed the possible beginnings of yet another outbreak – an outbreak which, the duke feared, might unleash forces capable of blowing to smithereens everything he'd worked so hard to nurture and to safeguard.

From a twenty-first-century standpoint, of course, the Duke of Argyll's apprehensions seem wildly exaggerated. We know that he and his kind were ultimately to prevail; that they were to make their world safe for themselves and for their successors; that the threat posed to the duke's position, whether by James Stewart or by the beliefs James held, was, in the end, of no great consequence. But it is easy to overlook, and absolutely vital to remember, that the Duke of Argyll, in September 1752, knew none of this. Our past was his future. And that future, from the duke's perspective, appeared anything but secure.

After all, though the constitutional structures dating from Duke Archibald's 'happy revolution' of 1688 had been in place for more than sixty years when Colin Campbell met his death in the Wood of Lettermore, there continued to be many people – the Ardshiel factor's killer, or killers, prominent among them, the duke believed – who wanted that revolution reversed. Their key objective was to restore to power the heirs of the Stuart king whose dethroning had been the principal outcome of the events of 1688. The supporters of a Stuart restoration were called Jacobites. That title derived from the Latinised name of the monarch, known in England as James II and in Scotland as James VII, who had fled to France rather than do battle with the army landed in Devon – towards the end of 1688 – by the Dutch-born Prince William of Orange, whom King James' enemies had invited to take charge of what had been James' kingdoms. During 1689, a challenge to the new dispensation, in the shape of a largely Highland rebellion in the former King James' interest, was seen off – after some fierce fighting – by William's followers. But Jacobitism as a cause, an ideal, even, in some respects, an ideology, survived this initial setback. In 1715, 1719 and 1745, Scotland's Jacobites mounted further insurrections which, had they gone as planned, would have led to the now-dead King James' son (in 1715 and 1719) or grandson (in 1745) occupying Britain's throne. Since the Duke of Argyll would have been among the casualties of any such Jacobite comeback, and since the Jacobite attempt of 1745 had come closer to success than its predecessors, there was every reason for Archibald Campbell – just seven years after that attempt's commencement – to be hostile to Jacobitism. There was particular reason, as already noted and as he himself now stressed, for Duke Archibald to harbour a profound dislike, even hatred, of the Stewarts of Appin – a clan whose territories included James Stewart's native Duror and whose leading men included James' half-brother, the exiled Charles Stewart of Ardshiel.

In 1715, the Duke of Argyll told James Stewart, his clansmen had joined 'the rebel army' which had besieged Inveraray that autumn and which, at Sheriffmuir some weeks later, fought a pitched battle with a pro-government force.[9] Although he made no explicit mention of this on Monday, 25 September 1752, that force had included, as all the duke's audience that day in 1752 knew, the young Archibald Campbell – who'd sustained at Sheriffmuir a leg wound sufficiently serious to have left him with a permanent limp.

'In the year 1719', Duke Archibald next informed James Stewart, 'your clan . . . did again rise in rebellion, and assisted a foreign enemy in an invasion; in this you are said to have acted a part, though at that time very young.'[10]

Afterwards James would deny that he'd been involved in the events of 1719 – when, despite the presence in the West Highlands of the Spanish troops who'd constituted the duke's 'foreign enemy', a further Jacobite uprising had quickly fizzled out. But there was no denying James Stewart's active participation in the more far-reaching, and more recent, events to which Archibald Campbell next turned. 'In the year 1745', the duke observed, 'the restless spirits of the disaffected Highlanders again prompted them to . . . rebellion. You and your clan formed a regiment in that impious service . . . in which you persevered to the last. The Divine Providence at first permitted you to obtain some advantages . . . [But] at last heaven raised up a great prince, the son of our gracious king, who, with courage equal to that of his ancestors, and with conduct superior to his years, did, at one blow, put an end to all your wicked attempts.[11]

Thus the duke summarised, for the benefit of his courtroom audience, the cataclysmic events in which James Stewart had become caught up during 1745, and which came close to dislodging William of Orange's latest successor, King George II, whose father, George I, had earlier been brought to Britain from his native Hanover with a view to keeping the country out of Jacobite clutches. In the summer of 1745, James Stewart had become a rebel officer in a rebel, and Jacobite, army. In the space of just three or four months, that army managed to conquer Hanoverian Scotland and to advance so far into Hanoverian England as seriously to menace London. But then, from a Jacobite perspective, everything went wrong. In April 1746 on Culloden Moor near Inverness, the Duke of Cumberland – George II's son and Archibald Campbell's 'great prince' – routed what remained of the Jacobite force, which, the previous autumn, had looked to be on the verge of a shattering military victory.

But what, the Duke of Argyll went on to speculate, if there had been no Culloden? What if the Jacobites, as they'd come so close to doing, had managed to defeat their Hanoverian opponents and gone on to take control of the United Kingdom? 'If you had been successful in . . . rebellion,' Archibald Campbell remarked almost musingly to James Stewart, 'you had been now triumphant . . . You might have been giving the law where you now have received the judgement of it; and we, who are this day your judges, might have been tried before one of your mock courts of judicature.'[12]

In reaching their verdict on James Stewart, the Duke of Argyll thus sought to emphasise, he and his High Court colleagues had been mindful of the danger posed by James, and by men like him, to Britain's civilisation – this civilisation being identical, from the duke's perspective, with the country's governing class. In order to defend that class from its Jacobite enemies, the duke reminded his Inveraray listeners, it had been necessary on occasion for the country's ruling establishment to have recourse to measures owing absolutely nothing to humanity and justice. As long as it was certain – and it seemed so to the Duke of Argyll – that Colin Campbell's death had resulted, even in part, from pro-Jacobite and anti-Hanoverian sentiment, it was perfectly proper, Archibald Campbell came close to hinting, for humanity and justice to be set aside again. Hence the significance of the Duke of Argyll's final words to James

Stewart: 'Though you don't now stand accused as a rebel ... yet I may say, with great force of truth, that this murder has been visibly the effect and consequence of the late rebellion.'[13]

James Stewart would have been vehemently at odds with much of the rest of the duke's long speech. But he might well have agreed with this last comment. Had he and so many other Duror men not become Jacobite soldiers in 1745, then James Stewart, as the man himself must have known better than anyone, never would have become entangled in the happenings that brought him to that courtroom on Monday, 25 September 1752, and caused him to be hanged.

CHAPTER TWO

'What,' cried I, 'were you in the English army?' 'That was I,' said Alan. 'But I deserted
to the right side at Prestonpans, and that's some comfort.'

Robert Louis Stevenson, *Kidnapped*

On the evening of the day he got word of the event which was ultimately to bring about his execution, the chances are that James Stewart was in the company of Donald Carmichael, the man then in charge of Duror's dramshop, Taigh na h-Insaig. This establishment – where, seven years later, he would be arrested by the troops sent to seize him in the aftermath of Colin Campbell's murder – was certainly one of James' favourite haunts. And it was the place where Duror's menfolk – eighteenth-century women being left out of such discussions – would have gathered when, as was the case this evening towards the end of July 1745, there was important news to debate. The news in question concerned the arrival in Moidart, just forty or fifty miles from Duror, of Prince Charles Edward Stuart, whose aim in coming to the Highlands, as he'd immediately announced, was to obtain the armed backing he needed to retake the throne his grandfather, James II and VII, had abandoned in 1688. Charles Edward's plans, it would have been agreed on all sides that night in Taigh na h-Insaig, were bound to have serious consequences for Duror. And so it proved. Not only were developments in Moidart to lead to the hanging in 1752 of James Stewart, they were also to lead to the deaths, on Culloden Moor in April 1746, of numerous Duror men – among them, as things turned out, Donald Carmichael, who, this July evening, was within two or three weeks of quitting Duror for the last time.

Taigh na h-Insaig stood on a little piece of flat, though slightly elevated, ground on the north bank of Duror's westward-flowing river at a point about three-quarters of a mile from the river's junction with Loch Linnhe. Although it is no longer so, the dramshop's site was a congested one. In 1745, Taigh na h-Insaig, Donald Carmichael's home as well as his business premises, was one of several dwellings constituting Insaig township. This township, whose tenants jointly worked the few acres of arable land in their immediate vicinity, has long gone. It was replaced, perhaps thirty or forty years after the battle in which Donald Carmichael died, by a single farm of the same name. In the 1950s, this farm, too, ceased to exist – its lands merged then with those of an adjacent holding. But Insaig's former farmhouse, still bearing the name of the township of two or three hundred years ago, has survived into the twenty-first century. And if you know where to look in the present-day Insaig's neighbourhood, you'll come across the crumbling, nettle-buried remnants of buildings that date from the time of Donald Carmichael and James Stewart.

The Gaelic term *taigh*, as in Taigh na h-Insaig, means simply 'a home'. But when attached in this way to the name of a settlement, or some other easily recognisable feature, it denoted – advertised almost – an alehouse, a dramshop, a drinking-place of some sort. Such *taighean*, some of them offering overnight accommodation as well as endless streams of home-brewed beer and locally distilled spirits, were to be found throughout the Highlands of the eighteenth century. Among their customers was Edmund Burt, an Englishman who travelled extensively in the Highlands during the 1720s and who wrote – with some feeling – of a night spent in a hostelry of the Taigh na h-Insaig variety. On arrival at this particular taigh as night was falling, Burt recalled, he first had to stable his horses in an outbuilding so 'weak and small' he feared the animals 'would pull it about their ears'. 'My next care', Burt went on, 'was to provide for myself, and to that end I entered the dwelling house. There my landlady sat, with a parcel of children about her, some quite, and others almost, naked, by a little peat fire, in the middle of the hut; and over the fireplace was a small hole in the roof for a chimney. The floor was common earth, very uneven, and nowhere dry, but near the fire and in the corners, where no foot had carried the muddy dirt from without doors. The skeleton of the hut was formed of small crooked timbers . . . The walls were about four feet high, lined with sticks wattled like a hurdle, built on the outside with turf.'[1]

In Highland taighean, Burt reported, 'the chamber pot' generally consisted of 'a hole in the ground by the bedside'. As for dinner, it was typically 'two or three eggs' – there usually being 'nothing else to be had'. During dinner, Burt continued, 'the landlord not only sits down with you . . . but, in some little time, asks leave and sometimes not, to introduce his brother, cousin, or more, who are all to drink your honour's health in whisky – which, though a strong spirit, is to them like water. And this I have seen them drink out of a scallop shell.'[2] Whether or not it was imbibed from scallop shells, plenty of whisky would certainly have been consumed in Taigh na h-Insaig. Hence the dim view taken of all such establishments by an eighteenth-century minister of Appin, the wider district of which Duror was part. 'These houses', this minister commented of the nine or ten taighean his parish contained, 'cannot be supposed to improve the morals of the people.'[4]

Perhaps not. But rough and ready though it probably was, Donald Carmichael's Taigh na h-Insaig, on the July evening with which this chapter began, can safely be assumed to have been packed with people eager for the latest information as to Charles Edward Stuart's intentions. Carmichael's customers would have belonged to one or other of Duror's several townships: Dalnatrat, Keil, Cuil, Achara, Insaig itself, Acharn, Achindarroch, Lagnaha. And among those customers there must have been plenty – the always talkative James Stewart for one – anxious to unburden themselves of their opinions as to what the unlooked-for happenings in Moidart might portend.

Lagnaha, Achindarroch, Acharn, Insaig, Achara, Cuil, Keil, Dalnatrat: all have altered enormously in appearance during the last 250 years, but all, as placenames, continue to exist. Dalnatrat, Keil and Cuil are located on the shores of Loch Linnhe. Achara, Insaig, Acharn, Achindarroch and Lagnaha are to be found in a three-mile-long valley known in the eighteenth century as the Strath of Duror. In the vicinity of Achindarroch, this strath – running parallel to Loch Linnhe but separated from it by a hill which rises to the north of Cuil – makes a right-hand junction with Glen Duror. A much deeper valley than the strath it opens onto, Glen Duror is flanked to the south by Fraochaidh, to the north by Beinn a' Bheithir – mountains which rise to just under 3,000 feet in Fraochaidh's case and well over 3,000 feet in the case of Beinn a' Bheithir. Duror's river, called the Water of Duror in eighteenth-century documents, flows swiftly down Glen Duror, slows slightly as it passes between Achindarroch and Acharn, then meanders close to Insaig before emptying itself into Loch Linnhe at the eastern end of a south-west-facing inlet called Cuil Bay.

Anne Grant, one of the first Highlanders – certainly one of the first Highland women – to write about the Highlands in English, glimpsed Duror when sailing up Loch Linnhe from Oban to Fort William in May 1773. 'I never saw a place that had more attractions for me,' she commented. 'It is wild without being savage; woody, but not gloomy; and fertile, but not flat.' Dorothy Wordsworth, who visited Duror in September 1803 in the company of her poet brother, William, was equally complimentary. Riding north by way of Dalnatrat and Keil, the Wordsworths – at this point in the vicinity of Insaig – found themselves, as Dorothy noted, 'in a retired valley scattered over with many grey huts'. There were 'hay grounds' in the middle of this valley, she went on, and everywhere there were trees 'growing irregularly or in clumps'. From the homes the Wordsworths rode by came the din of dogs barking, but such folk as they encountered were friendly enough: 'We met a very tall, stout man, a fine figure, in a Highland bonnet, with a little girl, driving home their cow ... He told us that the vale was called the Strath of Duror, and when we said it was a pretty place, he answered, "Indeed it was."'[4]

Duror has been inhabited for a long time. The township of Achara – *Achadh a' charraigh*, in Gaelic – owed its name to a twelve-foot-high standing stone which can still be seen a hundred or so yards to the east of the modern Ballachulish–Oban road. This stone was erected by the Duror people of some 5,000 years ago. And for all that few of its subsequent residents left monuments on such a scale, the locality has been inhabited ever since.

During the sixth, seventh and eighth centuries AD, Duror was one of the more northerly territories of the kingdom of Dalriada, whose principal families, immigrants from Ireland, introduced both their Gaelic language and their Christian religion to the Highlands. At the centre of Dalriadan Christianity was the monastery founded by Colmcille, St Columba, on the island of Iona. And since Duror's medieval church at Keil – disued even in James Stewart's day and now a ruin – was dedicated to Columba, it is by no means inconceivable that this most prestigious of Highland saints, who certainly sailed close to Keil when voyaging on Loch Linnhe, came ashore on occasion in Duror.

By the ninth and tenth centuries, Duror, like most of the West Highland seaboard, was dominated by the Vikings. Later, in the course of the fourteenth and fifteenth centuries, the district was incorporated into the Lordship of the Isles. This was a part-Norse, part-Gaelic principality ruled by the leading men of the MacDonalds – one of the numerous clans which took shape in the course of the middle ages. These clans were to be central to Highland society until, in 1746 and subsequently, clanship was systematically dismantled by Culloden's victors. The Lords of the Isles, it seems, came regularly to Duror – or so, at least, a nineteenth-century collector of Gaelic lore was told by one of his North Argyll informants. 'In those times', this man said, 'MacDonald of the Isles was wont to go on a tour once a year ... There were houses which belonged to him in certain places, and those houses, with bits of land, were given to certain persons who paid no rent – but they had to entertain MacDonald and his retinue when they came the way.' Three such establishments were named by the tradition-bearer from whom this statement was taken down. One, it appears, was located at Dalness in Glen Etive, some twelve miles east of Duror. A second was situated in Glen Creran – on Appin's southern boundary. The third lay somewhere in the vicinity of Cuil Bay.[5]

If, or when, the Lords of the Isles visited their Cuil residence – all trace of which has vanished in the 500 years that have elapsed since the lordship's collapse – they could not have been other than impressed by Cuil's outlook. From this part of Duror, the view is little short of panoramic. To the east and north-east are the high peaks of Beinn a' Bheithir, Fraochaidh and their outliers. To the west and south-west, across the wide expanse of Loch Linnhe, are the hills of Ardgour, Kingairloch, Morvern and Mull. There are many days, of course, when winds blowing off the Atlantic conceal this vista behind impenetrable curtains of rain and mist. But there are days, too, when sky and sea alike are the deepest of deep blues, when the visibility is little short of perfect, when the sun is warm and when the only sounds to be heard at Cuil are the mewing of gulls and the rattling drag of waves on shingle. On days like that – and such a day invariably comes if you wait long enough – Duror has always been one of Scotland's finest places.

Towards the close of the fifteenth century, the Lordship of the Isles gradually fell apart. This was greatly to the disadvantage of those clans, notably the MacDonalds, who'd been in charge of what had come close at times to being an independent state. But to the other clans who had been rendered marginal by the success of the Lordship, its demise created an opportunity – an opportunity which was seized above all by the Campbells, who, from their once diminutive heartland in the neighbourhood of Loch Awe, began to expand their territories and influence across mainland Argyll and into the Hebrides.

Among the early victims of Campbell expansionism is were the Lords of Lorn. Their family name was Stewart and – since their ancestry was traceable to a continental immigrant who'd come to Scotland, by way of England, in the twelfth century – the Stewarts are sometimes described as alien incomers. But if the Stewarts began as foreigners, they quickly became Scottish. Following a fortunate marriage, a member of the senior branch of the family became Scotland's monarch – a position his successors were to occupy for as long as the country possessed its own kings and queens. A number of the more junior lines of Stewarts, meanwhile, managed to equip themselves with extensive landholdings. The Lords of Lorn, whose title derived from their control of the mid-Argyll district of that name, belonged to one such grouping. On moving into Lorn during the fourteenth century, this particular set of Stewarts had done very well for themselves. When, in the 1440s, John Stewart – Gaelic-speaking and better known in that language as *Iain Mourach*, Leper John – took over from his father, this latest Lord of Lorn looked to be in a strong position. As events were soon to show, however, he was not.

Well before the end of the fifteenth century, much of Lorn had passed under the jurisdiction of the Campbells. For the next 300 years a branch of this family, operating out of a most formidable stronghold, Barcaldine Castle, was to dominate lands that the Stewart Lords of Lorn had expected to be theirs indefinitely. This development might easily have signalled the end of the Stewarts as a force in West Highland affairs. However, in the person of John Stewart's son, Dougal, they fought back – retreating out of Lorn to the north, but stubbornly refusing, either in the fifteenth century or subsequently, to subordinate themselves to their former territory's new masters.

On the map, the area where Dougal Stewart and his relatives now set up home is roughly rectangular in shape. To the west, it's bounded by Loch Linnhe; to the south and east are Loch Creran and Glen Creran; to the north is Loch Leven. Since early medieval times, this entire district had been known as Appin – a designation which points, or so placename experts assert, to its having been managed for a period by monks of the monastery founded in Columban times on the nearby island of Lismore. Be that as it may, neither Appin nor its component divisions, Duror included, were initially settled by the Stewarts who moved there in the years around 1500. Duror, as already mentioned, had then been populated for thousands of years. The same was true of the rest of Appin. And though the Stewarts, for the next two or three centuries, were to provide this district with its rulers, they were always to be in a small minority numerically. In Duror, as in Appin at large, from the sixteenth to the eighteenth centuries, the majority of the population consisted of families named Carmichael, Livingstone, Black, MacInnes, MacIntyre, Colquhoun or MacCombie, MacLaren, MacCorquodale and MacColl. This latter name was easily eighteenth-century Duror's commonest one, and its possessors were Duror's most well-entrenched residents, a fact reflected in a remark made by the nineteenth-century tradition-bearer quoted earlier. 'The MacColls were a long time in Appin,' this man said, 'before the Stewarts . . . came there.' As often with oral tradition, this was absolutely correct.[6]

The comings and goings of the various individuals who exercised authority over Duror residents in the middle ages and after can be followed – up to a point – in the charters which, from the late-medieval period onwards, Scotland's kings were in the habit of granting to their more powerful subjects. One such charter, dating from 1354, makes Duror over to the Lords of the Isles and another, of 1476, confirms this. Charters of 1500 and 1538 tell a different story, however. These mention, among other Duror localities, 'the seven merk-land of Coule [Cuil]', 'the seven merk-land of . . . Lagynhall [Lagnaha]', 'the three merk-land of Auchincar [Achara]', and 'the five merk-land of Auchnandarroch [Achindarroch]'. The nature of a 'merk-land' (a measure, in effect, both of a holding's value and of its extent) need not detain us. What matters is that everything of consequence in Duror – its woods, mosses, morasses, waters and mills as well as its farming townships – were part, as is stated by those charters of 1500 and 1538, of the domains presided over by Duncan (in 1500) and Alan (in 1538) Stewart.[7]

Duncan (the elder of the two) and Alan were sons of Dougal Stewart, who'd made Appin his base after failing to retain the Lordship of Lorn. But for all that the royal charters granted to Duncan and Alan may appear to convey ownership of Appin to them, neither man was Appin's laird or landlord in the modern sense. From the first, to be sure, the Appin Stewarts had something of the character of later lairds. And they were to become more, not less, laird-like as time went on. But no family aspiring – as the Stewarts definitely were – to influence and leadership in the sixteenth-century West Highlands could depend on charters of the sort bestowed by monarchs in faraway Edinburgh. Charters dealt wholly in legalities. And legalities counted for little in an area where – until the era of Culloden – a man's standing was directly proportionate to the amount of armed force at his disposal. What Dougal Stewart required from the moment of his setting foot in Appin was a mechanism capable of generating a supply of fighting men. Like everyone else who aspired to wield power in the Highlands of their time, Dougal and his successors found such a mechanism in clanship. They became, in other words, clan chiefs.

The Alan and Duncan Stewart who feature in the charter record were not known by those names to the MacColls, the Livingstones, the MacCombies, the MacInneses, the Blacks and the Carmichaels who followed Duncan and Alan into the numerous battles and skirmishes it took to keep Duror, and the rest of Appin, under Stewart control. In Gaelic-speaking Duror (and the place was wholly Gaelic-speaking down to the eighteenth century, partly Gaelic-speaking into the twentieth) Dougal was *Mac Iain Stiùbhairt na h-Apainn*, meaning the son of John Stewart of Appin. This was no more than a statement of fact in Dougal's case, his father having been the John Stewart in question. But exactly the same title would be given to Duncan, Alan and all their successors. In the lineage-obsessed Highlands of the sixteenth, seventeenth and eighteenth centuries, this indicated that all of Appin's Stewarts were – through any number of intervening generations – the progeny of their clan's founder. And although the clan in question – when compared, say, with the Campbells to the south, or the Lochaber Camerons and the MacDonalds of Glencoe to the north – was of recent birth, no Stewart of Appin thought himself other than on a par with neighbouring chiefs. Each Mac Iain Stiùbhairt – saluted in verse by Appin's Gaelic bards, honoured by his Stewart kin, followed by those MacColls, Carmichaels and MacCombies who'd been swept into his retinue – expected the undeviating obedience all Highland chieftains took as their due. Such obedience, to successive Stewart chiefs or their designated representatives, was almost invariably forthcoming. At Culloden it would result in many Duror men going unprotestingly to their deaths.

Scotland's kings and queens had adopted the French version of their name (Stuart rather than Stewart) during the sixteenth century, but that change didn't alter their family history. Like every other Stewart in Duror and Appin, therefore, James Stewart was related to the Jacobite prince whose landing in Moidart led to Culloden and its consequences. James and his kinsmen were well aware of this – having been hailed habitually by their bards as members of the 'mighty race' who had for so long worn 'the royal crown' of Scotland. Of itself, however, this connection, so distant by the eighteenth century as to be little better than theoretical, doesn't come anywhere near explaining why so many Duror men, James Stewart among them, joined the army which Charles Edward Stuart managed to assemble during the summer of 1745.[8]

Jacobitism's origins have been much debated, but perhaps the most decisive of the various causes of Jacobite feeling – in the case of Duror anyway – are to be found in the sphere of religion.

The inhabitants of eighteenth-century Duror were overwhelmingly Episcopalian. They adhered, in other words, to a variant of Protestantism which, for a time in the seventeenth century, was Scotland's established faith. Even when so established, however, this faith had never enjoyed the backing of the country's Presbyterians who had earlier exercised control over ecclesiastical matters and who resumed such control after the departure of Charles Edward Stuart's grandfather, James II and VII, to France in 1688. Episcopalians differed from Presbyterians on key points of doctrine and, unlike Presbyterians, continued to entrust church government to bishops during the post-1688 period. They duly found themselves subjected to oppression by the new ruling establishment. With the established Church of Scotland now Presbyterian in creed, as it has since remained, Episcopalian clergy were ordered both to renounce their beliefs and to take oaths of allegiance to the country's new – and pro-Presbyterian – king, William of Orange. Some Episcopalians conformed; others did not. This latter group, called non-jurors because of their refusal to swear loyalty to William, enjoyed strong support in several parts of the Highlands, including Duror. And since the exiled King James, despite being Catholic, had been supportive of the pre-1688 Episcopalian supremacy in Scotland, the non-juring clergy naturally favoured the restoration of James or his successors – hence the strong linkage which many contemporaries discerned between Episcopalianism and Jacobitism.

Edmund Burt, when travelling through the Highlands in the 1720s, met many Episcopalians, 'of whom,' he commented, 'I do not remember to have known one that is not a professed Jacobite'. Highlanders of this persuasion, it was reported by Burt and others, commonly swelled the congregations of the many non-juring preachers who, in defiance of the law, operated outside the framework of the established church and who, an anti-Jacobite observer alleged, 'poison the people and debauch them to rebellion'. Prominent among such preachers was John MacLachlan who ministered to Duror's Episcopalians, including James Stewart, and who was to become a chaplain in Charles Edward Stuart's rebel army in 1745. MacLachlan's parishioners, one of the British government's Highland agents reported, were 'the most deeply poisoned with disaffection . . . of any people I ever knew. They idolise the non-juring clergy and can scarcely keep their temper when speaking of presbyterians.'[9]

What exactly made any man or woman Jacobite in his or her politics is impossible to determine, of course. Religion – those Highland Jacobites who were not episcopalian being usually Catholic – clearly played a major role, but other factors loomed large also. And of those, by no means the least significant – especially in a Duror or Appin context – was the extent to which the Jacobite cause overlapped, from the start, with anti-Campbell sentiment.

In the 1640s, the Stuart monarchy found itself simultaneously at odds with England's parliamentarians and with Scotland's Covenanters, a politically influential group of Presbyterian extremists. Clan Campbell took the side of parliament and the Covenanters, resulting in the several other clans who considered the Campbells their enemies being propelled into the Stuart camp. Such clans, the Stewarts of Appin to the fore, consequently rallied to the Marquis of Montrose when, during 1644 and 1645, he raised a military force in the Highlands with a view to removing the Covenanters, together with their Campbell allies, from government. Montrose's campaign, despite his winning a series of smashing victories over both the Covenanters and the Campbells, was ultimately a failure – the Stuart dynasty's comeback in 1660, after Oliver Cromwell's brief supremacy, being due to English, not Scottish, developments. But the alignments of 1644 were broadly to be repeated in 1689 when the Stuart monarchy again got into serious trouble – the Stewarts of Appin taking their tenantries into battle on behalf of the recently fled King James and in opposition to the newly installed William of Orange. In 1689, as before, the Campbells were anti-Stuart. They were to be so again in 1715 when – with the backing, as always, of the Appin Stewarts – the Jacobites launched a rebellion against the Hanoverian king, George I, who had acceded to the throne of the United Kingdom of Scotland and England the year before.

The 1689 and 1715 risings were to founder as completely as the Montrose insurrection of 1644–45, and so was the much smaller scale Jacobite outbreak of 1719. By the 1720s, then, Jacobite prospects – on the face of things –

appeared hopeless. Armed revolt after armed revolt had been suppressed. The chances of breaking with this pattern seemed slight. From permanently garrisoned strongpoints like Fort William, less than twenty miles from Duror, the British army's red-coated infantry patrolled the Jacobite Highlands. In glen after glen, too, there were taking shape the highways which military engineers – trying further to limit Jacobite freedom of manoeuvre – were pushing into places where such highways had previously been unknown. Throughout the Scottish Highlands, according to Edmund Burt who travelled north to assist with this construction programme, 'the old ways (for roads I shall not call them) consisted chiefly of stony moors, bogs, rugged . . . hills, entangling woods and giddy precipices'. Now, where there had formerly been only the roughest of tracks, Burt boasted in the 1730s, thoroughfares 'as smooth as Constitution Hill [in London]' had been created. 'And I have galloped on some of them,' Burt added, 'for miles together in great tranquillity'.[10]

And yet, despite so much effort on the part of eighteenth-century Britain's Hanoverian monarchy; despite the existence of Fort William and several similar installations; despite the gradual development of a road network connecting those installations with the south; despite the ceaseless activities both of British army regulars and of the Highland militias the army raised to supplement its own battalions; despite all of this, localities like Duror remained persistently and unshakeably Jacobite.

Notwithstanding the Duke of Argyll's suggestion to the contrary at his trial, James Stewart is unlikely to have taken part in the fighting of 1719 – fighting which didn't last long enough for the Appin Stewarts to have been drawn into it. But James certainly came to maturity in a community where Jacobitism, together with the anti-Campbell sentiment with which it had always been linked, continued to flourish. In early-eighteenth-century Duror, tales were doubtless still told of how the Stewarts had lost Lorn to the Campbells of Barcaldine more than 200 years earlier. Tales were surely told, too, of the exploits (featured in a Gaelic verse which has survived into the present) of those Duror men who, under the Marquis of Montrose's command, had burned their way through Campbell-controlled Argyll prior to overwhelming a predominantly Campbell army at the Battle of Inverlochy. And as well as hearing tales of Campbell brutality and Stewart heroism, James Stewart would have been exposed when growing up in Duror to the recollections and reminiscences of Duror veterans of 1689 and 1715 – among them veterans, it is certain, men who had formed part of the Jacobite army which, as the Duke of Argyll recalled at James' trial, had laid siege in the autumn of 1715 to the Campbell capital of Inveraray.

When, in the early 1740s, after an unusually long period of peace between the two countries, Hanoverian Britain became embroiled in hostilities with France, the ensuing conflict was greeted with delight by Jacobites – to whom Hanoverian difficulty always represented opportunity. This Franco-British war was especially welcome to the then 23-year-old Charles Edward Stuart, who, in January 1743, left the Rome residence of his father – whom Highland Jacobites habitually dignified with the title of King James VIII of Scotland – and made his way north in the hope of taking part in a planned French invasion of England. The activities of the British Royal Navy, combined with the impact of some exceptionally ferocious gales, dashed all possibility of a French landing on the English south coast. But Charles – whom the French had intended to restore to his grandfather's throne, had their descent on England gone ahead – promptly looked for another means of getting to Britain. By the spring of 1745, he'd found just such a means in the somewhat unlikely guise of a Nantes-based privateer and slave-trader of Irish extraction, Antoine Walsh. At the beginning of July (in one of Walsh's vessels, *La Doutelle*) Prince Charles Edward Stuart sailed for the Highlands, anchoring off Moidart on Thursday, 25 July.[11]

Charles had been in communication for many months with Highland Jacobites. They had repeatedly warned him that there was no point in his coming to Scotland without a large supply of arms, a still larger supply of hard cash and several thousand French troops. In the event, the prince – who'd entrusted such soldiers and weapons as he had managed to scrape together to another ship which had fallen victim to the Royal Navy – stepped ashore in Moidart with next to nothing in the way of guns, money or men. This confronted Jacobite clan chiefs with a dilemma. Some of them, notably the Skye chieftains Sir Alexander MacDonald of Sleat and Norman MacLeod of Dunvegan, resolved the difficulty by refusing to have anything to do with Charles Edward. Having received one of the prince's emissaries in what a Jacobite source calls 'a very cool [and] unbecoming manner', the Sleat and Dunvegan chiefs hastened to assure Duncan Forbes, the British government's leading representative in the Highlands, that, as MacLeod put it in a letter to Forbes, they'd given 'no sort of countenance' to Charles' messenger. Several other supposedly Jacobite chieftains took the same line. Duncan Forbes, who'd hurried to Inverness from Edinburgh on hearing of the Jacobite prince's arrival in Moidart, duly began to relax a little. 'I am confident', Forbes had written of Charles Edward's prospects before leaving for the north, 'that the young man cannot with reason expect to be joined by any considerable force in the Highlands.' Now it looked as if Forbes' confidence was justified.[12]

However, Charles Edward – despite the setback he'd suffered at the hands of MacLeod of Dunvegan and MacDonald of Sleat – was having more success than Duncan Forbes had anticipated. In Moidart, Charles had been joined by MacDonald of Clanranald, MacDonell of Glengarry and MacDonald of Keppoch. Admittedly, they were marginal figures of a sort best described – in a phrase of Duncan Forbes' – as 'loose, lawless men of desperate fortune'. But no such description could be attached to Charles Edward Stuart's next recruit, Donald Cameron of Lochiel. A middle-aged, highly cultured man who dabbled extensively in overseas trade, Donald Cameron had exchanged his ancestral castle for a well-situated mansion at Achnacarry in the southern part of the Great Glen. He was as far removed from the stereotypical Highland chieftain, then, as it was possible for any mid-eighteenth-century Highlander of his class to have been. So why did Donald Cameron – without whose backing Charles Edward's uprising would immediately have stalled – decide, at Prince Charles' behest, to take what he knew to be a desperate gamble with his lands, his life and the lives of his clansmen? Cameron of Lochiel's sense of honour – deriving from his fervent Episcopalianism and equally fervent Jacobitism – had much to do with his throwing in his lot with that of Charles Edward. But the prince's undoubted charisma, which would play an important part in succeeding events, was also a factor in persuading Donald Cameron to set aside his many doubts. So, at least, an early historian of Jacobitism, the Edinburgh writer John Home, was told years afterwards by John Cameron of Fassifern, one of Donald Cameron's younger brothers. 'Brother,' John of Fassifern said to the Cameron chief as the latter set out to meet Charles Edward Stuart for the first time, 'I know you better than you know yourself. If this prince once sets his eyes upon you, he will make you do whatever he pleases.'[13]

With Clan Cameron's backing secured, Charles Edward raised the Stuart standard at Glenfinnan, about fifteen miles east of his Moidart landing-place, on Monday, 19 August 1745. Among the several hundred fighting men now under the Jacobite prince's command, there were, at this point, none from Duror. But that was shortly to change as a result of Prince Charles' contacts with leading representatives of the Appin Stewarts. Of those representatives, one proved disappointingly undependable (from a Jacobite point of view) during July and August 1745, as well as during the equally critical months that followed. This, ironically enough, was Appin's chieftain, Dougal Stewart.[14] Appin and Duror tradition later had it that Dougal responded to Charles Edward's pleas for assistance by remarking: 'I would rather spend the inheritance of Appin among the gay women of Edinburgh than risk its being lost striving to recover the crown for the prince, which I know cannot be done.' While there is no contemporary proof that Dougal actually used such words, the sentiments thus attributed to him are very much in accord with other pointers to the generally negative stance he took up in relation to Prince Charles' plans.[15]

An early exemplar of a type soon to become much commoner in the Highlands, Dougal Stewart was a clan chief who'd fallen out of sympathy with the people over whom he nominally presided. Remembered traditionally as 'very drunken', Dougal was assuredly – as surviving evidence demonstrates – a spendthrift. Though his father, Robert Stewart, had commanded a Duror and Appin detachment in the Jacobite army of 1715, Dougal, as he admitted freely, was without 'any notions of clannishness'. While in the Highlands, he lived grandly in Appin House, a compact but stylish home situated on rising ground a little to the east of the Sound of Shuna and equipped, very much in the Georgian manner, with ornate chimney-pieces and a purpose-built wine cellar. While in Edinburgh, where he spent rather more time than he did among his clan, Dougal Stewart occupied a flat in the Lawnmarket. There he subscribed to that most fashionable of London journals, *The Spectator*; there he bred canaries; there he involved himself in freemasonry; there he maintained a black African servant, or slave, named Orinocco. And there, most tellingly of all, this heir to men who'd made war their pastime as well as their profession, kept his broadsword in his attic.[16]

Openly regarded as 'a disgrace' by his Appin Stewart relatives, Dougal Stewart, from Prince Charles Edward's standpoint, was very much a broken reed. Hence the speed with which the prince turned to Dougal's close kinsman, Charles Stewart of Ardshiel.[17]

Charles Stewart was everything that Dougal, his chief, was not. Known to Duror folk as *Tearlach Mòr*, Big Charlie, the laird of Ardshiel was described by one contemporary as 'a very worthy, sensible man, but of a prodigious bulk'. To another, Charles in 1745 seemed 'a big, fat man, troubled with a lethargy'. But despite his size, when action was required Charles Stewart could muster plenty of energy. He was also an expert swordsman – as was shown by his having fought, and won, a duel with the famed Balquhidder freebooter, Rob Roy MacGregor.[18] Although MacGregor was getting on in years when this encounter took place, Charles Stewart's courage in tangling with so feared a fighter – to say nothing of his having succeeded in drawing Rob Roy's blood – provided Duror story-tellers with a tale which, several generations later, they were still recounting.[19]

The Ardshiel laird's Jacobite antecedents were every bit as impressive as his duelling skills. His father had fought in the Jacobite army of 1715; his grandfather had seen action in the same cause in 1689; his great-grandfather had stood alongside the Marquis of Montrose in 1644 and 1645. Like that of

Donald Cameron of Lochiel, who was the Ardshiel laird's close friend and whose own forebears were key figures in the Jacobite pantheon, Charles Stewart's Jacobitism, then, may be said to have been inherited. But it was none the less passionate for that. As far back as 1739, Charles had received – from the exiled court of Prince Charles Edward's father in Rome – a commission entitling him to command rank in any Jacobite army that might one day be formed in Scotland. And during 1744, when the Highlands were awash with rumours to the effect that a French invasion of Britain was imminent, Charles Stewart visited Edinburgh more than once with a view to making contact with Prince Charles' leading Scottish agent, one John Murray. 'About this time I received a letter from Stewart of Ardshiel,' Murray afterwards noted of a rendezvous which took place in the summer of 1744, 'telling me . . . he had come to town purposely to meet with me . . . and that he had seen [Cameron of] Lochiel lately. I went to town a day or two after and dined with him. His errand was to know of me . . . what hopes I had.'[20]

His lifelong Jacobitism notwithstanding, it must have been with mixed emotions that Charles Stewart received the news of Prince Charles Edward's arrival in Moidart. The sheer recklessness of the prince's plans would have been as evident to the Ardshiel laird as it was to Donald Cameron, his fellow conspirator of the year before. What Cameron and Stewart had anticipated was a French force which – when supplemented by several thousand Highlanders – would be strong enough to strike south with a reasonable prospect of securing an eventual victory. What they got was a penniless and weaponless young man who by all appearances believed that, by force of personality alone, he could change the course of history.

Despite their many doubts as to the wisdom of his campaign, many Jacobites, to be sure, felt obliged to ally themselves with Charles Edward. But they did so, very often, with feelings of foreboding. In Perthshire during August 1745, Lord George Murray, a veteran soldier soon to command Prince Charles Edward's army, wrote: 'My life, my fortune, my expectations, the happiness of my wife and children are all at stake (and the chances are against me), and yet a principle of (what seems to me) honour, and my duty to king and country, outweighs everything.' That same month, Charles Stewart of Ardshiel must have been prey to a similar swirl of emotions.[21] Duror tradition has it that, in the days prior to his setting off to join Prince Charles, Charles Stewart's anxieties reached such a pitch that his wife remarked in some exasperation: 'If you, Charles, are not willing to become commander of the men of Appin, stay at home and take care of the house, and I will go myself and become their commander.'[22]

Isabel Stewart, Charles' wife, came of a family, the Haldanes of Lanrick, every bit as steeped in Jacobitism as his own. Isabel's father – a laird whose lands were located in the Highland–Lowland border country between Callander and Stirling – was to serve Charles Edward Stuart as one of the prince's few cavalrymen. Isabel's two brothers were also active Jacobites in 1745 and 1746. One brother fought alongside his father in the mounted detachment known as Lord Kilmarnock's Horse. The other – destined to die at Culloden – joined the regiment his brother-in-law, Charles Stewart, was endeavouring to muster at the point when Isabel reportedly made her fire-eating threat to take over from him.When she'd married Charles Stewart in 1732, Isabel had been 19. In 1745, then, she was in her early thirties. Her family – six sons and four daughters – was well on the way to completion. Her August 1745 tiff with her husband, if it occurred, would almost certainly have taken place in the Stewart family home, Ardshiel House, located towards the northern tip of the hilly promontory lying between the Strath of Duror and Loch Linnhe.

Heading inland from Cuil and travelling through the Strath of Duror, south to north by way of Insaig, you come finally to Lagnaha. Just past Lagnaha, the land, which has risen gradually for two or three miles and which is now a couple of hundred feet above sea level, drops away steeply – with the result that, not much more than half-a-mile further on, you find yourself once again beside Loch Linnhe. Here there's a narrow inlet called Kentallen Bay, which Dorothy Wordsworth in 1803 described as 'perfectly sheltered'. On approaching Kentallen Bay, Dorothy added, she found a 'cluster of huts at the water's edge, with their little fleet of fishing boats at anchor, and behind, among the rocks, a hundred slips of corn, slips and patches, often no bigger than a garden such as a child, eight years old, would make for sport'.[23]

Dorothy Wordworth's 'slips' and 'patches' were some of the so-called lazybeds – artificially constructed mounds of seaweed-fertilised earth – on which, when the terrain permitted no more productive alternative, Highlanders of her time grew crops. Although such lazybeds can still be seen in the Outer Hebrides, those that formerly fringed Kentallen Bay are long gone. The inlet's surroundings have altered in other ways, too. Today, on Kentallen Bay's eastern shore, a busy main road – one that also bisects the modern Strath of Duror – takes traffic north in the direction of the Ballachulish Bridge and Fort William. A mile or two along this road is Lettermore – where Colin Campbell was murdered in May 1752. But if, instead of going in that direction, you take a left turn just before Kentallen Bay, you'll find yourself driving on a narrow, tree-lined road which eventually terminates among a set of wide, grass-covered fields sloping gently towards the sea. In the 1740s, Ardshiel House – home to Isabel Stewart, Charles Stewart and their children – stood at the top of those fields and at the foot of the thickly wooded hill which rises behind them.

Overlooking Loch Linnhe and commanding fine views of Onich and

Ardgour, Ardshiel House occupied a most attractive spot. Since the house was also sizeable, well appointed and of recent construction, it must have had the appearance, in 1745, of belonging to a man of considerable means. However, this wasn't so. By eighteenth-century standards, Charles Stewart was by no means poor, but he wasn't wealthy either. Ardshiel Estate – which one of Charles' grander contemporaries described a little sniffily as 'very small' – ran, in the mid-1740s, to 5,090 acres.[24] But of those acres, a mere 90 were in cultivation and only 640 counted as 'grass' or 'good pasture' – the bulk of the remainder consisting, apart from the scrubby woodland to be found here and there on the property, of what a surveyor of the period categorised as 'hill and moss'. It is not surprising therefore that his rents brought Charles Stewart less than £50 annually. Even allowing for the price inflation of the last 250 years, this was a less than lavish income. True, it would have been supplemented by profits from the cattle-rearing and other commercial activities in which Charles dabbled. But even when supplemented by these activities, Charles Stewart's revenues clearly weren't big enough to cover his outgoings – Charles' debts being reckoned, in 1746, at around £700. In any age, to owe a sum equivalent to several times one's yearly earnings is to be in a very parlous situation. It's possible, therefore, that Charles Stewart of Ardshiel, when he went off to war in August 1745, did so partly in the hope that, should the Jacobite cause triumph, his share of the ensuing spoils would serve to put him back on his feet financially.[25]

By 1745, the typical clan chief (turning his back, in the process, on clanship's quasi-tribal origins) was well on the way to being recognised, in law at least, as outright owner of the area his clan inhabited. The bulk of the estate to which the chief had thus established title was usually rented out by him to tacksmen – a tacksman being, in effect, a tenant. In their role as tenants, tacksmen were clearly subordinate to their chiefs. But because they also tended to be those chiefs' close relatives, tacksmen ranked just one step down from clan chieftains in the Highlands' overall pecking-order. This is evident in tacksmen's universally recognised status as something of a Highland gentry. It is evident, too, in the vital role a clan's tacksmen performed when war threatened; then tacksmen had the responsibility of mobilising, and taking charge of, the fighting men on whom each chief relied – those fighting men often doubling, in their day-to-day lives, as subtenants of the tacksmen to whom they answered militarily.

The Appin area was a bit of an exception to this standard pattern. Dougal Stewart, Appin's chief, shared power with a series of cadet families who, some generations back, had branched off from Dougal's own line. This meant that the families in question were headed, in 1745, by men who were – even if a little distantly – Dougal's cousins. Those men, however, were not (as might be expected on the basis of what happened elsewhere) the Appin chief's tacksmen. Perhaps because their clan's origins were not quite the same as those of other clans, Appin's cadet families had managed, at some stage in the sixteenth or seventeenth centuries, to obtain legal titles to segments of the territory which the original Dougal Stewart had appropriated in the wake of his father's losing Lorn to the Campbells of Barcaldine. Among the beneficiaries of these titles to various pieces of the first Dougal Stewart's lands were the Stewarts of Ardshiel. Among those beneficiaries, too, were four other families of similar standing: the Stewarts of Fasnacloich, Invernahyle, Achnacone and Ballachulish.

But for all that Charles Stewart was thus a property-owner in his own right, the property of which he was laird was nothing like a modern – or even a nineteenth-century – Highland estate. In 1745, for example, Charles' possessions did not constitute a single entity of the sort that would later become more or less obligatory. They consisted, rather, of five different landholdings, only two of which adjoined one another.

At the heart of Charles Stewart's estate was Ardshiel township. A couple of miles to the north (separated from Ardshiel by the lands of Lagnaha) was Lettermore, where Colin Campbell was to meet his death. At a similar remove to the south-east (with Lagnaha's lands again intervening) was Achindarroch township, its hill pastures extending along the southern flank of Beinn a' Bheithir as far as the swiftly flowing hill stream called Allt nam Meirleach, Thieves' Burn. Beyond this stream was the quite distinct holding of Glen Duror. Finally, to the south both of Achindarroch and Glen Duror (and separated from them by the lands of Acharn) was Charles Stewart's fifth piece of property, the township of Achara.

Lettermore, extending to 785 acres, consisted entirely of rough grazing and, according to a contemporary document, 'was always in the hands of [Stewart of] Ardshiel himself'. The much larger holding of Glen Duror, running to 2,170 acres but equally bereft of cultivable land, also seems to have been, like Lettermore, in Charles Stewart's direct occupancy in 1745. But in Ardshiel, in Achindarroch and in Achara – settlements with access to reasonable acreages of arable land – matters were more complex. In 1745, Achara, Ardshiel and Achindarroch were occupied by several tenants – their total number, across the three townships, probably in the region of fifteen or twenty. From those tenants, Charles Stewart derived the cash revenues mentioned already. From the same tenants, Ardshiel's laird also received a more old-fashioned type of rent, paid not in money but in kind. To Ardshiel House, as a result, Charles' Duror tenants regularly delivered stipulated quantities of butter, cheese, oatmeal, calves and cattle.[26]

The Duror townships which were not part of the Ardshiel Estate – namely Lagnaha, Acharn, Insaig, Cuil, Keil and Dalnatrat – had traditionally been under the direct control of Appin's chiefs. Four townships – Dalnatrat, Cuil, Insaig and Lagnaha – remained in this position in 1745. But at some point a little prior to that date, presumably by way of easing financial problems which were analagous to, but even more pressing than, those afflicting Ardshiel's laird, Dougal Stewart had sold Duror's two remaining townships, Keil and Acharn. To this transaction is owed at least some of the bad feeling which, by 1745, was jeopardising relations between Dougal and his senior clansmen – the new laird of Acharn and Keil being a Campbell.

The laird in question was Donald Campbell of Airds, whose principal landholdings were in the district known today as Port Appin. Because the Airds Estate was the one piece of Campbell territory to the north of Loch Creran, which they saw as something of a natural boundary between themselves and their Campbell enemies, the Stewarts of Appin viewed the Campbells of Airds with particular suspicion. Donald Campbell's acquisition of Keil and Acharn must have intensified that suspicion. It would have been intensified further when the laird of Airds also persuaded Dougal Stewart to sell Achabhlar and Bealach to him. Lying a mile or two east of Dalnatrat, those were pasture-based holdings of the Lettermore type. His possession of them, together with his ownership of Acharn and Keil, meant that Donald Campbell – nominally at any rate – was master, by 1745, of a large slice of Duror.

This, admittedly, had resulted in no very dramatic changes. In Bealach, Achabhlar, Keil and Acharn, the tenants who had previously been in place appear to have been left mostly undisturbed. Their rents now went to Donald Campbell. But some of them being Stewarts by name and others belonging to families with longstanding Stewart affiliations, the residents of Acharn, Keil, Achabhlar and Bealach – just like Duror's other inhabitants – continued to identify much more with the Stewarts of Appin than with the Campbells of Airds. This explains the extent to which – despite their new laird being on the opposite side of the Hanoverian–Jacobite divide – Donald Campbell's Duror tenants permitted themselves to be drafted into the regiment which, in early August 1745, Charles Stewart of Ardshiel raised to fight for the prince who'd landed the previous month in Moidart.

On purely livestock-rearing holdings such as Achabhlar, Bealach, Glen Duror and Lettermore, there would have been found, in 1745, no more than a handful of homes. Places like Keil, Cuil, Insaig, Achindarroch, Lagnaha and Ardshiel, on the other hand, were relatively substantial settlements. Its tenants occupied the lion's share of such a settlement's arable land and paid their rents directly to its laird. In addition to their tenants, however, places like Cuil or Achindarroch were usually populated by numbers of subtenants, so called because they rented little plots of land from their tenant neighbours. Subtenants often doubled as labourers. And tenants or subtenants, while primarily agriculturalists, might also be blacksmiths, weavers, joiners or the like. Communities of the Achindarroch or Cuil type, then, contained as many as fifteen, twenty or even more families. And in contrast to the modern Highlands, where households tend to be scattered across the landscape, all of an eighteenth-century settlement's inhabitants – its tenants, labourers and the rest – lived cheek-by-jowl in the sets of tightly clustered homes that contemporaries called (in Gaelic) a *baile*, (in Scots) a *toun* or (in English) a township. The ever-observant Edmund Burt provided his southern readers with a detailed account of the standard baile and, though it is slightly derogatory in tone, Burt's account rings true: 'A Highland town . . . is composed of a few huts for dwellings, with barns and stables, and both the latter are of a more diminutive size than the former, all irregularly placed, some one way, some another, and, at any distance, looking like so many heaps of dirt.'[27]

Both the interior and exterior appearance of one of Burt's 'heaps of dirt' – typically containing two, three or four adults and as many as ten children – were described in some detail by another eighteenth-century visitor to the Highlands, Samuel Johnson: 'A hut [or house] is constructed with loose stones . . . It has no floor but the naked ground. The wall, which is commonly about six feet high, declines from the perpendicular a little inward. Such rafters as can be procured are then raised for a roof, and covered with heath [or heather], which makes a strong and warm thatch, kept from flying off by ropes of twisted heath, of which the ends, reaching from the centre of the thatch to the top of the wall, are held firm by the weight of a large stone. No light is admitted but at the entrance, and through a hole in the thatch, which gives vent to the smoke. This hole is not directly over the fire, lest the rain should extinguish it; and the smoke therefore naturally fills the place before it escapes.'[28]

As already indicated, lairds like Dougal Stewart of Appin or Charles Stewart of Ardshiel did not inhabit houses like these. Nor did such lairds' immediate subordinates – James Stewart, for example. But although there would have been variations between one dwelling and the next – with a township's tenants doing better than its subtenants, for instance – the majority of Duror people undoubtedly lived in homes of the type described by Johnson and Burt. Their portrayal of Highland living conditions may be supplemented by the writings of a third eighteenth-century traveller, Thomas Pennant, who concentrated less on buildings than on their occupants: 'A set of people worn down with poverty: their habitations scenes of misery . . . The furniture perfectly corresponds: a pothook hangs from the middle of the roof, with a pot pendant over a grateless fire, filled with fare that may rather be called a permission to exist than a support of vigorous life: the inmates, as may be expected, lean, withered, dusky and smoke-dried.[29]

Judged by modern criteria, then, life in mid-eighteenth-century Duror – for most of the locality's population at any rate – was almost unimaginably hard. And it must have been even harder than usual in the summer of 1745, the previous winter having been so severe that throughout Argyll there had been a 'very great and universal . . . loss' of the cattle which were the county's only agricultural product of any real value.[30]

But if conditions in eighteenth-century Duror were tough, they may not have been significantly tougher than those in many other parts of the United Kingdom. On the whole, eighteenth-century Highlanders were healthier and lived longer than residents of then growing urban centres in the Lowlands and in England. This fact goes some way to account for the comparative ease with which Prince Charles Edward Stuart's mostly Highland army was to perform tremendous feats of physical endurance. It also helps to explain the positive note struck by the one description of Duror residents to have survived from the period of Charles Edward's rebellion: 'The people of the country are tall, strong and well-bodied.'[31]

The necessary raw material was readily available, then, when Charles Stewart of Ardshiel started trying to turn Duror men into soldiers fit for action in the Jacobite cause. From settlements on Charles' own estate, and from elsewhere in Duror, recruit after recruit came forward. The names of some, though not all, of those recruits have survived the lapse of more than 250 years: Duncan MacInnes, Donald MacColl, Duncan MacColl and Malcolm Carmichael from Ardshiel; Ewen MacColl, John MacColl and Duncan MacColl from Lagnaha; John MacColl, Duncan MacCombie, Archibald MacCombie, John MacCombie, John Stewart, Alan Stewart and Duncan Stewart from Achindarroch; John Stewart, Samuel MacColl and Duncan MacIntyre from Acharn; the already mentioned Donald Carmichael from Insaig; John MacLaren, Donald MacLaren, Duncan Henderson, Duncan MacColl and Alexander Stewart from Achara; Alan Stewart, John Stewart, Duncan Carmichael, Duncan MacCombie, John MacCombie junior, John MacCombie senior, Samuel MacColl, Donald MacIntyre and Robert Stewart from Cuil; Archibald MacCombie, John Cameron, Donald Cameron, Duncan Black and Lachlan MacLachlan from Keil; Duncan MacLaren and Hugh MacLaren from Achabhlar; John MacKenzie and Donald MacCorquodale from Bealach.[32]

Did they go willingly to war, these men? On this point, commentators of the time were divided. One leading British soldier of the eighteenth century considered that Highlanders rushed to the Jacobite colours simply because they thought it 'a most sublime virtue' to 'pay a servile and abject obedience' to men such as Charles Stewart of Ardshiel. Other contemporaries tell a very different tale, concentrating, for example, on how recruiting sergeants acting on behalf of Charles Stewart's close ally, Donald Cameron of Lochiel, dragooned at least some of the Cameron chief's clansmen into the Jacobite army by telling those clansmen 'that, if they did not forthwith go with them, they would that instant proceed to burn all their houses'.[33]

Although there is no evidence of similar threats having been issued in Duror during 1745, the fact remains that in any era men are generally reluctant to become soldiers. Some degree of coercion is almost invariably required to fill an army's ranks: a press-gang in the United Kingdom of the eighteenth century; a conscription law in twentieth-century Britain. It is unlikely, then, that when in August 1745 Charles Stewart and his colleagues came calling on Duror household after Duror household, they left each one accompanied by eager volunteers. But even if intimidatory methods were used, and some such methods certainly would have been, the results – numerically anyway – were undeniably impressive. 'Stewart of Appin, chief of that branch of the Stewarts, was not personally in the late rebellion,' a British government agent reported from the Duror area in Culloden's aftermath, 'but the gentlemen and commons of his clan rose to a man with a very uncommon zeal.'[34]

Men can be bribed as well as forced to fight, of course. Dougal Stewart's estate manager, the United Kingdom authorities were informed, told prospective recruits they would receive rent reductions on joining the Jacobite army. If this were so, it opens up the possibility that the Appin chief, despite his studied non-belligerence, was himself more pro-Jacobite than suggested earlier – a possibility strengthened by the suggestion, in a British intelligence report, that Dougal Stewart attended 'meetings' with Stewart of Invernahyle and Stewart of Ardshiel in the course of the August weeks when the latter was taken up with 'raising the men of his [Dougal's] country'.[35]

Be that as it may, his Invernhayle, Fasnacloich, Ballachulish and Achnacone counterparts were clearly of far more use than his chief to Ardshiel's laird during this critical period. Alexander Stewart of Fasnacloich, a man of 73 who had fought in both the 1689 and 1715 risings, considered himself too old to participate in the latest Jacobite rebellion. But he 'took an active part', it is said, 'in raising men for the expedition'. Equally involved in Charles Stewart's recruiting effort were Alexander Stewart of Invernahyle and his namesake, Alexander Stewart of Ballachulish, another veteran of the 1715 campaign. Although in his sixties, the Ballachulish laird was to serve as one of Charles Stewart's officers in what would become, by the end of August 1745, the

Jacobite army's Appin Regiment. Alexander Stewart of Invernahyle would also be one of Charles' officers, and so would yet another Alexander Stewart, a brother of the laird of Achnacone, together with a further Charles Stewart, a son of Fasnacloich's elderly – but still staunchly Jacobite – proprietor.[36]

Also holding high rank in the Appin Regiment was James Stewart. In 1746 James featured on an officially compiled list of prominent Jacobites as 'an officer in the rebel army'. Six years later, he was described by the government lawyers who drew up the High Court indictment detailing the offences for which he was tried in Inveraray, as 'the natural [or illegitimate] brother of Charles Stewart of Ardshiel'.[37] Responding in 1752 to the Duke of Argyll's claim that he had been involved in one or more of the Jacobite insurrections preceding that of 1745, James Stewart said: 'I was a schoolboy in the year 1715, and was but little more in the year 1719.' This suggests that James was born around the middle of the eighteenth century's opening decade – which, if correct, would make him around 40 when he joined the Appin Regiment.[38]

The father of both James and Charles Stewart was John Stewart of Ardshiel. But while John had married Charles' mother, whose maiden name was Elizabeth Stewart and who was the daughter of a Perthshire laird, he hadn't married the mother of James, whose identity is nowadays unknown.

His illegitimacy, of course, deprived James of any chance of inheriting any part of his father's estate. Otherwise, it doesn't seem greatly to have disadvantaged him, for, presumably at his father's expense, James was given a good education by the standards of the time. Like every other inhabitant of the Duror of his day, Gaelic was James' first language. While a boy, however, he'd been taught English – which he spoke fluently. James had also been taught (and this was by no means common in the eighteenth-century Highlands) to write. Whether or not he was literate in Gaelic is unclear, but as is proved by those of his letters which have been preserved among the records of Scotland's High Court, James wrote English clearly and well.

Probably in the mid-1720s, James married Margaret Stewart, who may have grown up in the vicinity of Fort William – where her brother William was a merchant – and who was James' cousin as well as his wife. Margaret and James had at least three children, Alan, Charles and Elizabeth. Like their father, Alan and Charles could read and write. Literacy being commonly judged of no great use to girls or women, Elizabeth, like her mother, couldn't even sign her name. It is probable for reasons touched on later that James and Margaret Stewart had at least two more children. Their names, however, have not survived, nor is it certain where exactly in Duror the family were living in 1745 – though evidence relating to James' post-Culloden activities points, as will be seen, to their home at this period having been in Achindarroch. If so, the Alan Stewart from that township who served in the Appin Regiment may conceivably have been James' son. Though James' Alan would probably have still been in his teens at this stage, teenagers, as Culloden casualty lists would show all too starkly, were very definitely not exempt from fighting (and dying) in the cause of Charles Edward Stuart.

At his trial, one of James Stewart's lawyers described him as 'sensible'. 'All who know him,' this same lawyer commented, 'will say he is a humane, peaceable, good-natured man.' While some of this can be discounted as the stuff of a soundly argued defence case, none of it contradicts what is known of James from other sources. For example, and this was also stressed in the course of James' trial, 'strangers' were 'happy to get their children under his care'. James had a well-deserved reputation as a caring and conscientious foster-father, being 'tutor and curator', at the time of his arrest in 1752, to 'several orphans who have not the smallest relation to him'.[39]

James is known to have been a tenant of land, at different times, in Glen Duror, Achindarroch, Acharn and Keil. Because of his connection with the first of these places, James was known throughout Duror and beyond as *Seumas a' Ghlinne*, James of the Glen.[40] This nickname served to distinguish James from the rest of Appin's numerous James Stewarts. It also indicates that his association with Glen Duror was a fairly lengthy one.

As well as being a farmer, James was a dealer in cattle. And in the Duror of the nineteenth century, when memories of him were comparatively fresh, James was also said to have been something of a trader – keeping, in this capacity, 'a large store . . . in the lower part of Glen Duror'.[41] Nineteenth-century tradition (which there is no reason to reject) supplies one or two further snippets of this sort. In years if not in status, it was said, Seumas a' Ghlinne had the advantage over his half-brother, Tearlach Mòr. And Tearlach, it seems, held the older man in high esteem. James Stewart, Duror's tradition-bearers insisted, was someone in whom Ardshiel's laird 'had great confidence'. What occurred in Duror during 1746 and subsequently was to demonstrate as much.[42]

Prince Charles Edward Stuart had landed in Moidart on 25 July. When, a few days later, Charles Edward met, and managed to get the active backing of, Donald Cameron of Lochiel, Cameron, on being sent back home 'to raise his men' was also instructed to do what he could to ensure that the Stewarts of Appin undertook 'to raise theirs'. Letters to this effect were sent from Prince Charles' Moidart base to Appin and Duror at about the same time. The ensuing mobilisation must have taken about a fortnight – for, on the afternoon of 19 August, within an hour or two of the Stuart standard having been unfurled at Glenfinnan, an emissary, or so it was afterwards recorded, 'came from Appin' in order 'to acquaint the prince' with the information that Stewart of Ardshiel's newly formed regiment 'would join him in a few days'. Accordingly, on 21 August, by which point Charles Edward had left Glenfinnan and was advancing in the direction of the Great Glen, 'expresses' were dispatched to the Ardshiel laird with a view to ordering him and his men to rendezvous with the main body of what was now a growing Jacobite army in the vicinity of Invergarry – which the prince was to reach on 26 August.[43]

The Appin Regiment had already seen action of a sort, tangling briefly with their ancient enemies, the Campbells of Barcaldine, who, needless to say, were vehemently opposed to any notion of a Stuart restoration. Not the least significant outcome of this August 1745 skirmish, according to a Campbell account of it, was that Barcaldine's laird, John Campbell, became 'the first man in Britain [to] draw his sword against the rebels'.[44]

In order to boost their numbers, it appears, some of Stewart of Ardshiel's recruiters had ventured across Loch Creran to Campbell of Barcaldine's lands, where they hoped to make contact with Jacobite sympathisers who would otherwise have remained outside their net. What happened next is recounted in a Campbell document of the period: 'A party of them [the Appin Stewarts] crossed an arm of the sea and carried away some people from the side where his [John Campbell's] estate is, in order to force them into the rebellion. Mr Campbell with his servants and some of his nearest tenants pursued them in his own boat so close, though in the night, that, upon landing, they abandoned their prisoners and he brought them back with him.'[45]

This was not, perhaps, an auspicious start to the Appin Regiment's campaign. But it did nothing to halt Charles Stewart of Ardshiel's overall progress. His success in recruiting Duror's menfolk into his regiment's ranks has already been noted. That success was quickly to be replicated in other parts of Appin.

At this time, Clan Stewart's total military manpower was thought by two external but well-informed observers, one of whom was Duncan Forbes, to be around 300. By the end of the third week in August, Charles Stewart had 260 of these men under his command. And on or around 23 August 1745, he marched the Appin Regiment out of Duror and headed north, by way of Lettermore, for Ballachulish. There, or in that area, it is probable that the Appin men fell in with their immediate neighbours, the MacDonalds of Glencoe, another traditionally Jacobite clan whose fighting men now accompanied the Appin Regiment into the Great Glen. The precise route selected by Stewart of Ardshiel is not certain. But by one means or another, the Appin Regiment avoided contact with the government troops still holding Fort William, and on the evening of Tuesday, 27 August, in the neighbourhood of

Aberchalder, a township at the northern end of Loch Oich, they joined the rest of Prince Charles Edward Stuart's forces – whose total strength they brought up to some 2,000.

British government ministers in London considered the rebel army to be at this point 'a despicable rabble' which would be 'crushed with all the ease in the world'. This, however, was seriously to underestimate Jacobite capabilities. Worse, it was entirely to overlook the difficulties confronting Britain's senior commander in Scotland, General Sir John Cope. Since Cope could, on the face of things, call on the services of a British army which had more than 60,000 troops at its disposal, he should, in theory, have been able easily to see off Charles Edward's 2,000 Highlanders. But as the general well knew, practically all of Britain's frontline formations, then in action against France in the Low Countries, were wholly unavailable to him. Scotland, in fact, was held by no more than 4,000 soldiers – and many of them were of the poorest quality.[46]

With hindsight, John Cope's best bet might have been to remain in the Lowlands and wait for the Jacobites to come to him. This possibility was rejected, however. Instead, from his forward base at Stirling, Cope moved into the Central Highlands. By 26 August, he had crossed the Pass of Drumochter and was in Badenoch, from where he'd intended to advance into the Great Glen.

In 1745, this strategically vital valley, connecting the Moray Firth to the north-east with Loch Linnhe to the south-west, could most readily be approached from Badenoch by way of one of the military roads which Edmund Burt had helped construct a few years earlier. This road – today abandoned and unused except by walkers – traversed the 2,500-foot Corrieyairack Pass which it approached, from the south, by means of a long series of steeply ascending hairpin bends. Each of these 'traverses', as their builders called them, could readily be held against Cope's advancing army, or so the general feared, by the tiniest of Jacobite detachments. On 26 or 27 August, convinced – mistakenly – that Charles Edward was already in possession of the Corrieyairack, Cope decided to outflank the Jacobites, as he thought, by marching out of Badenoch in the direction of Inverness.

This strategy would have made sense if Prince Charles had been aiming only to hold the Great Glen. As it was, the prince's objectives being hugely more ambitious, Cope's push for Inverness was a strategic blunder of monumental proportions – for the simple reason that it left unprotected the main route from the Highlands to the south. The Jacobites now proceeded along this route at a rapid clip. By the end of August, they were at Blair Castle in Atholl. By 3 September they'd reached Dunkeld and, on the following day, took Perth – where a bystander, as was afterwards noted, glimpsed Charles Stewart of Ardshiel 'at the head of his men'.[47]

Like Cameron of Lochiel and several of the other clan chiefs who'd thrown in their lot with Prince Charles Edward, the Ardshiel laird had been made a member of the prince's council of war, the Jacobite army's decision-making forum. At Perth, and during much of what ensued, this council's foremost personality was Lord George Murray, younger brother of the Duke of Atholl and a highly skilled tactician who had joined the Jacobites in the course of their advance through Perthshire. By one of his Jacobite colleagues, Murray was said to have 'possessed a natural genius for military operations'. A further comment from the same source helps account for the high regard in which Lord George, whom Prince Charles promptly made his field commander, was held by the Duror and Appin men whose movements he was personally to direct at more than one critical moment in 1745 and 1746: 'He [Murray] was tall and robust, and brave in the highest degree; conducting the Highlanders in the most heroic manner, and always the first to rush, sword in hand, into the midst of the enemy. He used to say, when he advanced to the charge, "I do not ask you, my lads, to go before, but merely to follow me."'[48]

Since John Cope and his men were still far to the north, nothing more than a scratch force of a few hundred troops now stood between Edinburgh and the Jacobites – who, from Perth, were soon pressing on southwards. On the night of 14 September, the Appin Regiment was one of the units dispatched by Lord George Murray to mount an attack on Edinburgh's defenders, then somewhere in the vicinity of Linlithgow. Outnumbered and demoralised, their Hanoverian opponents melted away into the darkness before Stewart of Ardshiel's men could engage with them.

And by 17 September, together with the rest of the Jacobite army, the Appin Regiment was in Edinburgh. Next morning, an Edinburgh newspaper, *The Caledonian Mercury*, observed bemusedly: 'Affairs in this city and neighbourhood have taken the most surprising turn since yesterday, without the least bloodshed or opposition; so that now we have in our streets Highlanders and bagpipes, in place of dragoons and drums.' The Highlanders in question, an Edinburgh eyewitness reported, universally favoured the age-old dress of the hills. Instead of jackets and trousers, in other words, they wore kilted plaids of tartan cloth, belted at the waist and thrown, sash-like, across the shoulder. From a Lowland perspective, the same eyewitness wrote a little excitedly, their plaids turned the Jacobite soldiers into exotics: 'The Highland garb favoured them much, as it showed their naked limbs, which were strong and muscular; that and their stern countenances, and bushy uncombed hair, gave them a fierce, barbarous and imposing aspect.'[49]

While Prince Charles Edward Stuart had been hastening south, General Sir John Cope had been marching his battalions from Inverness to Aberdeen, from where he planned to transport them south by sea. The outcome was that at the same time as the Jacobites were occupying Edinburgh, the Hanoverian commander and his troops were landing at nearby Dunbar. Marching east to confront the threat thus posed to their possession of the capital, Prince Charles, Lord George Murray and the Jacobite army encountered Cope's formations at Prestonpans, near Tranent, on 20 September. There was no fighting that day. But following an overnight manoeuvre which enabled them to attack from a direction other than the one John Cope expected, the Jacobites, just as the sun was rising, came hurtling down on the general's lines.

The previous evening, or so it is said, MacDonald of Keppoch, one of the Jacobite chiefs, in the course of a debate as to the state of morale among the Jacobite army's Highland soldiers remarked to Charles Edward 'that, as the country had been long at peace, few or none of the private men had ever seen a battle, and it was not very easy to say how they would behave'.[50]

MacDonald's concerns were rapidly assuaged by events at Prestonpans on Saturday, 21 September 1745. They were particularly set to rest, perhaps, by the achievements of the Jacobite left. There Charles Edward's front line consisted mainly of the Appin Regiment and the Lochaber Camerons. Nor was there anything accidental about this arrangement. The Stewarts of Appin had long been allies of the Camerons – whose chief, as already indicated, was also a personal friend of Charles Stewart of Ardshiel. Thus it came about that when lots were drawn in the Jacobite camp to determine the Prestonpans battle-order, 'the Camerons and Stewarts, inclining . . . to be in a body, drew one lot'.[51]

Under the feet of the Duror men – but not noticeably impeding them – when they charged the waiting Hanoverians was a 'thick stubble' left just a day or two before by the Prestonpans harvesters. Seconds into the battle, in response to the Jacobite charge, Cope's cannons – a terrifying novelty from a Duror perspective – opened fire. 'The line seemed to shake,' it was afterwards recalled of the still rapidly advancing Jacobite army at this moment, 'but the men kept going on at a great pace.' And so tremendous was the impetus of their attack, it seems, that, 'in a very few minutes . . . the whole [Hanoverian] army, both horse and foot, was put to flight'.[52]

Near the heart of the Appin Regiment as it crashed into the Hanoverian right was Alexander Stewart of Invernahyle. In later life, the Invernahyle laird, who had moved by then to Duror, was to be well known to the young son of Stewart's Edinburgh lawyer. This lawyer was named Walter Scott. So, too, was his son – a boy who, on growing up, would become one of the nineteenth century's most renowned novelists. In 1786 or 1787, Walter Scott junior left his father's Edinburgh home to undertake, as he subsequently remembered, 'the first excursion I was permitted to make on a pony of my own'. Scott's destination was Alexander Stewart's Duror home. 'He was a noble specimen of the old Highlander,' Walter Scott afterwards recalled of Stewart, 'far descended, gallant, courteous and brave, even to chivalry'. The Invernahyle laird also possessed – in full measure – the Highland knack of telling a good story. And what the teenage Scott heard during his visit to Duror of Alexander Stewart's Prestonpans exploits would provide the eventual writer with the basis of his first – and arguably best – novel, *Waverley*.[53]

Towards the end of his life, Walter Scott acknowledged his debt to Stewart of Invernahyle and retold one of Stewart's Prestonpans tales. Scott's retelling starts thus: 'When [at Prestonpans] the Highlanders made their memorable attack . . . a battery of four field-pieces was stormed and carried by the Camerons and the Stewarts of Appin . . . Alexander Stewart of Invernahyle was one of the foremost of the charge and, observing an officer of the king's forces, who, scorning to join the flight all around, remained with his sword in his hand, as if determined to the very last to defend the post assigned to him, the Highland gentleman commanded him to surrender.'[54]

Stewart, Scott goes on, 'received for reply a thrust'. This the Invernahyle laird skilfully blocked (or, in Scott's parlance, 'caught') by instantly raising the leather-bound targe, or shield, which every Highland soldier then carried on his left arm. Such was the power behind the Hanoverian officer's swordswing that his blade, on encountering Alexander Stewart's targe, became embedded in it. Scott continues: 'The officer was now defenceless, and the battleaxe of a gigantic Highlander (the miller of Invernahyle's mill) was uplifted to dash his brains out, when Mr Stewart, with considerable difficulty, prevailed on him to yield. He [Alexander Stewart] took charge of his enemy's property, protected his person and finally obtained him liberty on parole.'

Alexander Stewart's prisoner was Colonel Alan Whiteford, a British artillery officer who was by coincidence on leave in Edinburgh in August and September 1745. On first hearing of Prince Charles Edward Stuart's 'invasion', Whiteford, as he informed one of his army colleagues, believed the prince's plans would 'end in smoke'. But when this didn't happen, Whiteford felt obliged to report to General Cope, who put the colonel in charge of his field guns – of which, incidentally, the general possessed six and not, as Walter Scott thought, four. On the morning of 21 September, Whiteford, despite having been 'deserted', as he put it, 'by the whole people who were to assist him', managed somehow to discharge five of those small cannons. This duty attended to, the colonel was left to confront the Appin Regiment whose leading ranks, he said after his capture by Alexander Stewart, 'advanced on me with a swiftness not to be conceived'.[55]

Colonel Alan Whiteford was the most prominent of the 'great number of prisoners' taken at Prestonpans by the Appin Regiment. How many Hanoverians died at the regiment's hands is not recorded, but it's known that for the loss of under thirty of their own troops, the Jacobite army as a whole slaughtered more than 300 of Cope's soldiers. How those soldiers perished is perhaps neither here nor there, but the type of warfare in which eighteenth-century Highlanders specialised would have meant that many of John Cope's men died gruesomely. 'The field of battle', a Jacobite eyewitness recalled of Prestonpans, 'presented a spectacle of horror, being covered with heads, legs, arms and mutilated bodies; for the killed all fell by the sword.'[56]

From start to finish, the Battle of Prestonpans lasted for no more than five or ten minutes. Shortly after its close, as Sir John Cope's surviving troops fled for their lives into the surrounding countryside, there emerged cautiously from among remnants of the Hanoverian army a young man who – taking care, no doubt, to identify himself in Gaelic to any approaching Highlander – immediately expressed a wish to change sides. Like Alexander Stewart of Invernahyle, Jacobitism's newest recruit had connections with Duror. Also like the Invernahyle laird, he was to inspire a great novel – the novel, in this instance, being Robert Louis Stevenson's *Kidnapped*. In Stevenson's novel, this deserter from Cope's forces is called Alan Breck, and by way of introducing him, Stevenson has his novel's narrator, David Balfour, provide some initial impressions of the man who, in *Kidnapped* as in real life, was to be hunted across Scotland as Colin Campbell's murderer: 'He was smallish in stature, but well set and as nimble as a goat; his face was of a good open expression, but sunburnt very dark, and heavily freckled and pitted with the smallpox; his eyes were unusually light and had a kind of dancing madness in them, that was both engaging and alarming; and when he took off his great-coat, he laid a pair of fine, silver-mounted pistols on the table, and I saw that he was belted with a great sword. His manners, besides, were elegant . . . Altogether I thought of him, at the first sight, that here was a man I would rather call my friend than my enemy.'[57]

The non-fictional Alan was perhaps not quite so appealing. James Stewart, Alan's foster-father and the man hanged in his stead, would be driven eventually to calling his foster-son 'a desperate foolish fellow'. And James would have been less than human if, as he sat in the Fort William cell where he spent the last weeks of his life, the thought didn't cross his mind that it might have been better for him if he'd never set eyes on Alan or if, failing that, Alan had met with a Jacobite bullet on the Prestonpans battlefield.[58]

For better or for worse, however, James' foster-son – as was shown by his conduct at Prestonpans, and as was to become still more obvious in the years ahead – was nothing if not a survivor. But if every bit as tough as Robert Louis Stevenson made him out to be, Alan was not, as Stevenson claimed, 'smallish'. In 1752, in fact, he was described by James Stewart as 'a tall . . . lad' whose other distinguishing characteristic was his 'very black hair'.[59]

Alan's surname, like that of his foster-father, was Stewart. In Gaelic he was known as *Ailean Breac*. Anglicised to Alan Breck in the wanted notices circulated after Colin Campbell's killing, Alan's nickname derived, as Robert Louis Stevenson hinted, from his having had smallpox. *Breac*, meaning speckled or spotted, was the adjective commonly applied to those whose faces, following encounters with that then common disease, were left cruelly pocked and pitted.

One of the numerous 'fatherless children' James Stewart was said at his trial to have found space for in his Duror home, Alan had been born in Rannoch, a famously lawless corner of the hard-to-access hill country where Argyll and Perthshire meet. Several Stewart families had moved from Appin and Duror to the Rannoch area over the years and Alan's father, Donald Stewart, who farmed in the Rannoch township of Invercomrie, seems to have belonged to one of these.

Donald was certainly 'a distant relation' and 'a particular friend' of James Stewart, Seumas a' Ghlinne, whom the Invercomrie farmer, not long before his premature death, made responsible for his children's upbringing. How many children were involved in this transaction is not specified in any surviving record. But James, it was observed in 1752, 'faithfully executed [Donald Stewart's] trust, took care of the children's education and managed their effects to the best advantage'.[60]

Alan, however, caused difficulties from the first. As he 'grew up to man's estate', it was said, he became 'extravagant'; first spending 'what was left him by his father'; next becoming a constant drain on James, 'who used to supply him with money and pay little debts for him'. It is possible, then, that when Ailean Breac declared that he wanted to become a soldier and went off to sign up with the British military, his foster-father considered himself rid of an increasingly burdensome obligation. How James reacted to Alan's defection at Prestonpans is not recorded. But Alan, for his part, surely felt he'd staged – in typically dramatic style – something of a prodigal son's return. And while there's no absolute proof that following Alan's desertion he was attached to the Appin Regiment, this seems – given that Alan is known to have served in the Jacobite army – by far the most probable outcome. Among the Appin Regiment's officers was Alan's foster-father. At the regiment's head was Charles Stewart of Ardshiel, his foster-father's half-brother. And in the Appin Regiment's ranks were many Duror men – MacColls, MacCombies and others – who would have been Alan's boyhood friends.[61]

It is safe to bet that Alan celebrated his reunion with his Duror contemporaries in one of Edinburgh's many taverns when the Prestonpans victors got back to the capital on Sunday, 22 September. There Alan and possibly James as well – for the foster-father was as frequent and as rowdy a drinker as the foster-son – may have gazed out on Edinburgh's ever-congested High Street and, being far from Duror, wished themselves back, as one ale followed on another, in Taigh na h-Insaig.

Chapter Three

'When the men of the clans were broken at Culloden, and the good cause went
down, and the horses rode over the fetlocks in the best blood of the north, Ardshiel
had to flee like a poor deer upon the mountains.'

Robert Louis Stevenson, *Kidnapped*

At the end of October 1745, Prince Charles Edward Stuart's army
marched out of Edinburgh and headed for the English border. By
then James Stewart, as is shown by the regiment's surviving order
book, held the rank of captain and, as such, was entitled to an income –
assuming the funds were there to pay it – of two shillings and sixpence a day.
Under James' immediate command at this point was a company consisting of a
lieutenant, a second-lieutenant, two sergeants and twenty-nine men. None of
those soldiers can be identified with certainty. But it is by no means impossible
that one of the sergeants answering to Seamus a' Ghlinne was Taigh na h-
Insaig's Donald Carmichael, who is known to have held that rank. And it is
probable that most, maybe all, of the men in James' company came from Duror
– just as it is likely that the majority of men in Alexander Stewart of
Invernahyle's comparable unit belonged to Alexander's own immediate locality
on the northern shores of Loch Creran.

The Appin Regiment's numbers were to fluctuate throughout its seven-
month existence. The 260 or so men who had linked up with Charles Edward
at Aberchalder in August were joined on their way to Edinburgh by several
dozen more – many of these latecomers drawn from the Balquhidder area with
which, as a result of family associations going back to medieval times, the
Appin Stewarts had always had close connections. However, when quartered in
or around Duddingston (on Edinburgh's southern outskirts) during the weeks
following Prestonpans, the Appin Regiment, like several other Jacobite
formations, appears to have lost many of its men to desertion. This was a

universal problem in armies of the eighteenth century. Since most soldiers were also farmers or peasants, it was inevitable that, come September, they were anxious to ensure that their families had got the harvest safely in. If at all feasible, therefore, such soldiers tended simply to go home each autumn – and there's no doubt that a number of Duror men did just this within days of Prestonpans. That much is clear from a letter sent to Duncan Forbes by Norman MacLeod of Dunvegan in mid-October. MacLeod was reporting to Forbes – who, from his Inverness base, was doing everything he could to keep powerful figures like the Dunvegan chief in the Hanoverian camp – on conversations he'd had with Charles Stewart of Ardshiel, the Appin Regiment's colonel. 'We know here by a visit of Ardshiel who was in the battle [of Prestonpans]', MacLeod wrote, 'that the desertion after it was very great, and that several of their [the rebel army's] officers are come home to drag them [the deserters] out again.'

The Ardshiel laird had visited Skye, in the aftermath of Sir John Cope's shattering defeat, to try to persuade Norman MacLeod and Sir Alexander MacDonald – from both of whom Charles Edward had hoped for much on his arrival in Moidart – to rally, even at this late stage, to the Jacobite cause. He failed. But while on his way south again in the closing weeks of October 1745, Tearlach Mòr would no doubt have taken the opportunity to spend a day or two in Duror. There he'd have rooted from their homes in Lagnaha, Achindarroch, Acharn, Insaig, Achara and other townships, such of his troops as may have hoped that, with Prestonpans won, they would be permitted to spend the coming winter with their mothers, their wives and their children. This group, and it may well have been a large one, Charles Stewart now ordered back to Duddingston. The result was that when the Jacobite army set out for England on 31 October, the Appin Regiment's total strength was once again over 250.

The Appin Regiment had a command structure very similar to that of an equivalent formation in the British military of the time, with a colonel, captains, lieutenants, sergeants and the rest – something that makes an important point about the force which marched through the Scottish border country in the opening week of November 1745. This force certainly relied heavily on Highlanders drawn from those clans whose leaders had been prepared to commit themselves to Charles Edward Stuart. But for all that Hanoverian writers – and many subsequent historians – were to describe Highlanders like James Stewart and his Duror contingent in terms which suggest they constituted nothing more sophisticated than a tribal war-party, this was far from the case. James and his subordinates were not professional soldiers, admittedly, but, as the structure of their regiment reveals, neither were they the wholly unsoldierly ruffians of anti-Jacobite legend. Clans like the

Stewarts of Appin had not maintained their semi-independent existence through several centuries without intensively drilling their boys and young men in the business of war. This is evident from what was remembered, more than a hundred years later of how Charles Stewart of Ardshiel went about preparing Duror lads for the fighting in which they might one day be involved. 'It was the custom in the Highlands of Scotland before the year 1745', a North Argyll tradition-bearer was to recall in the 1860s, 'that the gentry kept schools to give instruction to youths in sword exercise, and the laird of Ardshiel kept a school for the instruction of the youth of his own district.'[2]

Real swords, of course, were not dished out willy-nilly to boys barely able to hold them. Instead the skills of swordsmanship – slashing, cutting, parrying and the like – were imparted by exercises in which ash and hazel staves, or cudgels, took the place of the razor-sharp weapons to which eighteenth-century Duror's youngsters were gradually introduced as they grew older.

'He stored the cudgels behind his house,' the same tradition-bearer said of Charles Stewart, 'and lads and laddies went every day to receive instruction on the cudgel from the laird. After the laddies had received their day's instruction, each got a bannock [or oatcake] and lumps of cheese. They were then sent to try who would soonest ascend a mountain and eat the bannock and cheese; and whoever was first got another bannock and lumps of cheese home with him.'

The 'mountain' mentioned here was probably the hill which rises behind Ardshiel. This hill is almost 900 feet high and its northern flank, immediately above the site of Charles Stewart's home, is extremely steep. Running from Ardshiel House to its summit and back, then, would have been no small test of a boy's endurance. It's not at all surprising, therefore, that the Jacobite army's Highland units – all of them composed of men who had been subjected to a similar régime from childhood – were capable of getting across country at speeds which astonished observers accustomed to the much more leisurely pace of the United Kingdom's red-coated troops. Nor is it surprising – given the way the Duror men had been trained, when boys in his sword school, to do whatever Ardshiel's laird might ask of them – that Charles Edward Stuart's staff officers were totally confident of their ability to keep the Jacobite army under strict control. This was a force expected both to take orders and to behave in what was – by the standards of that era – an altogether exemplary fashion.

There was to be no looting, no disorderly conduct of any kind, the Jacobite army was instructed. 'It is seriously recommended to all the officers', company commanders like James Stewart were told, 'that the most exact discipline be observed . . . It is forbid, above all things, to shoot sheep, hens, etc, or to break open the country people's houses.'[3]

'An officer of each regiment is to be in the rear of all the [army's] columns', runs one of numerous such injunctions entered in the Appin Regiment's order book, 'to hinder stragglers to go about the country.' 'The majors of each regiment are to answer upon their peril for all disorders that may be committed upon the march,' states a further such entry, 'it being their particular business that the men should march in order and keep their ranks.' 'The officers are to be very alert this night,' a third instruction reads, 'and they are to visit . . . the soldiers' quarters [to see] that they may not strip [meaning undress] but keep themselves always in readiness.'[4]

Mostly, it appears, these orders were observed; so was a refreshingly non-hierarchical directive that 'colonels and other officers are forbidden to have any wheeled carriages'; and so – though maybe not quite so conscientiously – was a command to the effect that Jacobite officers were 'forbidden to suffer any woman to follow their regiment but the women they really know to be married'.[5] Any eighteenth-century army on the march was followed everywhere by shoals of so-called washerwomen whose livelihoods tended to derive from services that went well beyond laundering, and this decree was aimed at preventing that practice. It is unlikely, of course, that Charles Edward's staff succeeded in outlawing prostitution. But what is interesting about their anti-prostitute ordinance – because of the way the ordinance's existence undermines the still-prevalent notion of the Jacobite army as a rowdy and unruly horde – is that they even made the attempt.[5]

From a Lowland or English perspective, to be sure, the Appin Regiment, with or without an accompanying cavalcade of Edinburgh street women, must have looked outlandish. The Duror men who marched from Duddingston through Dalkeith and Kelso on 31 October and 1 November 1745 wore heavy plaids, instead of uniform coats and trousers. And where the eighteenth-century British army favoured high-peaked caps or tricorn hats, the headgear of Duror's Jacobite soldiers would have consisted of woollen, handwoven bonnets decorated – if decorated at all – with nothing more than the oak twigs which had long been the distinguishing badge of fighting men in Appin Stewart service.

Imagine, too, how folk living in a Lowland rural district where the sound of bagpipes had never been heard before would have reacted to the ear-splitting consequences of this late-night order to the Appin Regiment's non-commissioned officers: 'The army decamps tomorrow [morning]. The pipes are to play at four [a.m.] that all may be ready to [de]part at five.' To the many Lowlanders and English people who were to encounter Highland troops for the first time in the closing weeks of 1745, by no means the least frightening characteristic of such troops was that they were preceded everywhere by pipers.

The bagpipe, if not quite the Jacobite army's secret weapon, was certainly its most distinguishing – and, to southern ears, most alien – attribute.[6]

But although there was, from an English or a Lowland standpoint, much that was intrinsically exotic about Prince Charles Edward Stuart's Highland troops, the several weeks they had spent in and around Edinburgh had at least enabled most of them to acquire more conventional armaments than those they'd carried when first taking the city in mid-September. Then it had been noted that only half of the Jacobite Highlanders were 'completely armed', the others having to be content with 'pitchforks, scythes, a sword or a pistol, or . . . only a staff or a stick'. To be 'completely armed', by the criteria of the time, was to possess a musket. Some of Charles Edward's Highlanders had done so from the outset of his campaign. But the firearms in question were, to begin with, singularly ill-assorted – one Edinburgh eyewitness observing of his city's Jacobite invaders 'that their firelocks were not similar or uniform, but of all sorts and sizes, muskets, fusees and [even] fowling-pieces'.[7]

Once installed in Edinburgh, however, 'the Highland army', as the *Scots Magazine* commented indignantly, 'seized all the cannon, arms and ammunition belonging to the city'. Thus it came about that a Duror man, John MacColl, 'received in Edinburgh', as he afterwards recalled, the gun which he 'used . . . when in England' during November and December 1745. Thus it came about, too, that a British agent, in the course of one of his reports to his superiors, observed of the Jacobite troops he managed to get sight of at this time: 'The men are all pretty well armed. There is scarce any but has . . . gun, sword and pistol. Some few have bayonets and some few targets [or shields].'[8]

To Britain's politicians and military men, all of whom had previously viewed Charles Edward Stuart as nothing more than a tiresome distraction from what they saw as altogether more important battles on the continent, the news from Prestonpans came as an extremely unpleasant shock. 'This thing is now grown very serious,' commented one professional soldier, Sir John Ligonier, 'the rebels, to the great dishonour of Scotland, having taken possession of [that country] with three or four thousand beggarly banditry.'[9]

Ligonier's feelings mirrored those of the majority of English people. In advance of Prestonpans, a Church of England clergyman complained, his congregation had been utterly unmoved by events in the north: 'I have endeavoured to awaken them with the notion of their religion, their laws, their liberties and their properties being at stake; at which they yawn and ask if they do not pay soldiers to fight for them.' The Jacobite prince's capture of Edinburgh and – still more – his routing of Sir John Cope altered such attitudes overnight. 'When the news of the surrender of the city and the defeat of the army reached them, it spread a universal consternation and concern. It awakened them out of their stupidity. They saw their religion, liberty and lives in the utmost danger, and popery and slavery approaching near to their borders.'[10]

Although Charles Edward Stuart, like his father and grandfather, was a Catholic, the largest part of his Highland soldiers (including all, or almost all, the Duror men in the Jacobite army's ranks) adhered, as already stressed, to Episcopalianism. Theologically speaking, therefore, they had a good deal in common with the Anglican parson whose remarks are quoted above. But that, needless to say, mattered nothing to the propagandists responsible for the barrage of abuse and vilification directed at the Highlanders who so suddenly threatened, in the autumn of 1745, not just to overthrow King George II but to destroy, in the process, the entire political and financial establishment whose power and privileges George was thought to guarantee. Badly frightened men of influence in England failed to recognise the different religious views of the Jacobites. Since it suited the rulers of what was then a highly sectarian country to call their opponents papists, all Highlanders were so called. They were called a lot of other things as well: 'animals', 'vermin', 'monsters', 'beasts'; 'robbers' and 'bandits'; 'the scum of the world'; 'a hellish band'; 'swine'; 'a parcel of rabble'; 'filthy, farting, pissing, shitting' primitives who 'let fall their ordure . . . wherever they rested' and who were, in consequence, fit only to be 'hunted down', wiped out, exterminated.[11]

Exposed over several weeks to these and similar portrayals of Highlanders, it is perfectly understandable that when the real thing was finally encountered in the south, 'the terror of the English', as a Jacobite soldier wrote subsequently, 'was truly inconceivable'. Hence the hysterical reaction of one Englishwoman to that most cultivated of Highland chieftains, Donald Cameron of Lochiel: 'One evening as Mr Cameron . . . entered the lodgings assigned to him, the landlady . . . threw herself at his feet, and, with uplifted hands, and tears in her eyes, supplicated him to take her life but to spare her two little children. He asked her if she was in her senses . . . She answered that everybody said the Highlanders ate children and made them their common food.'[12]

Prince Charles Edward Stuart's army of supposed savages and cannibals waded across the River Esk and entered England on Friday, 8 November 1745. The autumn had been rainy. 'There never was such dismal weather as we have had constantly here,' one of Duncan Forbes' informants had complained a couple of weeks before. The Esk, in consequence, was high and getting from one side to the other must have been a perilous undertaking. The crossing, however, was made safely.[13]

On gaining the Esk's English bank, or so accounts of the time assert, the soldiers of each Jacobite unit drew their broadswords, wheeled to the left and, facing Scotland, saluted the country which many of them – certainly most of the cold, wet Duror men clambering heavily onto English soil – were leaving for the first time. Quite why this gesture was made is a matter for debate. But there is no doubting the interpretation placed by Charles Edward's Highland troops on the fact that Donald Cameron of Lochiel, in the act of pulling his sword from its scabbard, managed somehow to cut his hand. Universally, this was reckoned a bad omen. And when things shortly began to go wrong for the Jacobites, the Cameron chief's shedding of his own blood would be remembered as a grimly ominous portent.

From the Esk, the Jacobite army advanced smartly towards the walled town of Carlisle, which was taken after a short siege. Then the Highlanders pressed on through Penrith, Kendal, Lancaster, Preston, Wigan, Manchester, Stockport, Macclesfield, Leek and Ashbourne, reaching Derby just before noon on Wednesday, 4 December.

The autumn's rains had given way by now to frosts and blizzards. At night, it was observed, 'many of the soldiers were obliged to lie on the ground, though covered with snow'. And sometimes the same men 'could get nothing to eat after marching thirteen hours'. But even in the most atrocious weather and on deeply rutted roads that were covered in mud, water and ice, the pace of the Jacobite army continued to amaze the Hanoverian government's spies. At a time of year when Britain's regular soldiers seldom got on the move before nine o'clock in the morning, Charles Edward's Highlanders, it was reported, frequently set out four hours earlier; taking advantage, while their government counterparts waited for sunrise, of such moonlight or starlight as was available and covering, entirely on foot, an astonishing 30 or 35 miles each day.[14]

In the aftermath of the Jacobite descent on Derby, a local 'gentleman' – writing in the town's newspaper – described his encounters with the six Highland officers and forty soldiers who'd been quartered briefly in his fine home. Comparing his uninvited guests to 'a herd of Hottentots or wild monkeys', he told how they'd managed to consume a side of beef, eight joints of mutton, four cheeses, six hens and an 'abundance' of both white and brown bread, to say nothing of huge quantities of strong ale, tea and other drinks. If this particular set of 'fierce and desperate' Highlanders included men from Duror, then such men, it is clear, lived far, far better while in Derby than they ever had at home.[15]

As the afternoon of Wednesday, 4 December, wore towards an early dusk, Derby's streets filled gradually with men from the six clan units who constituted the core of Prince Charles Edward Stuart's highly mobile force: the Appin Regiment; the Lochaber Camerons; Cluny MacPherson's men from Badenoch and Strathspey; the MacDonalds of Clanranald, of Keppoch, and of

Glengarry. They were 'a mixture of every rank', it was noted of those universally Gaelic-speaking Highlanders, 'from childhood to old age, from the dwarf to the giant'. And as late as the start of the twentieth century, old people in Derby would recall hearing from their grandparents of how Charles Edward's Jacobite Scots had once upon a time come swarming into town, demanding food, it was said, in a strange and incomprehensible tongue.[16]

The British government's generals had ordered the demolition of Swarkeston Bridge on Derby's southern outskirts. But so rapid was the Jacobite advance that this strategically vital river crossing was seized on 4 December before it could be blown up. Beyond the bridge lay a well-paved road to London – just 120 miles, or four days' march, away.

In London, eighteenth-century Europe's most populous city and the capital of what was then one of the world's most powerful states, something approaching panic was beginning to become apparent. 'There never was so melancholy a town,' noted that usually unflappable diarist, Horace Walpole. Among politicians, meanwhile, there was – as a senior government minister, the Duke of Newcastle, admitted privately – 'a good deal of consternation'.[17]

Reflecting years later on Prince Charles Edward Stuart's rebellion, the Edinburgh writer John Home, who personally saw service on the Hanoverian side during 1745 and 1746, commented: 'The conclusion of this enterprise [in other words, the Jacobite prince's ultimate defeat] was such as most people both at home and abroad expected; but the progress of the rebels was what nobody expected; for they defeated more than once the king's troops; they overran one of the united kingdoms [i.e., Scotland] and advanced so far into the other [i.e., England] that the capital trembled at their approach; and during the tide of fortune, which had its ebbs and flows, there were moments when nothing seemed impossible; and, to say the truth, it was not easy to forecast, or to imagine, anything more unlikely than what had already happened.'[18]

Of all the points in 1745 at which 'nothing seemed impossible', December's opening days were easily the most critical. On 25 July, when Charles Edward arrived in Moidart, no outcome had appeared 'more unlikely', as John Home put it, than the prince being in a position, just four or five months later, to menace London from deep inside the English Midlands. This remarkable accomplishment, and the earth-shattering possibilities it opened up, has resulted in impassioned debate ever since about what might have happened if Charles Edward, as was the prince's own strong inclination, had ordered his Highlanders – James Stewart's Duror company among them – over Swarkestone Bridge prior to sending those same Highlanders striding off along the high road south.

In the present context, however, what matters is not what *may* have occurred on 5 December. What matters is what *did*; for in the course of what turned out to be a long, fraught day of argument, Charles Edward Stuart, usually so effortlessly persuasive and manipulative, finally ran out of credibility.

During the previous winter, while still in France, Charles Edward had repeatedly been told that the French, discouraged by the setbacks they had experienced at the start of 1744, would not make a renewed attempt to invade the United Kingdom until Britain's Jacobites organised an internal insurrection. This might have been acceptable to the prince had he not also been informed – just as regularly – that no British insurrection was possible until French troops came ashore. As it was, Charles Edward found himself locked into an unendingly circular dispute as to who exactly – France or Britain's Jacobites – should move first. Seeing no other way to break out of this impasse, Charles had decided, in the early part of 1745, to come, practically alone, to the Highlands. On reaching Moidart, the prince was told by almost everyone he met that his chosen course of action was madness. He persevered nevertheless. And by so persevering, Charles Edward quickly achieved what had been widely believed to be unachievable without French intervention. He got an armed uprising underway. Better still, he managed, by mid-September, to annihilate a British army and to install himself in the city from which so many of his Stuart ancestors had ruled Scotland. Unfortunately, this unlooked-for triumph had the effect of convincing Charles both that destiny was on his side and that he could do no wrong. In Edinburgh, when more sceptical members of his army council tried to dissuade the prince from initiating an immediate attack on England, Charles had accordingly responded – telling himself, perhaps, that his lies were simply a means to the final victory he had begun to take for granted – by wildly exaggerating the numbers of, and the extent of his contacts with, England's Jacobites. Thousands of new supporters, Charles Edward Stuart had insisted, would join him as soon as he had moved across the border into England. On news of this reaching Paris, the prince had added, his good friend and ally, King Louis XV of France, would immediately order a cross-channel invasion and thereby administer the death blow to a Hanoverian regime which Charles Edward, in the aftermath of Prestonpans, optimistically supposed to be already tottering.

Lord George Murray, the most prominent figure in Charles Edward's council, found this scenario implausible. In Edinburgh he had reluctantly agreed to do what Charles asked. But now, Lord George having brought a Scottish army further into England than anyone had ever done before, Lord George believed himself to have put Prince Charles's theories fully to the test, and in the process to have found them badly wanting. At Derby on 5 December, according to an eyewitness, Lord George told Charles Edward that his soldiers 'had now done all that could be expected of them; that they had marched into the heart of England ready to join any party that would declare for him [the prince]; that none had and . . . that there was no French landed'. Backed by every other council member except Prince Charles himself, Lord George announced that – with British formations closing in from all sides on a Jacobite force totalling not much more than 5,000 men – the time had come to retreat. Accordingly, on 6 December, which Jacobite sympathisers ever after called 'Black Friday', Charles Edward's army left Derby for the north.[19]

Nothing testifies more amply to the sheer quality of Lord George Murray's generalship than what happened next. Since 21 November, the government's forces in England had been under the command of George II's younger son, William, Duke of Cumberland, who assumed that as a result of the Jacobite pull-back from Derby, he would shortly have Charles Edward Stuart in his grasp. But for all that his little army was deep in hostile territory, and for all that his men were massively outnumbered and outgunned by the many crack troops which Britain's badly rattled politicians had brought back from the continent and placed at Cumberland's disposal, Lord George Murray ensured that neither Prince Charles (whom Murray increasingly despised) nor the prince's Highland soldiers (whom Murray increasingly esteemed) fell into Cumberland's clutches. On 18 December, at Clifton, just south of Penrith, Jacobite units – one of them the Appin Regiment – under Lord George's personal direction successfully fought off Cumberland's pursuing cavalry. And on 20 December, Charles Edward's army recrossed the River Esk – now so heavily in spate that 'the heads of the Highlanders [were] generally all that was seen above the water'.[20]

Once back in Scotland, the position of the Jacobite army – despite its withdrawal from England – was by no means hopeless. Among the army's commanders, however, morale was crumbling. A potentially significant Jacobite victory at Falkirk on 17 January 1746 was not followed up aggressively. Instead it was concluded – very much at the instigation of Charles Stewart of Ardshiel, Donald Cameron of Lochiel and other senior representatives of the army's clan regiments – that with Cumberland now in control of Edinburgh, it would be best to withdraw still further to the north with a view to regrouping and reorganising in or around Inverness. At the beginning of February in the vicinity of Crieff, therefore, the Jacobite army was split into two columns. One, under Lord George Murray, was to make for Inverness by way of Montrose and Aberdeen. The other, commanded by Prince Charles Edward and including the Appin Regiment, was to take the more direct route through Atholl and over Drumochter.

To start with, it looked as if Cumberland might follow Charles Edward into the Central Highlands. From Crieff on 5 February, however, one of his officers, Joseph Yorke, wrote gloomily: 'Every step we take here grows worse and worse, and ever since we left Stirling we have gone up hill, and I see nothing but snowy mountains above us.' Next day, conditions had deteriorated further and it was concluded that 'the Highlanders cannot be pursued by reason of the great fall of snow'.[21]

The 'cold, stormy weather' which features constantly in such correspondence as survives from February 1746, impeded Jacobite, as well as Hanoverian, mobility. Writing subsequently of the climatic horrors encountered in the course of that month's march to Inverness, John Daniel, one of the few recruits Prince Charles had gained in England, remembered: 'When we marched out of Aberdeen, it blew, snowed, hailed and froze to such a degree, that few pictures ever represented winter . . . better than many of us did that day; for men were covered with icicles hanging at their eyebrows and beards; and, an entire coldness seizing all their limbs, it may be wondered at how so many could bear up against the storm, a severe contrary wind driving snow and little cutting hail bitterly down upon our faces, in such a manner that it was impossible to see ten yards before us. And very easy it now was to lose our companions; the road being bad . . . and the paths being immediately filled up with drifted snow.'[22]

James Stewart and his little band of men from Duror, making for Inverness by way of passes reaching altitudes of well over a thousand feet, faced conditions even more extreme than those John Daniel confronted in Aberdeenshire. Snowfalls, of which the Highlands got more in the eighteenth century than the region does today, were measured by Gaelic-speakers according to the height they reached on a man's leg. Ankle-depth snow was common; knee-depth snow less usual; thigh-depth snow exceptional. But it was snow in this latter category, or even deeper, that Duror men were said to have encountered when tramping through Badenoch and Strathspey in February 1745. 'In some places,' it was said, 'the snow reached their haunches.'[23]

Although his movements must have been slowed drastically by that month's bitter weather, word of the Appin Regiment's progress was regularly brought back to Duror at this time by a young man called Duncan MacColl. Duncan – who appears to have lived with his uncle, John MacColl, in the Duror township of Achara, where John both worked a piece of land and ran a blacksmith's business – is featured in one of the several lists of Jacobite sympathisers produced by the pro-Hanoverian officials who were to pour into Duror and adjacent localities following the Jacobite rebellion's eventual collapse. The document in question refers to Duncan MacColl having served as 'post' – a letter-carrying runner, in other words – 'between this country and the rebel army'. During February and March 1746, Duncan, who shared his duties with another runner, Donald Carmichael, from Kinlochlaich near Achnacone, would have had no shortage of news to impart to the many mothers, wives and girlfriends in Duror for whom this must have been a period of almost incessant strain and worry.[24]

The Appin Regiment, as Duncan MacColl would have told inquirer after inquirer on his return to Duror with news from Charles Edward's headquarters, reached Inverness safely. There the Jacobites found both the town and its principal military strongpoint, Fort George,[25] abandoned by the pro-government force which had been holding them since the previous autumn. Rather than defend Inverness, this force (commanded by the Earl of Loudoun, a professional soldier who'd served with the British army on the continent) had withdrawn to the north. First crossing the Beauly Firth, then the Cromarty Firth and finally the Dornoch Firth, Loudoun and his men had taken refuge in the south-eastern corner of Sutherland. By various routes, a number of Jacobite formations – among them the Appin Regiment – promptly left Inverness in pursuit. 'We all joined at Dingwall,' one of the pursuers recalled, 'and marched from that to the town of Tain . . . opposite to Lord Loudoun's headquarters.' Soon those headquarters were under Jacobite attack – with the result that Loudoun, accompanied all the while by Duncan Forbes, now retreated to Skye, which was still being held for the government by Forbes' correspondent of the previous autumn, Norman MacLeod of Dunvegan.[26]

More than a hundred miles to the south, meanwhile, Lord George Murray was mounting a remarkably successful attack on the British army's forward posts in his native Perthshire. Having carefully plotted the widely separated locations of as many as thirty Hanoverian detachments, Lord George divided his available troops into small, commando-like bands whose members, at dead of night and amid intermittent squalls of hail and snow, descended more or less simultaneously on practically every one of the army's Perthshire positions. Over 400 prisoners were taken by Lord George's exultant men. And the total would have been still higher had not some British soldiers chosen, as inquiries afterwards revealed, to absent themselves – without permission – from their posts. One of those absentees, because he held an officer's commission, attracted particular censure from his superiors, some of whom wanted to have the offender court-martialled. In the event, this did not happen. But the errant officer's 'disgraceful behaviour' had been noted all the same, and it would thereafter constitute something of a black mark in the military record of a man whose name, some six years later, would be noised across Scotland – Colin Campbell of Glenure.[27]

With Perthshire thus secured, the Earl of Loudoun effectively neutralised and Fort George already in their hands, the Jacobites set out to consolidate their command of the mainland Highlands by capturing the two remaining Hanoverian strongpoints in the north: Fort Augustus in the middle reaches of the Great Glen, and Fort William at the same glen's southern end.

After a siege of a week or so, Fort Augustus was taken on 5 March. As Lord George Murray had shrewdly suspected from the start, however, Fort William proved a much more difficult proposition: 'The resolution of besieging Fort William, I did not approve, as I always had heard it was a strong place and regularly fortified. But [Cameron of] Lochiel, [MacDonald of] Keppoch and the other Highlanders who had their homes in that neighbourhood were very keen.' Among the 'other Highlanders' Lord George had in mind was the Appin Regiment's colonel, Charles Stewart, whose Ardshiel home, as would shortly become all too apparent, was extremely vulnerable to attack from Fort William. Hence the Appin Regiment's prominent role in the month-long siege which now began.[28]

Fort William was a set of fortifications which had first been constructed by Oliver Cromwell's invading troops in 1654 and which had been taken over, in 1690, by the fervently anti-Jacobite forces of King William of Orange – the monarch whose name the place has borne ever since. Thomas Pennant, who passed this way in 1769, noted – as many others have done since – that Fort William, being 'surrounded by vast mountains', was afflicted by 'almost perpetual rain'. Anne Grant, some four years later, was equally unenthusiastic, observing of the fort: '[It] looks just like a place to kill people in, it is so gloomy and uncouth: it [the fort] is triangular; the soldiers' barracks are of wood, grown black with the constant rains.' Outside the original Fort William's three-sided perimeter and a little to the south, there had developed, as eighteenth-century visitors observed, the settlement which later grew into today's town – a town which Gaelic-speakers, in recognition of Fort William's military beginnings, still call 'An Gearasdan', the garrison.[29] With a view to distinguishing this settlement from the fortress to which it owed its existence, it was named Maryburgh in honour of William of Orange's queen. 'Maryburgh,' according to a 1770 account, 'is a pretty large town, well inhabited, [consisting] of a principal street and two side-streets, and some lanes. Ships of some burden can come up to it, or to the fort, which is hard by.'[30]

Fort William had been built in 1654 at the northern tip of Loch Linnhe with a view to its being supplied by sea. And the fact that it could be so supplied was of critical importance in 1746. Recognising this, the Jacobites, during February, strongly occupied both shores of the Corran Narrows. At this point (where a ferry connected, as it still connects, Nether Lochaber with Ardgour) Loch Linnhe is only a few hundred yards wide. At Corran, as a result, naval vessels regularly came under Jacobite musket fire, with one such vessel actually falling into Jacobite hands. At the beginning of March, however, this potential stranglehold on Fort William was eased when Hanoverian troops from among the several hundred stationed at the fort were put ashore in strength at Corran. Having killed two of their Jacobite opponents and put the remainder to flight, those troops, in order to impress on local residents that it would be best for them if Jacobite activity was not resumed at Corran, first burned the homes occupied by Corran's ferrymen and next set fire to 'a little town[ship], with about twelve houses in it, a quarter mile distant from the ferry house on the north side'.[31]

All this was reported to the Duke of Cumberland who, in mid-February, had brought his army north to Aberdeen. 'I look upon Fort William to be the only fort in the Highlands that is of any consequence,' Cumberland was to inform his subordinates during March. 'I have taken all possible measures,' the duke added, 'for the security of it.' Foremost among Cumberland's 'measures' was his appointment of Captain Caroline Scott as Fort William's commander. Scott was a Lowland soldier in whose 'courage, zeal and skill', the duke commented, he placed 'great confidence'.[32]

Announcing that he 'was determined to defend the fort to the last extremity', Scott reached Fort William by sea on 13 March, just as the Jacobite attack on the garrison was getting properly underway. Aiming to deprive Fort William's besiegers of cover, the fort's new commander – with the single-minded ruthlessness that would be his hallmark for as long as he remained in the West Highlands – began by ordering that 'the town of Maryburgh', together with nearby 'garden walls', 'were all [to be] levelled'. Since any close approach henceforth faced an unobstructed and withering barrage of musket fire, Fort William's Jacobite attackers – against whom Scott also mounted a number of daring night-time raids – were kept mostly at a distance. Despite Scott's best efforts, Fort William came under Jacobite artillery bombardments several times and these bombardments, it was recorded at the time, were sufficiently accurate to ensure that 'the roofs of the fort were exceedingly damaged'. But because the Jacobites lacked really heavy guns and because 'Captain Scott had been indefatigable . . . in erecting new works', Fort William's stoutly constructed outer walls remained both intact and unassailable. A contemporary story claims that when a sentry patrolling one of the fort's perimeter bastions called to a comrade inside that all was well, a Highlander lurking some two or three hundred yards away was heard to yell: 'Yes, God damn you, too well!' From this exchange, when he was told of it, Caroline Scott no doubt derived much satisfaction. He would have been still more pleased when it became apparent on 3 April that the Jacobite siege of Fort William had been abandoned, because Charles Edward Stuart was concentrating his forces to meet Cumberland's anticipated advance on Inverness.[33]

Duror – by way of Ballachulish Ferry – was no more than a morning's walk away for those of its menfolk who took part in the siege of Fort William. Many of the Appin Regiment's Duror soldiers consequently took the chance, during March 1746, to spend some time at home. Among them was the regiment's commander, Charles Stewart, who managed, as Caroline Scott noted on 14 March, to spend several days 'at his own house'. Because of the possibility of a seaborne attack of the sort made earlier on Jacobite positions at Corran being launched against Tearlach Mòr's home at Ardshiel, the Appin Regiment's colonel, Scott went on, had surrounded himself with 'a guard of fifty men'. Intelligence reaching Scott also told him that a number of 'married men' had 'come home [to Duror] to labour the ground' – March being the month when, weather permitting, Duror's fields were made ready for sowing with the oats and barley that were then the locality's staple crops. Duror's 'single fellows', Scott thought, had mostly remained with the Jacobite battalions deployed around Fort William. On word reaching the West Highlands that the Jacobite army was being readied for battle in the vicinity of Inverness, Duror's younger men were rejoined at Fort William in early April by their older comrades – Charles Stewart, having again turned those men out of their townships before leading them off once more to war.[34]

During the early days of April 1746, then, the Appin Regiment, having come north by way of the Great Glen, returned to Inverness. On their arrival there, the regiment's soldiers, in the company of Moidart men commanded by MacDonald of Clanranald, were immediately sent east into Moray. Their destination was the River Spey, which the Duke of Cumberland's army – four days out of its winter quarters in Aberdeen and keeping up a fast pace on 'a good hard road' – reached on 12 April. 'If the rebels had defended this river,' one of Cumberland's officers commented, 'we should have found some difficulty . . . I never saw a stronger pos[ition] in my life.' Jacobite tactics, however, were in growing disarray, not least because Lord George Murray, the Jacobite commander most likely to have disputed Cumberland's crossing of the Spey, had fallen increasingly out of favour with Charles Edward Stuart in the months following the retreat from Derby. Instead of being held in strength, therefore, the line of the Spey wasn't even contested by the Jacobite army's forward troops. On 12 and 13 April, those troops, the newly arrived Appin Regiment among them, simply pulled back ahead of Cumberland who, on 14 April, reached Nairn – less than twenty miles from Inverness.[35]

Expecting the duke's advance to be resumed next day and determined to retain possession of the town that had long been – and remains – the Highland capital, Charles Edward, on the morning of 15 April, got his army into battle-order on Culloden Moor, a flat and featureless expanse of bog and heather on the summit of the ridge which separates Inverness and the Moray Firth coastline from the shallow valley of the River Nairn. Culloden Moor, 500 feet above sea level and with steadily falling ground on three of its four sides, commands impressive views: of Ben Wyvis and other mountains to the north, and of the hills beyond Strathnairn to the south. As a piece of terrain on which to give battle, however, Culloden has little to commend it. Lord George Murray, who would ideally have preferred merely to draw Cumberland deeper and deeper into the Highlands, where his formations could be harried at will, was strongly of the opinion that if King George's son had to be confronted at all, he should definitely not be confronted on Culloden Moor. 'I did not like the ground,' Lord George commented of Culloden. 'It was certainly not proper for Highlanders.' But Murray's views were disregarded by Prince Charles Edward, now looking elsewhere for advice. Rejecting Lord George's last-minute pleas to move the Jacobite army across the River Nairn, where there was at least some prospect of its making one of the downhill charges which had long been a favoured Highland battle tactic, Prince Charles determinedly lined up his regiments on Culloden Moor and waited for the Duke of Cumberland to come to him.[36]

The Hanoverian commander, however, did not oblige. Tuesday, 15 April, was Cumberland's twenty-fifth birthday and, by way of celebration, his troops were – in effect – given the day off. Instead of marching on Inverness that morning, they remained encamped at Balblair, a mile or so to the west of Nairn, which they'd reached the previous evening. There, as one of Cumberland's English soldiers afterwards recalled, 'every man had a sufficient quantity of biscuit, cheese and brandy allotted him at the sole expense of the duke'.[37]

At Culloden, meanwhile, as morning gave way to afternoon and afternoon to evening, Charles Edward was gripped by the notion that, if the Duke of Cumberland was not going to attack him, he ought to seize the initiative by attacking Cumberland. As dusk fell, then, the men of the Appin Regiment – despite being badly in need of sleep, because they'd been more or less constantly on the move for several days – found themselves ordered, with the rest of the Jacobite army, to march on Balblair. This march was made across rough country in darkness. As such, it was an enormously difficult undertaking which Lord George Murray, for one, countenanced only on the basis that it was 'better', as he put it, to brave the well-known hazards of marching by night 'than to fight upon that plain muir', about which, from the moment he glimpsed it, Lord George had the gloomiest of forebodings.[38]

Murray himself – at the head of the advancing Jacobite force and accompanied by the Appin Regiment – set a cracking pace along the north bank of the River Nairn. But several other Jacobite units failed to keep up with him, and it gradually became apparent, at a point when even the Appin Regiment were still two or three miles short of Balblair, that there was no possibility of Charles Edward's straggling formations reaching Cumberland's camp before dawn deprived them of the chance to descend on the duke's forces while the bulk of those forces were still asleep. The morning of Wednesday, 16 April, therefore, found James Stewart and his Duror subordinates back with the rest of the Jacobite army on Culloden Moor. Like every one of the other 5,000 or so men arrayed across the moor's bleak surface, Duror's contingent knew that, with the Duke of Cumberland's army again advancing steadily in their direction, no more than a few hours separated them from what was bound to be a brutal, terror-filled encounter with a force outnumbering theirs by nearly two to one.

Reflecting at the start of the nineteenth century on his many years with one of the numerous regiments which the British army was to raise in the post-Culloden Highlands, David Stewart of Garth, a Perthshire laird who was distantly related to his Appin namesakes, observed of Gaelic-speaking troops: 'The common soldier of many other countries has scarcely any other stimulus to the performance of his duty than the fear of chastisement, or the habit of mechanical obedience to command . . . With a Highland soldier it is otherwise . . . He is surrounded by the companions of his youth and the rivals of his early achievements; he feels the impulse of emulation strengthened by the consciousness that every proof which he displays, either of bravery or cowardice, will find its way to his native home . . . It is thus that, in a Highland regiment consisting of men from the same country, whose kindred and connections are mutually known, every individual feels that his conduct is the subject of observation, and that . . . he has to sustain a separate and individual reputation . . . [A Highland soldier] acts from motives within himself . . . He goes into the field resolved not to disgrace his name.'[39]

There is an element of romance in this account, perhaps. But it's true, as David Stewart claimed, that the gruesome physical punishments, involving regular whippings and the like, on which British military discipline depended, both in his time and in the era of Culloden, were scarcely ever inflicted on Highland soldiers of the type Stewart commanded. This, as David Stewart contended, is evidence that units composed of such soldiers possessed much more internal cohesion than was usual at that time. And since the units in question were the direct successors of the clan-based corps mobilised to fight for Charles Edward Stuart, it is probable that much of what David Stewart wrote about the Highland troops of a slightly later period could equally well have been written about the Duror men who, keeping close to James Stewart, their company commander, stood waiting, on the morning of 16 April 1746, for the Battle of Culloden to begin.

As David Stewart remarked of the Highland infantry he commanded towards the close of the eighteenth century, those men were all each other's neighbours and close relatives. To James Stewart, for example, his regiment's colonel, Charles Stewart, was more familiar, in James' own words, as 'a very affectionate, loving brother'. And the company James captained at Culloden may well have included – as noted previously – one of his own sons. Even if that were not so, this company would definitely have consisted very largely, maybe entirely, of men James had known all his life. As a contemporary writer observed of Jacobite officers more generally, James Stewart, then, was 'supported by his nearest relations and most immediate dependants'. And what applied to the Jacobite army's higher echelons, this same writer continued, applied equally to its lower ranks: 'The private men were also marshalled according to consanguinity. The father, the son and the brother stood next to each other.'[40]

During any age, of course, men who find themselves fighting side by side tend to develop extraordinarily strong feelings for each other. But in the western world at any rate, modern warfare – because it usually involves units composed of officers and men drawn from widely separated localities and from very varied social groupings – offers little or no insight into the emotional and psychological ramifications of being surrounded, when going into combat, by one's kith and kin. As far as David Stewart of Garth was concerned, and he was clearly in a position to know, those ramifications were, from a purely military perspective, wholly positive in that they led to soldiers such as those of the Appin Regiment developing especially powerful feelings of mutual solidarity. Maybe so. But if it helps, when staring death in the face, to have around you folk who are as close to you as anyone on earth, it must also make a battle all the more horrific if that battle culminates in your father, your son, your brother, your uncle, your nephew or your cousin dying violently and bloodily beside you.

To the Jacobite survivors of Culloden, it sometimes seemed in retrospect that the weather of 16 April 1746 was among the grimmer features of that desperately grim day. '*As an adhar bha trian ar lèiridh,*' one such survivor was to write. 'From the sky came a third of our misery.' 'It rained very sore as I ever seed,' commented one of the Duke of Cumberland's troopers, 'both hail and rain, and strong wind.' But because this wind came out of the east or south-east, Cumberland's men had the advantage of having their backs to the worst of what another of them described as 'a very cold . . . morning'. Things were worse for Charles Edward Stuart's soldiers. Lined up across Culloden Moor to meet an enemy advancing along the route they themselves had followed in the course of the previous night's debacle, they stood and stared for hours into an icy, energy-draining, morale-sapping gale. 'It was a dark, misty, rainy day,' one Jacobite staff officer remembered, 'and the wind blew in the faces of the prince's army.'[41]

That Wednesday morning, then, James Stewart and the men around him were wet, chilled and miserable. They were also desperately tired and very hungry. 'They had been several weeks without any pay and without any provisions but a scrimp allowance of oatmeal,' a London newspaper, the *National Journal*, was later to observe of the Jacobite army's troops. Those troops, on the evening of Tuesday, 15 April, after many hours spent at battle stations and with provisions consisting of a 'single biscuit each', had set out on what proved to be a pointless night march of more than twenty miles. Newly returned from this march, Prince Charles Edward Stuart's soldiers 'were obliged to engage in battle', as the *National Journal* commented, 'before they had either sleep or refreshment, which was enough to dispirit any troops in the world. Yet notwithstanding all this, their front line, especially their right, attacked with a fury next to madness'.[42]

The Jacobite right, on which the *National Journal* chose to focus, was under the overall command of Lord George Murray. Accounting for between a quarter and a third of Jacobite strength, this wing of the army consisted of three distinct formations: the 700 men of the so-called Atholl Brigade from Lord George's own part of Perthshire; the 600 men answering to Donald Cameron of Lochiel; and the 250 or 300 men of the Appin Regiment.

The Jacobite army first caught sight of their Hanoverian opponents at around eleven o'clock on the morning of Wednesday, 16 April. The Duke of Cumberland's force totalled 9,000, nearly double the numbers available to Prince Charles Edward. Unlike their Jacobite counterparts, and much to their advantage, Cumberland's men were well fed and well rested. Also to their advantage was the further circumstance that the duke's men, in contrast to Charles Edward's, belonged to an army equipped with plenty of heavy guns in the care of highly trained gunners. The extent of this particular discrepancy between the two contending forces become apparent when, at around two p.m., 'the rebels', in the words of a contemporary report, 'began firing on the king's army . . . with their cannon'. Being few, small and 'ill-served', the same report continued, those cannon 'did little execution'. Cumberland's field artillery, in contrast, was soon being deployed 'with such success as [quickly] put the rebels in great disorder'.[43]

The incessant rain and sleet had eased off a little, but the wind continued south-easterly. In other words, it blew from behind Cumberland's front line which, when the duke's pre-battle manoeuvrings had been completed, was five or six hundred yards away from the spot where James Stewart and his men were standing. On Cumberland's artillery opening up, therefore, James and his subordinates were promptly blanketed in dense clouds of drifting fumes and smoke. 'Their nostrils filled with sulphur', it was subsequently recalled of what the Jacobite army's front-line troops now experienced. More tormentingly still, those same troops were exposed to wind-propelled and still smouldering fragments of the wadding which separated cannon balls from gunpowder in the fieldpieces of the time. As a result, many of the Jacobite soldiers had 'their faces burnt'.[44]

This continued for between 20 and 40 minutes. Every few moments the evil-smelling smog enveloping the still stationary Appin Regiment was lit up by a flash from one or other of the field guns which Cumberland had positioned on his army's left. And more than once, it may be assumed, a cannonball fired by such a gun ploughed into a group of men, including those from Duror, blowing apart the bodies of those individuals unfortunate enough to be directly in its path, ripping away the limbs of others, drenching unscathed bystanders in a gruesome, stomach-wrenching mix of flesh, blood, bone and entrails.

Eventually, while Prince Charles Edward dithered hopelessly as to what orders he should issue, the Jacobite front line began to move of its own volition – not to the rear, as would have been more than pardonable in the circumstances, but in the direction of the now largely invisible Hanoverian army. This movement began in the Jacobite centre. Almost immediately, however, it spread to the Jacobite right where it was given shape and direction by Lord George Murray who promptly instructed the Atholl men, the Camerons and the Appin Regiment to charge the Hanoverian left. 'They had ... a greater confidence and trust in me than I could deserve,' Lord George commented later of the men he now ordered forward. Such was Murray's reputation that those men obeyed him instantly, running as fast as they could towards the two British regiments drawn up in front of them.[45]

In accordance with eighteenth-century custom, these regiments, Barrell's and Munro's, were named after their colonels. And because the Jacobite right was the only part of Charles Edward's army to get effectively to grips that afternoon with the Duke of Cumberland's troops, Munro's and Barrell's, as the duke himself was subsequently to acknowledge, bore the brunt of the British army's Culloden casualties. 'They . . . came running upon our frontline like troops of hungry wolves,' one British soldier recalled of the Appin Regiment, the Camerons and the Atholl men. A second Hanoverian eyewitness wrote of how the Jacobite right 'advanced on us with great swiftness and great appearance of resolution'. A third told of the Stewarts and the Camerons, 'their glittering swords in their right hands', racing 'swiftly' out of the gloom and 'making a frightful huzza'. [46]

A Highland charge of the kind James Stewart and his comrades unleashed at Culloden was a carefully considered tactic which had evolved as a means of enabling sword-wielding Highlanders to come into close and potentially devastating contact with opponents whose principal objective was to keep their enemies at a distance and to subject them, all the while, to repeated volleys of musket fire. By advancing at breakneck speed and by screaming Gaelic warcries as they ran, the Jacobite right hoped to so unnerve the soldiers they bore down on as to cause those soldiers to discharge their firearms at too long a range to do much damage. Having thus minimised their own initial casualties, the still advancing Highlanders paused suddenly within three or four yards of the opposition's front line and, raising their own muskets to their shoulders, delivered a counter-barrage of heavy musket shot which, the range now being point-blank, was shattering in its impact. Next, having flung aside their firearms and drawn their broadswords, the clansmen resumed their pell-mell rush and smashed, still screaming, into men who were either caught up in the time-consuming task of fitting a fresh ball and cartridge into their muzzle-loading muskets or who, as had happened at Prestonpans, were already taking to their heels in terror.

But such was the chaos caused by the Duke of Cumberland's prolonged and brutally effective artillery bombardment at Culloden that these tactics didn't work. Lord George Murray, reflecting later on the performance both of the Appin Regiment and of the other Highland troops under his immediate command, conceded as much: 'Their custom has always been . . . to run upon the enemy with the utmost speed so as only to receive one fire [i.e., volley] or at most two before they mixt. In the present case, they were quite in disorder and received several fires before they could come up with the enemy . . . [Also] the Highlanders lost the benefit of their own fire, for only a few who ran in quickest actually fired upon the enemy. By far the greater number, who followed as fast as they were able, could not fire as some of their own men were betwixt them and the enemy. This was a vast loss, for the fire of Highlanders is more bloody than that of any regular troops whatever.'[47]

From the perspective of the waiting infantrymen of Barrell's and Munro's regiments, the approaching Highlanders looked to be hurtling towards them, it was afterwards remarked, in 'large bodies like wedges'. Glimpsing this onrush, Cumberland's gunners switched to grapeshot. This meant that instead of loading their guns with the cannonballs they'd formerly been using, they began loading them with previously prepared canisters containing a lethal mix of musket bullets, nails and scrap iron. The effect on the rapidly advancing Highlanders was catastrophic. 'Their lines were formed so thick', recalled one British soldier, 'that the grapeshot made open lanes quite through them, the men dropping down by wholesale.'[48]

But still James Stewart, his Duror men and those around them managed to retain their forward momentum. After firing very irregularly at a considerable distance, a Hanoverian officer commented of the Highland attack on Barrell's and Munro's, 'they [the Highlanders] rushed furiously in upon them [the British infantry], thinking to carry down all before them as they had done on former occasions. However, they found themselves grossly mistaken; for, though by the violence of the shock Barrell's regiment was a little staggered, yet Major-General Huske, who commanded the second line, perceiving where the weight was felt, rode up to the regiment and, bidding the men push home with their bayonets, was so well received by these brave fellows that hundreds perished on their points'.[49]

At his Ardshiel sword school and in the course of the repeated drills to which he had subjected the Appin Regiment during the months since he'd taken command of it, Charles Stewart had trained his troops in the mechanics of how to cope with bayonets, then a relatively new weapon. At Prestonpans and Falkirk, techniques like those Stewart favoured had been deployed to good effect. Later those techniques were to be described in detail by one of the Ardshiel laird's fellow Jacobites: 'When within reach of the enemy's bayonets, bending their left knee, they [the Highlanders], by their attitude, cover their bodies with their targets [or shields] [in order to] receive the thrusts of the bayonets, which they contrive to parry while, at the same time, they raise their sword-arm and strike their adversary.'[50]

Having, by those means, 'got within the bayonets and into the ranks of the enemy', Highland troops, according to this same Jacobite writer, were virtually irresistible: 'The [enemy's] soldiers have no longer any means of defending themselves, the fate of the battle is decided in an instant and . . . carnage follows.'[51]

During the time they'd spent in Aberdeen, however, the Duke of Cumberland's soldiers had received intensive training in how more effectively to cope with Highland broadswords. Instead of attempting to break through the guard of such sword-bearing Highlanders as appeared immediately in front of him, each soldier was instructed that he should thrust his bayonet under the uupraised sword-arm of the attacking Highlander immediately to his right. According to one battlefield dispatch from Culloden, this was exactly how the men of Barrell's and Munro's dealt with the Appin Regiment: 'Before [the adoption of those new methods], the bayonet-man attacked the sword-man fronting him; now the left-hand bayonet attacked the sword fronting his next right-hand man . . . This manner made an essential difference, staggered the enemy who were not prepared to alter their way of fighting, and destroyed them in a manner rather to be conceived than told.'[52]

The odds against a Jacobite victory were mounting as fast as the Jacobite casualty count. But another contemporary report from Culloden makes it clear that the Atholl Brigade, the Camerons and the Appin Regiment were by no means instantly disposed of: 'The enemy's attack on the left wing of the [British] army was made with a view to break that wing, to run it into disorder and then to communicate [this] disorder to the whole army. This could not be easily effected when a second and third line were ready to sustain the first. But it must be owned that the attack was made with the greatest courage, ardour and bravery. Amidst the hottest fire of small arms and continual firing of cannon with grapeshot . . . they [the Highlanders] ran in upon the points of the bayonets, hewed down the soldiers, drove them back and . . . possessed themselves of two pieces of cannon.'[53]

So many of their comrades had already been killed or brought down by repeated discharges of grapeshot and volley after volley of musket fire that the surviving men of the Appin Regiment, in order to engage with Barrell's and Munro's forward troops, had, in many instances, to jump or clamber over the bodies of their own dead and dying. Together with the rest of the Jacobite right, they neverless succeeded – as is evident from the Hanoverian sources already quoted – in silencing two of Cumberland's guns and breaking through the first of the three lines in which the duke's infantry had been deployed. This, though, was the high point of such small success as Charles Edward's troops achieved at Culloden. With no other part of the Jacobite army succeeding even in making contact with the Duke of Cumberland's front line, and with no reinforcements immediately available in their own sector, the Appin Regiment, the Camerons and the Atholl men were unable to make any further progress. 'There was scarce a soldier or officer of Barrell's and of that part of Munro's which engaged', runs a further Culloden dispatch, 'who did not kill one or two men each.' 'The Highlanders', another eyewitness account goes on, 'fought like furies . . . It was dreadful to see the enemies' swords circling in the air as they were raised from the strokes; and no less to see the officers of the [British] army, some cutting with their swords, others pushing with their spontoons, the sergeants running their halberds into the throats of their opponents, the men ramming their fixed bayonets [in] up to the sockets.'[54]

Two or three more minutes passed. On the British army's left, where

Barrell's and Munro's regiments were contriving to hold their ground, those Highlanders still on their feet 'at first made a short pause, [next] retreated a little, and then, turning round, fled with the utmost precipitation'. Soon, according to a Hanoverian observer, there 'followed a general carnage. The moor was covered with blood; and our men, what with killing the enemy, dabbling their feet in the blood, and splashing it about one another, looked like so many butchers.'[55] 'I never saw such a dreadful slaughter,' one of Cumberland's soldiers remembered. 'We . . . could hardly march for dead bodies,' another recalled. 'Sure, never such slaughter was made in so short a time.'[56]

Adding substantially to the number of Highlanders killed as the Jacobite right began to fall back were those ancient enemies of the Appin Stewarts, the Campbells. During the preceding winter, there had been raised on the extensive Campbell lands in Argyll some twenty companies of militia. Several of these companies served at Culloden. Among them was one commanded by Donald Campbell of Airds, who had not long before acquired the ownership of Duror townships like Acharn and Keil – and who was so passionately anti-Jacobite in his politics that, for several months past, he had insisted on serving King George without pay. 'There never was a more complete victory obtained,' Donald Campbell wrote within days of Culloden. The Appin Regiment and the rest of the Jacobite right, Campbell added, 'were received with such a close and hot fire from our small arms that they soon gave ground and fled outright – which, by the by, was the pleasantest sight I ever beheld.'[57]

With other units of the Argyll Militia, Donald Campbell's company had succeeded in outflanking the Jacobite army by occupying a piece of ground lying beyond a turf and stone boundary wall on Culloden Moor's southern fringes. Before the battle Lord George Murray, suspecting that the wall in question might provide Cumberland's soldiers with just this sort of cover, had wanted it levelled. But those who had replaced Lord George in Charles Edward Stuart's affections had seen no point to this. The wall was left standing. From behind it, Donald Campbell's troops were able to pour fusillade after fusillade into the withdrawing Appin Regiment. So smoke-filled was Culloden's air by this point that it is unlikely that Campbell and his subordinates could see their targets clearly. But among those targets were Duror men – such as James Stewart – whom the Airds laird certainly knew personally. Whether this made him more or less willing to gun down such fleeing Jacobites as came within range of his company's muskets, Campbell did not record. But it is evident that as a result of the actions taken by Campbell and his Argyll Militia associates, Culloden became one of the many Campbell–Stewart encounters constituting the hate-filled background to the murder for which

James Stewart would one day hang. The victim of this murder, Colin Campbell of Glenure, made this plain in his reaction to the battle. Although not actually present at Culloden on 16 April, Colin Campbell warmly welcomed the engagement's outcome when, five days later, he had occasion to to write to his brother, John Campbell of Barcaldine: 'The Argyllshire men by all accounts behaved gallantly and did great execution . . . It gives me great pleasure our friends behaved so well.'[58]

There was good cause for further Campbell gratification when the extent of the Appin Regiment's Culloden losses became apparent. In the course of a battle lasting less than an hour, 92 of the regiment's men were killed and a further 65 were wounded. Well over half the regiment's fighting strength had fallen victim to the Duke of Cumberland's troops, with a third or more of the regiment's total personnel being among the many hundreds of Jacobite dead.

A clan regiment's officers always led from the front, so the Stewart gentry of Duror and the rest of Appin suffered disproportionately. Six of the Appin Regiment's thirteen company captains died at Culloden. And though the regiment's colonel, Charles Stewart of Ardshiel, and his half-brother, James Stewart, escaped unscathed, no fewer than eight other members of Charles' family were killed. Alexander Stewart of Invernahyle – who was himself wounded – saw three members of his immediate family die. Also among the Appin Regiment's dead were eighteen men by the name of MacColl, thirteen MacLarens, six Carmichaels, five MacCombies, four MacInneses and four Livingstones – the latter including, or so his great-grandson claimed, the great-grandfather of David Livingstone, who, a hundred years later, would become one of Victorian Britain's most renowned missionaries and explorers.

'Everybody allowed who saw them dead in the field of battle', it was noted of the Jacobite slain by a Hanoverian commentator, 'that men of a larger size, larger limbs, and better proportioned, could not be found.' Maybe so. But neither their physical strength nor their almost unbelievable bravery were to keep two or three dozen Duror men out of the heaped-up and grassed-over mass graves which can still be seen at Culloden. Among the corpses consigned to one such grave was that of Donald Carmichael – in charge, until the previous August, of Duror's Taigh na h-Insaig. Among these corpses, too, was that of an Appin Regiment soldier who had been so agonisingly wounded by musket fire or grapeshot that he had begged his own younger brother to put him out of his misery. The brother of whom this final favour was asked, according to nineteenth-century tradition, was named Duncan MacColl. Duncan came from Duror, and when Culloden was fought, it is said, he was no more than sixteen years of age.[59] Coming across his horrifyingly maimed brother (only slightly older than himself) just as the Appin Regiment was starting to pull back from its bloody confrontation with Barrell's and Munro's, Duncan, with feelings that can scarcely be imagined, heard his brother – whose name has not survived – say that he would 'rather be despatched' than suffer any longer. 'On hearing this,' or so the story went a century later, 'Duncan dashed out his [brother's] brains with the butt-end of his musket.'[60]

At the point – around three o'clock on the afternoon of Wednesday, 16 April 1746 – when sixteen-year-old Duncan MacColl was killing his brother, much of the centre and left of the Jacobite army had so far disintegrated that the units composing those sectors had practically ceased to exist. This would make soldiers from such units easy prey for the Duke of Cumberland's cavalry, who, in the course of the next hour or so, were to kill scores, maybe hundreds, of the Jacobite troops in question. On the Jacobite right, however, Lord George Murray was typically managing to conjure some degree of order from the confusion all around him. While the remnants of the rest of Prince Charles Edward Stuart's army scattered chaotically northwards in the direction of Inverness, and while the prince himself fled westwards into Stratherrick with just one or two companions, Murray retreated in reasonably good order to the south. He crossed the River Nairn with what he hoped might still become the nucleus of a reconstituted fighting force, making for the comparative safety of Strathspey and Badenoch.

The rain and sleet which had so afflicted the Jacobite army on Culloden Moor had fallen as snow at higher altitudes. The enormously depleted ranks of the Appin Regiment accompanying Lord George Murray over the hills separating Culloden from Strathspey – many of those ranks consisting of the regiment's walking wounded – found themselves 'mid-leg deep' in wind-blown drifts. It would have been understandable if, facing this fresh misery, James Stewart and the rest of Culloden's Duror survivors – all of them worn out, traumatised and starving – had finally given up. But pausing only to snatch a few hours' sleep, their first for two days, they pressed on, falling in, en route, with three or four hundred Badenoch men who had come north too late for the battle and tramping on, in the company of those men, by way of Carrbridge, Aviemore and Kincraig, to Ruthven.[61]

At Ruthven, near Kingussie, the Hanoverian authorities had some years previously constructed a fortified barracks complex on a knoll which had earlier been surmounted by a medieval castle. This barracks, taken by the Jacobite army during its northwards march to Inverness in February, now became Lord George Murray's rallying point. Including the Badenoch contingent he'd picked up while bound for Ruthven, Lord George, on arriving there towards dusk on 17 April, had well over a thousand troops at his disposal. Some of those he at once sent to hold the various mountain passes giving access to Badenoch.

The remainder, he hoped, might yet provide him with the means of embarking on a further war, of the kind he had urged on Charles Edward Stuart prior to Culloden. Had a pitched battle been avoided, Lord George contended, his Highland soldiers 'could have made a summer campaign without risk of any misfortune; they could have marched through the hills . . . by ways that regular troops could not have followed . . . and might have fallen upon the enemy when least expected'. But Charles Edward, it soon became apparent, had lost his stomach for conflict. Intent only on getting back to France – which he reached some five months later – the prince's final communication with the remnants of his army was, in effect, an order to disband. There was appended no word of thanks or appreciation for what had been achieved by so many Highlanders on his behalf. Instead, the order read simply: 'Let every man seek his own safety the best way he can.'[62]

Recognising that 'all was [now] to no purpose', Lord George penned an embittered letter to the man for whom he had done so much. 'It was surely wrong', he told Prince Charles, 'to set up the royal standard [at Glenfinnan] without having positive assurance from His Most Christian Majesty [meaning Louis XV of France] that he would assist you with all his might.' Pro-Jacobite writers have ever since regarded those sentiments as amounting to little better than treachery; that most romantic of twentieth-century Jacobite romantics, Compton MacKenzie, going so far as to call Lord George's letter 'contemptible'. But Murray, who had more than earned the right to be critical of Charles Edward Stuart, was arguably not too far wide of the mark. By all thinking Jacobites, a category which included Charles Stewart of Ardshiel and Donald Cameron of Lochiel as well as Lord George, it had long been recognised that no Jacobite uprising was likely to succeed in mid-eighteenth-century Britain unless it had active and energetic backing from France. By constantly telling his followers that such backing would be forthcoming when he had not the slightest basis for supposing that it would, Charles Edward had been guilty of wishful thinking at best – of bad faith at worst. This accusation lay at the heart of Lord George Murray's letter from Ruthven. It is an accusation that has deservedly sullied Charles Edward Stuart's reputation ever since.[63]

At Ruthven, on or about Sunday, 20 April 1746, the remnants of the last non-government army to have existed in Britain began to disperse. The Appin Regiment's colonel, Charles Stewart, headed west for Lochaber, where he intended to link up with Cameron of Lochiel – who, despite having received temporarily disabling wounds at Culloden, continued to harbour notions of maintaining some sort of armed resistance to the Duke of Cumberland. The other Duror men who were at Ruthven – a category which presumably included James Stewart – wanted only to get home. This, however, was no straightforward task. In 1746, as today, anyone making a journey from Badenoch to Duror would be inclined to take a south-westward route by way of Laggan and Glen Spean. But straddling that route was Fort William, where the garrison's recently triumphant commander, Caroline Scott, was already sending out parties of troops to search for survivors of Culloden. It is probable, therefore, that the Appin Regiment's now demobilised veterans accompanied Lord George Murray south across Drumochter into Perthshire.

From Glen Garry, just beyond Drumochter, the Duror men may have trekked west by way of Glen Errochty and Kinlochrannoch. Lord Glenorchy, who headed the segment of Clan Campbell which included the Campbells of Barcaldine, reported as much from his base at Taymouth Castle – situated a little to the west of Aberfeldy and the place, incidentally, where Colin Campbell of Glenure illicitly spent the March night that saw Lord George Murray's capture of the soldiers Campbell was supposedly commanding. 'Upon the first news of this defeat [i.e., Culloden],' Glenorchy wrote on 23 April, 'I gave orders to watch the passes and to seize all who attempted to go through this country.' But to issue such a command was one thing, to enforce it quite another. 'A great many have crossed the country with their arms,' a rueful Glenorchy reported, in groups 'greatly too strong to be stopped'. The members of one such group, it is virtually certain, would have been bound for Duror. Probably they crossed Rannoch Moor and, dropping down into Glencoe, reached their own country by way of Ballachulish.[64]

Chapter Four

A little after we had started, the sun shone upon a little moving clump of scarlet close in along the waterside to the north. It was much of the same red as soldiers' coats; every now and then, too, there came little sparks and lightnings, as though the sun had struck upon bright steel. I asked my boatman what it should be; and he answered he supposed it was some of the red soldiers coming from Fort William into Appin, against the poor tenantry of the country.

Robert Louis Stevenson, *Kidnapped*

As often happened in the eighteenth century, the West Highland spring of 1746 was slow to arrive. John Daniel, the Englishman who had joined Charles Edward Stuart's army the previous November and who found himself in Lochaber during the fortnight following the army's disintegration, had to go to ground for 'several days' as a result of 'the prodigious quantity of snow that fell upon the mountains'. But even the most protracted of eighteenth-century winters – seasons always accompanied, in the words of a Duror clergyman of the period, by 'colds and coughs', 'fevers and fluxes' – had to give way eventually. As always, the end of April and the early part of May, when Duror's Culloden survivors were arriving home, would have brought higher temperatures and some at least of those astonishingly clear, sunny mornings when Duror hillsides seem visibly to be greening over and when Duror woods sound as if they've suddenly been colonised by half the world's cuckoos. Four or five months into 1746, then, Duror, if not quite the 'fruitful and beautiful country' one eighteenth-century visitor described it as, would certainly have been looking its best. And it would surely have appeared more than usually welcoming to men who, two or three weeks before, must have thought it unlikely that they would ever see Duror again.[1]

The veterans of recently ended conflicts had been returning to Duror from time immemorial, of course. And the men who arrived home from Culloden seem to have thought initially that the war they'd fought in, just like all the wars which had gone before, would sooner or later be followed by further hostilities of much the same type. The Marquis of Montrose's uprising in 1644 and 1645 had been succeeded by the rebellion of 1689, and that rebellion had itself been succeeded by the further fighting of 1715, so was it not conceivable, indeed probable, that the campaign in which they had participated might turn out – or so ex-members of the Appin Regiment's Duror contingent may have speculated in Taigh na h-Insaig – to be no more than the latest episode of a saga destined to go on unfolding far into the future? It was this kind of thinking, surely, that lay behind the fact that the Duror men who had been at Culloden took care, when on the battlefield and when fleeing from it, to keep hold of a remarkable number of broadswords, muskets and other weapons. This mentality, too, explains why so much effort went into rescuing and safeguarding that still-surviving relic of Culloden, the Appin Regiment's battle standard.

Consisting of a yellow saltire sewn on to a blue background, the Appin Regiment's banner had been carried from Culloden – where, tradition insists, both its original bearer and several of his successors died – by Donald Livingstone, another of the regiment's teenage soldiers. At great additional risk to his own life, Livingstone – with bullets whistling about his head – took time, at a point when everyone around him was in rapid retreat, to pick up the fallen standard, to rip the muddied yellow-and-blue banner from its pole and to wrap this banner round his waist. Thus it came about that in the course of May 1746, a month which saw the ceremonial burning in Edinburgh of the first of the sixteen Jacobite colours captured by the British army at Culloden, the Appin Regiment's battle standard was being carefully hidden away by Stewarts, who, despite the disaster of 16 April, expected this emblem of their clan's commitment to the Jacobite cause to be carried into action on some future occasion. In the event, it never was – Culloden proving to be merely the prelude to change so cataclysmic that first Jacobitism and second clanship itself were eliminated from the Highland scene.

In retrospect, this most far-reaching of transformations can be seen to have had numerous underlying causes – causes stemming from the inherent impossibility of an essentially tribal society continuing to exist indefinitely inside the boundaries of a state that was beginning to be comprehensively reshaped by the forces unleashed by eighteenth-century Britain's industrial revolution. Since those forces were to destroy equally deep-rooted ways of life all around the globe, it was inevitable that Highland clanship – because of its geographical proximity to industrialism's birthplace – would become one of the earliest victims of the new order. But what was by no means inevitable was that the United Kingdom's assault on clanship would acquire the uncompromising, brutal and unforgiving character it took on during 1746. This was wholly due to circumstance; it was due, in particular, to the apprehensions induced, and the antagonisms engendered, by Highland clans like the Appin Stewarts having played so major a role in Prince Charles Edward Stuart's indubitably reckless, but nonetheless remarkably successful, attempt to engineer the violent overthrow of Britain's Hanoverian establishment.

The men who mattered in the United Kingdom of the mid-eighteenth century were badly rattled by the events of 1745. And because they knew that the inhabitants of places like Duror had played an influential role in those events, the same men were united in their determination to ensure that Highlanders, when opportunity allowed, were treated harshly. In part, this was because frightened people tend to lash out at the source of that fright. But longer-term calculations were also involved. By teaching Highlanders that rebellion led to pain and misery, the British government aimed to make Highland uprisings less likely. By eradicating the bonds of clanship which had enabled Charles Stewart of Ardshiel, Donald Cameron of Locheil and others to provide Charles Edward with a ready-made army, the government hoped ultimately to make such uprisings impractical.

From his friend and close colleague, the Earl of Chesterfield, the Duke of Newcastle, one of Britain's most influential politicians, received pointer after pointer as to appropriate policy priorities for the Highlands. 'There must be alertness and vigour in crushing of this [the rebellion],' Chesterfield advised in December 1745, 'and unrelenting severity in punishing it afterwards.' It had to be kept firmly in mind, Chesterfield commented three months later, that Highlanders were 'not enemies but criminals'. What the government should do, therefore, was 'starve the whole country [meaning the Highlands] indiscriminately, put a price upon the heads of the chiefs and let the Duke [of Cumberland] put all to fire and sword'.[2]

Joseph Yorke, a military man serving on Cumberland's staff, was of much the same opinion. 'The want of several necessities has obliged us to stop here,' Yorke wrote from Perth on 8 February. 'But I hope soon we shall be able to move forward and extirpate the race [of Highlanders] . . . I hope we may not be deprived of the power to revenge the nation on the beggarly wretches . . . The thing [meaning rebellion] must be put an end to so effectually that it will never be able to break out again . . . I don't doubt that it will be at least a summer's work to clear those parts of 'em [rebels] and to destroy their clannism, but it must be gone though with.'[3]

Those were the Duke of Cumberland's sentiments exactly. They had been sent north, the king's son told his soldiers at the end of January, 'to crush the insolence of a set of thieves and plunderers'. So ingrained was this 'insolence', Cumberland appears to have concluded at one stage, that 'the only sure remedy for establishing quiet' might lie in the wholesale 'transporting of particular clans' to Britain's colonies in America. 'It is feared', the duke explained, 'that while they [the clans in question] remain [in Scotland] . . . their rebellious and thievish nature is not to be kept under without an army always in reach of them.' Mass deportations would have involved huge costs as well as other difficulties, however. And the closer he got to the Highlands, the more convinced Cumberland seems to have become that the region's recalcitrant inhabitants could rapidly be brought to heel by 'some stroke of military authority and severity'. When in Aberdeen, the duke accordingly made known that 'all methods' might legitimately be 'used for disarming the disaffected people in the hills'. And by way of making clear exactly what methods he had in mind, Cumberland, prior to advancing on Inverness, ordered troops into the Angus and Deeside glens with instructions that they were 'to burn the habitations of all those . . . [suspected of being] with the rebels'. 'Parties were immediately sent out through the country,' it was duly reported. 'Most of the rebel gentlemen's houses on Deeside were plundered, and some burnt.'[4]

Word of those events would have reached Duror in the weeks preceding Culloden. Still more alarming would have been news of simultaneous occurrences in Morvern – just a few miles away on the other side of Loch Linnhe. There, on 10 March 1746, soldiers and marines put ashore from a most appropriately named British warship, *The Terror*, embarked on an orgy of destruction across a wide area. In a single day, according to one of the officers involved, 'near 400 houses, amongst which were several barns well filled with corn, horses, cows, meal and other provisions, were destroyed by fire and firearms'.[5]

Soon the Morvern burnings were rumoured to have been accompanied by other atrocities – including, it was claimed in a letter reaching Alexander Stewart of Invernahyle from Donald Cameron of Lochiel towards the end of March, 'stripping of women and children and exposing them to the open fields and severity of the weather'. An outraged Alexander Stewart duly fired off a letter of his own to one of the many pro-Hanoverian soldiers the Invernahyle laird knew personally. 'I am heartfelt sorry that the burning of houses and destruction of cattle is . . . begun in our country,' Alexander Stewart wrote. 'If my friends and I should differ about the government of the nation, I always thought it was better we decided in the [battle]field than bring our sentiments upon innocent wives and children.' As ensuing weeks were all too amply to demonstrate, however, old-fashioned chivalry of the type by which Stewart of Invernahyle set such store meant nothing either to the Duke of Cumberland or to his subordinates.[6]

On and around Culloden Moor, both on 16 April and during the following two or three days, Cumberland's troops shot and bayoneted substantial numbers of the Jacobite wounded. This was by way of signalling that Highlanders – being both rebels and primitives from the British government's perspective – were not entitled to the consideration that would automatically have been extended to the soldiers of a more 'civilised' enemy, such as France. The same message was to be rammed home across the West Highlands when, in mid-May, the Duke of Cumberland marched his army out of Inverness – which had been his base since the evening of the day of the Battle of Culloden – and headed for Fort Augustus.

From Fort Augustus, during the rest of May and into June, the British army was unleashed on the lower part of the Great Glen, Lochaber and adjacent districts. An early target was Donald Cameron of Lochiel's home at Achnacarry. 'The order was to set fire to his [Cameron's] mansion,' one of Cumberland's soldiers recalled. 'His fine chairs, tables and all his cabinet goods were set a-fire and burnt with his house. His fine fruit garden, above a mile long, was pulled to pieces and laid waste. A beautiful summerhouse that stood in the pleasure garden was also set on fire, and everything valuable burnt or destroyed.' Soon the homes of several other Jacobite chiefs had also gone up in flames. 'Vast numbers of the common people's houses or huts are likewise laid in ashes,' a southern periodical was informed by a military correspondent. 'All the cattle, sheep, goats, etc. are carried off; and several poor people, especially women and children, have been found dead in the hills, supposed to be starved.'[7]

'There's still so many more houses to burn,' one of Cumberland's senior officers, General Henry Hawley, lamented in the course of a letter sent to England from Fort Augustus in June, 'and, I hope, still some [rebels] to be put to death. Tho' by computation there's about seven thousand houses burned already, yet all is not done.'[8]

'We get great quantities of cattle and burn and destroy some of the country,' Hawley's colleague, Joseph Yorke, reported on 26 May, 'but I hope we shall destroy much more; was it left to me I would not trust one of the Highlanders.' Some of the latter were beginning to surrender their weapons, Yorke wrote on 3 June. 'Such as do not submit,' he went on, 'are pursued and put to the sword as rebels in arms, their cottages and husbandry gear burnt, and all their cattle drove away and disposed of.'[9]

The notion that every Highlander was by definition a traitor – and that any Highlander killed by the army deserved, therefore, to die – was made explicit in orders issued to the commander of the men sent to set fire to Cameron of Lochiel's residence. He was 'to destroy as many of them [the rebels] as he can', this officer was told, 'since prisoners would only embarrass him; and in case the country people did not come in immediately, deliver up all their arms and submit to the king's mercy, he was to burn and destroy their habitations, seize all the cattle, and put the men to death, being pretty well assured it will be difficult for him to shed innocent blood on that account'. [10]

Towards the end of May, the Duke of Cumberland sent another party, this one headed by a Major Lockhart, into Glen Moriston 'to do military execution'. 'He is just returned,' it was reported of Lockhart from Fort Augustus on 31 May, 'killed about 17, burnt above 400 houses and drove home 1,400 head of cattle. Some of the killed were hung up by their heels with labels expressing the reasons for it.' [11]

The man charged initially with the task of ensuring that the Duke of Cumberland's orders were carried out in Duror was General John Campbell, a professional soldier who'd been brought back from the continent in December 1745 to take command of the Argyll Militia. Since the latter was essentially Clan Campbell in another guise, the general was an obvious candidate for this position. Personally, he took no active part in Cumberland's pre-Culloden campaigns. But he did have something of a directing role, from his base at Inveraray, in the defensive operations which ensured the survival of the Hanoverian garrison at Fort William. And no sooner had news of Culloden's outcome reached him than the general began to move against those most longstanding of Campbell foes, the Stewarts of Appin. 'By Wednesday evening,' John Campbell informed the Duke of Cumberland on Saturday, 3 May, 'I shall have a body of 600 men encamped in [the] Appin country for [the purpose of] enforcing an order I gave out some time past to oblige the rebels in this country . . . to deliver up their arms.' [12]

Even at the height of Charles Edward's rebellion, the government had managed to retain something of a presence in Stewart territory – this presence taking the shape of the dozen or so troops, officered by yet another Campbell, holding Castle Stalker. Standing on a tiny island in Loch Linnhe, this little fortress (which remains in existence) had once been in the possession of the Appin Stewarts themselves. During the seventeenth century, however, it had been acquired by the Campbells of Airds – one of whom, or so tradition has it, was fortunate enough, in the course of an exceptionally drunken evening, to persuade a claret-filled Stewart of Appin to exchange Castle Stalker for an eight-oared galley. Be that as it may, Stalker remained in Campbell hands from the seventeenth century into the eighteenth. And though it posed no major military threat to the Jacobites during the winter of 1745–46, the castle's commander, an Islay man by the name of Donald Campbell, was able to keep the British authorities well informed as to what was going on in Charles

Stewart of Ardshiel's back yard.

Towards the end of the first week of May 1746, Donald Campbell's previously isolated soldiers, who had had to be supplied by sea for several months, found themselves in the company of the several hundred militiamen John Campbell brought with him to Appin. Mostly quartered in tents pitched on fields below Appin House, the home of that most ineffectual of Stewart chiefs, Dougal Stewart, Campbell's troops were ultimately responsible to the Duke of Cumberland. And his plans for them were clear from the outset. He was 'to distress the rebels by all the ways possible to bring them to a total submission', one of Cumberland's aides informed General Campbell. The duke, Campbell was further instructed, 'would have you make incursions into the country of those who have not brought in their arms'.[13]

From Inverness, where he spent the weeks immediately following Culloden, Donald Campbell of Airds wrote to the general to tell him that he, for one, was 'extremely glad to hear of you being in our neighbourhood'. Well aware that many of his Duror tenants had served with the Appin Regiment, whose destruction he had assisted with on the afternoon of 16 April, the Airds laird was naturally anxious that those tenants should cause the authorities no further trouble. General Campbell, it transpired, had some positive news in that regard. 'Some of . . . Airds's people have delivered in their arms to me,' he reported on 11 May. But this, the general went on to complain, was by no means the standard response, whether in Duror or in the rest of Appin, to his repeated calls for weapons to be handed over. 'The people in this country are very backward in obeying the order given for that purpose, but they will and must repent it very soon.'[14]

The means by which General Campbell intended to induce such repentance became apparent in Duror on Wednesday and Thursday, 21 and 22 May. '[On] Wednesday and Thursday', the general reported to Cumberland's headquarters on the Saturday following, 'I sent out two parties which brought in all the cattle that could be found upon the farms of Stewart of Ardshiel and Stewart of Ballachulish. The whole is sold to people who do not belong to this country, and a party ordered to see them over the ferries [at Shian on Loch Creran and at Bonawe on Loch Etive] to prevent them [the confiscated cattle] being brought back. The money which is near £200 [an enormous sum in eighteenth-century terms] is to be given amongst the private men.'[15]

Prudently, John Campbell did not reveal to Cumberland the contents of a letter he dispatched the same weekend to Isabel Stewart, Charles Stewart of Ardshiel's wife, whose cattle – together with the cattle of her husband's tenants – the general's men had appropriated only three or four days earlier. 'Madam,' Campbell wrote, 'your misfortune and the unhappy situation [Stewart of]

Ardshiel has brought you and your innocent children into, by being so deeply concerned in this unjust and unnatural rebellion, make my heart ache. I know the king to be compassionate and merciful. I know the brave duke, under whose command and orders I act, to have as much humanity as any man on earth; from which, and with my own natural inclination, I have taken the liberty of ordering back your milk cows, six wethers and as many lambs; the men who pretend a right to them shall be paid. I have taken the freedom at the same time of ordering two bolls of meal, out of my own stores . . . which I desire you to accept for the use of yourself and little ones; and if what I write can have any weight, I most earnestly entreat you to bring up your children to be good subjects to His Majesty [King George]. I wish your husband, by surrendering himself to the Duke of Cumberland, had given me an opportunity of recommending him to His Majesty's mercy. I feel for you, and am, madam, your most obedient and humble servant, John Campbell.'[16]

Despite his ritual affirmation of Cumberland's 'humanity', in extending this helping hand to Isabel Stewart and her family, General Campbell was acting in flat defiance of the duke's orders. When some of his soldiers – encouraged, it seems, by such military wives as managed to join their menfolk at Fort Augustus – had made oatmeal available to starving women and children who begged them for it, Cumberland had posted the following instructions: 'There is no meal to be sold to any person but soldiers . . . If any soldier, soldier's wife or any person belonging to the army is known to sell, or give, any meal to any Highlander or any person of the country, they shall be first whipped severely for disobeying this order and then put on meal and water . . . for a fortnight.'[17]

As he made clear in his letter to Isabel, Campbell had to buy back the cows, sheep and lambs he restored to her from the troops who had seized them. Similarly, he had had to purchase the oatmeal (more than two hundredweights in total) he sent her at the same time. John Campbell's charity to Isabel Stewart cost him no small sum. So why did Campbell rush so expensively and at such risk to the aid of a woman everyone, John Campbell included, had long known to be as fanatically Jacobite as anyone in the Highlands? Perhaps straightforward sympathy for an attractive and vulnerable woman in a desperate plight had something to do with the general's gesture. But bearing in mind that no such gesture was made by the Argyll Militia's commander to any of the other Duror residents who had been similarly deprived of their livestock, it may not be overly cynical to suggest an additional motive. Although he had managed to bring Charles Stewart of Ardshiel's neighbouring Jacobite chief, Alexander MacDonald of Glencoe, to account during May 1746, General Campbell had failed to discover the whereabouts of the Appin Regiment's former colonel. When coming to the help of Charles' hard-pressed wife, the general would certainly not have expected her to respond by betraying her husband – he knew Isabel too well for that. But it might have occurred to him that his investment in those returned cattle and that consignment of oatmeal might yield a worthwhile dividend in the form of some carelessness on Isabel Stewart's part – carelessness which, with a bit of luck, would provide John Campbell with a badly needed pointer as to Charles Stewart's hiding place.

Immediately following Lord George Murray's dissolution of the Jacobite army at Ruthven, during the closing days of April 1746, Charles Stewart had travelled to Lochaber. There the Ardshiel laird made contact with Donald Cameron of Lochiel, who, for all that he'd been semi-immobilised as a result of injuries caused by fragments of grapeshot taken in both ankles at Culloden, was still casting around for some means to keep Jacobite hopes alive. 'It was determined', or so it was afterwards recalled by someone present at the ensuing discussions, 'to attempt raising a body of good men, and with them to keep the hills, till such time as they [Cameron and Stewart] could be satisfied that the French either were, or were not, in earnest to support them.' There followed a further gathering at Murlaggan – deep in the mountains to the west of Donald Cameron's house at Achnacarry – on 8 May. Those who attended this meeting, including several Jacobite chiefs, agreed that a number of West Highland clans, including the Stewarts of Appin, should 'raise in arms . . . all the able-bodied men' available to them – with a view, as Cameron of Locheil informed a fellow conspirator on 15 May, to 'preparing for a summer campaign'. With the Duke of Cumberland's troops moving in strength into the West Highlands, however, the prospects for such a campaign, which had never been high, were rapidly reduced to zero. Before another week had passed, a now homeless Donald Cameron was hiding out, with just one or two trusted followers, in the hills to the south of Loch Eil – while Charles Stewart, for his part, was making his way back to Duror.[18]

Since Duror was awash with General John Campbell's men at this time, the Ardshiel laird's position was precarious in the extreme. If captured, Charles Stewart knew, he was very likely – as a rebel ringleader who had served on Prince Charles Edward Stuart's army council – to be executed. Admittedly, just as Charles Stewart got back to Duror General Campbell was telling Isabel, Charles' wife, that if her errant husband were to give himself up, he would personally be prepared to put in a good word with King George II on Charles' behalf. But neither Isabel nor Charles would have set much store by this offer. Many Jacobites of much less consequence than Charles Stewart had already been hanged on the Duke of Cumberland's orders. With Isabel's connivance, therefore, on reaching Duror Charles went instantly to ground.

The Ardshiel laird's determination to keep himself out of Hanoverian clutches must have been reinforced by the British parliament's adoption, in early June 1746, of a so-called Act of Attainder. This included a long list of named individuals, one of them Charles Stewart, who, in the words of the Act, 'did, in a traitorous and hostile manner, take up arms and levy war against his present most gracious majesty [George II] . . . and [who] are fled to avoid their being apprehended and prosecuted'. Anyone named by the Act of Attainder and still at large on 12 July, it was made clear, would then be 'adjudged attainted [or guilty] of . . . high treason'. And for high treason the automatic penalty was death.[19]

Just a year earlier, Charles Stewart had been living the life of a financially hard-pressed but outwardly comfortable man of means. Just a few months earlier, he had been helping to direct the operations of a conquering army and, however tentatively, looking forward to having a substantial role in the Jacobite régime this army was endeavouring to bring to power. Now he was a fugitive and an outlaw whose neck depended on his keeping always one step in front of his pursuers.

Throughout the summer and autumn of 1746, then, Charles Stewart was constantly on the run. In early June, he was joined briefly by Donald Cameron of Lochiel and one or two other Jacobite notables at 'a place', one of the men in question remembered later, 'a little above the ferry of Ballachulish'. At other times, the Appin Regiment's ex-colonel was said by the Hanoverian authorities to be 'skulking in the [Duror and Appin] hills' in the company of 'some other gentlemen [one of whom appears to have been Alexander Stewart of Invernahyle] who have about twenty men with them in arms'. Prominent among those armed men, according to a further Hanoverian report, was an Alan Stewart 'who deserted from Cope's army'. This, beyond doubt, was Ailean Breac, James Stewart's foster-son, who – as noted previously – had joined the Jacobites at Prestonpans and who was subsequently said by James to have 'kept close by my brother [meaning Charles Stewart] in his greatest distress'.[20]

Ailean's situation at this point was every bit as hazardous as that of his foster-father's half-brother. As the young man would have been well aware, deserters from the British army, if captured, faced precisely the same punishment as traitors. Already, both in Inverness and elsewhere, more than thirty such deserters had been summarily hanged at the Duke of Cumberland's personal instigation. And if Ailean Breac was to avoid an identical fate, he needed, like Charles Stewart, to escape as soon as possible to France, a country which, for all that it had failed to give military assistance to Charles Edward Stuart, was more than willing to accommodate Jacobite refugees. Meantime, Alan was happy to accompany Charles Stewart from one hiding-place to the next.

On occasion, Charles concealed himself in a cave on the west-facing flank of Beinn a' Bheithir above the township of Lagnaha. Since this particular cave is flanked by a waterfall which in wet weather flows over its entrance, even a short stay there must have been a damp and miserable experience. But the cave's location deep in an extremely hard-to-access gully made it virtually impossible for searchers to find. And it possessed the additional attraction of being within easy walking distance of Charles' home at Ardshiel – where, according to tradition, he visited his wife and family under cover of darkness more than once.

But although several Duror folk risked their own lives by supplying their runaway laird with food and other provisions, and although he appears to have retained at least the tacit goodwill of the rest of the locality's population, Charles' security depended on his keeping perpetually on the move. One day he might be found towards the head of Glen Duror; the next he would have slipped across the pass, a little to the north-east of Fraochaidh, separating Glen Duror from Glen Creran and Fasnacloich; a day or two later he'd be in Glen Stockadale, which contains some of the deepest, most inaccessible, caves in Scotland and which, from its opening on the Appin coast near Castle Stalker, runs north-eastward to Bealach, one of the more isolated stock-rearing townships on Duror's southern fringes.

More than once the Hanoverian authorities got word of Charles Stewart's whereabouts. By the time the army or the militia had organised a force big enough to take on Ailean Breac and the rest of Charles' escorts, however, he'd have decamped yet again – and not necessarily by foot. Because Duror fronts Loch Linnhe not far from that loch's junction with Loch Leven, it was a simple matter to get from Duror, by sea, to Ardgour or Kingairloch on Loch Linnhe's western shore. It was equally easy to to travel, again by sea, to Callart on Loch Leven's north coast, to Kinlochleven at the loch's furthest extremity or to Glencoe on its southern shore. Hence the significance of a military intelligence report of September 1746: '[Stewart of] Ardsheil has a small boat that is rowed by four servants and, when anyways alarmed, [he] steers off for Callart, Glencoe, Kinlochleven and sometimes to Kingairloch.'[21]

When General John Campbell and the men of the Argyll Militia were redeployed from Appin to Morvern and Strontian at the end of 17 May 1746, responsibility for security matters in Duror passed, in effect, to the Hanoverian garrison at Fort William and in particular to the garrison's commander, Captain Caroline Scott. This development coincided with a visit to Fort William – a visit undertaken in recognition of the garrison's having withstood the Jacobite siege of two months before – by none other than (to give King George's younger son his full title) His Royal Highness, William Augustus, Duke of

Cumberland. 'At three o'clock in the morning of the 30th [of May]', it was reported formally from Cumberland's Fort Augustus base, 'the duke, with a hundred [troopers] of Kingston's Horse as his guard, set out on horseback and, before nine, reached Fort William. A little after his arrival, all the officers were called upon, had the honour to kiss His Royal Highness's hand for their brave defence of the place during the late siege, and were ordered to acquaint the private men that he [Cumberland] gave them thanks for their good behaviour on that occasion.'[22]

It is likely that Cumberland spent much of 30 May in the company of Caroline Scott – whom the duke, as he had already made clear, rated highly and whom he was afterwards to make one of his aides-de-camp. But despite Scott's being regarded by his superiors as, in the words of one of them, 'a very pretty man and a diligent officer', he was viewed by most Highlanders in a very different light.[23]

When soldiers are permitted, or even encouraged, to engage in casual violence and brutality, it is inevitable that the nastier individuals among them will take full advantage of the opportunity thus offered. Hence the British army's involvement, during 1746, in some inexcusable episodes. At that time there existed no legal apparatus of the sort that would be used much later to bring war criminals to justice, and so no representative of the British military was obliged to account for what would now be seen as war crimes. But with a view to ensuring that the army's often appalling treatment of Highlanders would not be forgotten, one man made it his business to seek out, and take down statements from victims and first-hand witnesses of some of the worst of the many atrocities which occurred right across the West Highlands in the months following the Battle of Culloden. This man was Robert Forbes, an Episcopalian cleric. Since Forbes was himself a Jacobite whose politics resulted, at one point, in his imprisonment, his material is necessarily one-sided. But there exists more than enough corroborative evidence – not least in Hanoverian documentation of the type already quoted – to make clear that Forbes' indictments of soldier after soldier cannot simply be dismissed as Jacobite propaganda. In relation to what happened in Duror in the spring and summer of 1746, then, it is significant that one of the names to feature repeatedly in Robert Forbes' ten manuscript volumes of testimony is that of Caroline Scott.[24]

One testimony concerning Scott gives a flavour of the overall tenor of what Forbes recorded about him. This testimony relates to an incursion the captain made, shortly after Culloden, into Glen Nevis, not far from Fort William. There Scott was met by three men who had taken no part in the recently concluded rebellion and who had sought out Scott in order to obey the Duke of Cumberland's well-publicised order that all weapons of any kind – by whomsoever they were held – should be handed over to the military. Caroline Scott responded to this gesture, or so Robert Forbes wrote, by telling the men that 'as others had not done the same thing, they were to be hanged'. Forbes continued: 'The poor men said it would be hard to punish them for the fault of others; and so little did they think he [Captain Scott] intended any such thing, but that he intended [only] to frighten them, they were laughing when the soldiers were putting the ropes about their necks. But they were mistaken; for instantly they were hanged and had not so much time as to beg God to have mercy upon their souls.'[25]

More than a hundred years after his death in India, in 1754, the perpetrator of this crime was well remembered in Duror, where tradition-bearers and storytellers referred to him as 'governor of the garrison of Lochaber' or 'a king's man called Captain Scott'. 'Both rich and poor who rose in the cause of Prince Charles were plundered,' it was said of Scott and his troops in nineteenth-century Duror. 'Neither cow nor horse, sheep nor goat was left to them [the Duror people]. The blankets were taken off their beds; any part of their body-clothes that was worth [money] was taken from them; and even the skeins of yarn were taken out of the dye-pots, and their houses were put on fire.'[26]

Duror's year of burnings appears to have been launched in reprisal for the Jacobite siege of Fort William – to which the Caroline Scott responded, towards the end of March 1746, by ordering punishment raids on such communities as his men could reach by sea. 'This afternoon', it was reported of one such raiding party on 26 March, 'our boats returned with cattle and sheep from the country near Ardshiel. They also brought in four prisoners, one of [whom] was wounded. The party burned two rebel villages.' Other burnings followed, a military intelligence report of 30 October noting: 'There are six towns burned in Appin, viz., Laroch [where the modern village of Ballachulish later developed], Ballachulish [the township beside Ballachulish Ferry's southern terminus], Lettermore, Auchindarroch, Glen Duror, Keil.' Because Keil was in the ownership of Donald Campbell of Airds who, as noted previously, was serving with the Argyll Militia, its houses, as a nineteenth-century tradition-bearer was long afterwards to point out, should not have been destroyed. But such distinctions mattered little to Scott and his men who, the same tradition-bearer said, 'set fire to them [Keil's houses]' anyway.[27]

Among the occupants of the Duror township of Achindarroch in 1746 was James Stewart, newly returned from his months with the Appin Regiment. 'He had his whole stock of cattle carried away [in 1746] by the king's troops,' James was to swear in the course of a 1750 legal hearing concerning the administration of the Ardshiel estate. Another Duror man, John MacColl, told the same hearing 'that he was [a] tenant in the said town [of Achindarroch] for the years

1745 and 1746, that everything that belonged to him was burned in his house and barn which consisted of ten couples [meaning that it was of a size requiring ten sets of rafters], [and] that the whole of his cattle was carried away by His Majesty's troops'. A third Duror resident, also a MacColl, added 'that in the year 1746 he was herd to . . . Charles Stewart of Ardshiel in the lands of Glen Duror and saw the whole houses on the said farm [of Glen Duror] burnt and the cattle carried away by the king's troops'. His own home, this man went on, was among those torched – his 'furniture [being] all burned' in the ensuing conflagration.[28]

'The town[ship] of Ardshiel [was] not burned,' one of the British government's agents in the Highlands reported towards the close of 1746, 'but the mansion house [was] taken down and all the timber, freestone and slate and furniture . . . carried away to Fort William by order of Captain Scott and disposed of by him, which, by information, amounted to above £400 sterling.'[29]

The mansion house in question was, of course, the home of Charles Stewart. And that 1746 account of its fate – from a Hanoverian, not a Jacobite, source – accorded with what Robert Forbes was afterwards to write about Caroline Scott's systematic destruction of this fine home. 'The captain,' Forbes commented, 'after he had rummaged the house, took great care to have the slates and sarking [or timbers] taken from the roof. He gutted the house and office-houses [or outbuildings] of all the timber in them, with the least damage possible even to the [careful] drawing [out] of the nails. He then had all the walls cast down . . . all of which he sold, with the planting, which chiefly consisted of many large ash trees.'[30]

Testifying to a Hanoverian official two years after Scott's demolition of Ardshiel House, Isabel Stewart, Charles' wife, said: 'The kitchen garden and orchard at Ardshiel . . . were almost entirely destroyed by the king's troops in August 1746, the best of the fruit trees having been cut down and carried off, and what remains standing are broken and hacked round the stocks . . . There was an avenue of large ash and plane trees and other planting at Ardshiel, but . . . now very few of them remain, there having been cut down upwards of four hundred of the best of [these] trees and [the resulting timber having been] carried off by Thomas Johnstone, barrack master at Fort William, by order of Caroline Scott who also carried off the whole timber of the house of Ardshiel and [the] hewn stone [from] the windows and chimneys.'[31]

Following further interrogation of Isabel Stewart about what had occurred at Ardshiel during Caroline Scott's various searches for her persistently elusive husband, Isabel's questioner noted: 'She declares that in May and August 1746 his [Charles'] whole corns, cattle and household furniture and other goods, charter chest and papers, were all carried off by the king's troops, and nothing left [to] her but her own and [her] children's clothes.'[32]

The repeated humiliations to which Isabel Stewart was subjected by Scott and his men are evident from a letter she wrote to General John Campbell on 25 August 1746. Isabel informs the general, that she is 'troubling' him with this letter on account of his earlier 'sympathy with [her] misfortunes'. Bitterly, she asks Campbell to 'excuse the coarseness of my paper, my good friend Captain Scott having left me none better'. She mentions that the Ardshiel estate's tenants have been 'burned and harried'. And she attributes much of their suffering to Caroline Scott. Only 'my own [self] and my poor children being the unhappy instruments of his cruelty'. Isabel observes of the Fort William garrison's commander, 'could make me believe that any man, especially bred in a civilised country and [in] good company, could be so free of compassion and [could] . . . descend to such a low degree of meanness'. 'He [Scott] would not allow me when at Ardshiel,' she continues, 'so much as the smallest of my [cooking] pots to dress a little victuals for my children, nor spoon, or knife, or fork, or bed to lie on, or even a blanket.' The captain, Isabel adds, her grammar deserting her in her fury, 'keeped the whole of the keys [of Ardshiel House] from the time he came'. He took 'the horse I had for my own riding,' she goes on, 'and two small horses [kept] for carrying home any peats or any other little uses I had for them'. And when he had finally rendered her home uninhabitable, Isabel concludes, Scott 'ordered both myself and [my] children to leave the place'.[33]

The Duke of Cumberland left Fort Augustus for the last time on 18 July 1746. Before the end of the month the duke had reached London – where he was greeted by cheering crowds, bonfires and fireworks prior to being honoured by a series of formal balls and receptions organised in celebration of what had been achieved in Scotland. During August, the army Cumberland had left behind in the Highlands was placed under the command of William Anne Kepel, Earl of Albemarle, whose immediate priority was to demonstrate that his opinions of Highlanders were every bit as unyielding as his predecessor's. He was 'one of those', the earl told his political superiors in September, who thought 'nothing could effect' the pacification of the Jacobite Highlands 'but laying the whole country waste and in ashes, and removing all the inhabitants (excepting a few) out of the kingdom'.[34]

Having received instructions from London 'to be . . . vigilant in preventing the escape . . . of such of the principal rebels as still remain in Scotland', Albemarle responded: 'I shall be very diligent in apprehending such rebels as are still lurking about the hills.' But capturing those Jacobites who remained at liberty in the Highlands was, as Caroline Scott had informed the earl in a letter dispatched from the captain's temporary base at Ardshiel on 3 August, much easier said than done. 'I have been detained here [in Duror] longer than I expected,' Scott reported, 'by some information of rebels and their cattle being near to, but I find in general they had notice of our marching almost as soon as we left Fort William, and drove off what cattle the Campbells [i.e., the Argyll Militia] left them twenty miles . . . into the mountains.'[35]

Despite the best efforts of General John Campbell and Captain Caroline Scott, then, Duror showed not the slightest sign of abandoning its Jacobite convictions. Dozens of Duror men, it was reported over the summer of 1746, were quite openly disobeying instructions to surrender their weaponry. This was true, for example, of Duncan MacColl and Duncan MacCombie, both of whom lived at Ardshiel and were described as Charles Stewart's 'servants'. It was true, too, of four Lagnaha residents and eight of their Achindarroch counterparts. Among the more recalcitrant Achindarroch people, according to a document compiled in July 1746 by Archibald Campbell of Stonefield, sheriff of Argyll, was Alan Stewart – possibly James Stewart's elder son – whom the sheriff described as '[Stewart of] Ardshiel's baggage-keeper'. Also prominent among the Achindarroch folk known to be keeping swords and muskets firmly in their possession were John MacColl, the man whose burned barn had run to 'ten couples', John MacCombie, a drover, Angus MacCombie, a tailor, and a second John MacColl, whom Argyll's sheriff categorised as 'an idle man'.[36]

Nor was the population of the rest of Duror demonstrating any greater interest in acceding to the regularly repeated injunction that each and every Highlander had immediately to disarm himself. Two Acharn residents, Archibald Campbell of Stonefield reported, were stubbornly holding on to guns and other weapons. So were eleven men living at Cuil. And so were four Achara men – among them Duncan MacColl, who, as noted earlier, had been one of the Appin Regiment's letter-carriers and runners for the duration of Charles Edward Stuart's rebellion.

One cause of the difficulties the Hanoverian authorities continued to face in Duror was Duror folk's persistent 'expectation of great things from France'. Although no such thing was to occur, a French landing in the Highlands, the author of an army intelligence report drawn up at the end of October 1746 maintained, was confidently anticipated by lots of Duror men who, their Culloden experiences notwithstanding, had declared themselves ready to join Scotland's French invaders as soon as the latter put in their expected appearance.[37]

Defiant comments of this kind from Appin Regiment veterans were no doubt encouraged by the regiment's former colonel, Charles Stewart, who, for all Caroline Scott's increasingly desperate attempts to apprehend him, remained at large. In September it was rumoured that Charles – like Cameron of Lochiel and Charles Edward Stuart himself – had succeeded in escaping to

France. But this was quickly contradicted by Hanoverian agents who expressed themselves confident, on 30 October, that the Ardshiel laird was 'still in the bounds of the country'. That this was indeed the case seems likely from a 1752 statement by Charles' Duror tenants that they had paid their 1746 rents – which were due in November – directly to 'our master'. It seems probable, therefore, that it was not until the early part of 1747 that Charles Stewart at last managed to get a boat to France – where, as a loyal Jacobite, he was promptly awarded an annual pension of 3,000 livres by the French king, Louis XV, who also permitted him to set up home at Sens in Champagne.[38]

In Duror, meanwhile, the winter of 1746–47 was proving more than usually bleak and dispiriting. During snowy weather in December, Isabel Stewart is said to have given birth to her latest child, a daughter, in the 'hut' to which Caroline Scott had effectively confined her. As for the rest of Duror's population, they were doubtless among 'the inhabitants of the rebellious countries' who were reckoned that winter 'to be in misery for want of provisions'. At about this point, admittedly, the British military authorities noted that a number of Jacobite localities in the vicinity of Loch Linnhe had been 'supplied with meal and other provisions from Ireland, and that there are several boats come into that country, on the pretence of buying wood, [which] bring with them meal, butter, cheese, salt, spirits and tobacco'. For the Duror people's sake, it is to be hoped that this particular piece of intelligence was more soundly based than another which maintained that Duror was doing comparatively well as a result of so many of its menfolk having recently met their deaths: 'There was a great many inhabitants of this place killed at Culloden, which makes meal more plent[iful] in that country than [in] many others.'[39]

With even the well-provided for Hanoverian garrison at Fort William – where 'about two hundred men' had contracted 'an epidemical distemper' – suffering greatly from disease as cold weather returned to the West Highlands, it is improbable that Duror, its reduced numbers and Irish imports notwithstanding, was in other than a very bad state by Christmas. Its people, according to information reaching the Earl of Albemarle's Edinburgh headquarters, retained enough spirit to be busy 'repairing [the] houses burned by Captain Scott'. But as they laboured to replace the wall timbers, the rafters and thatch which had gone up in flames, Duror's families could not have been looking to the year ahead with much optimism.[40]

Chapter Five

Now the tenants . . . pay a rent to King George; but their hearts are staunch, they
are true to their chief; and what with love and a bit of pressure, and maybe a
threat or/ two, the poor folk scrape up a second rent for Ardshiel . . . And it's
wonderful to me how little pressure is needed. But that's the handiwork of my good
kinsman and my father's friend, James of the Glens; James Stewart, that is: Ardshiel's
half-brother. He it is that gets the money in, and does the management.

Robert Louis Stevenson, *Kidnapped*

At the start of 1747, with her home in ruins, her children and a new baby needing her constant attention and her husband – who had been in hiding for several months – about to take himself off to France, Isabel Stewart, whom life had favoured previously, was in an unenviable plight. At this time bad weather and poor harvests were bringing all sorts of difficulties to estate managements right across the West Highlands. Even on the Campbell lands in more southerly parts of Argyll – lands which were well administered and which had not been affected directly by Charles Edward Stuart's rebellion – large numbers of cattle were dying of hunger and rent arrears were accumulating. Since the Ardshiel estate, as observed earlier, had never provided its laird with a generous income, the widespread agricultural downturn of 1747 makes it probable that Charles Stewart, even if he had never taken the gamble which went so catastrophically awry at Culloden, would not have got through the 1740s without encountering some financial embarrassment. As it was, Charles' wife, whom he left to make the best of things at home when he fled abroad, was on the verge of destitution. 'Nor can it be expected', Isabel commented of her tenants in the wake of Caroline Scott's burning of their houses, 'that these poor people . . . will pay any rent . . . I doubt not that the poor people would give me some of their few remaining cattle . . . in lieu of it [rent], but I can't take them as I have no secure place for them.'[1]

During the winter of 1746–47, then, if she was to regain any kind of security, Isabel Stewart desperately required assistance. She got the help she needed from her husband's half-brother, James Stewart. In the course of James' trial at Inveraray in 1752, this development was interpreted by the Duror man's prosecutors as one he had engineered for entirely selfish reasons. 'When [Stewart of] Ardshiel was obliged to leave the country,' the Inveraray courtroom was told, 'his brother [James] set himself at the head of the [Ardshiel] family interest, and it not appearing in that part of the world a forced transition [because of James' connection with Ardshiel's refugee laird], he was allowed to take this authority upon him. In a short time, therefore, he came to be a leading man and to have the chief influence over the common people.'[2]

James Stewart saw matters differently. 'I . . . thought it my duty,' he said, explaining why he'd become so heavily involved in the management of the Ardshiel estate. It had been his particular responsibility, James insisted, to do what he could for his half-brother's sons and daughters – 'to whom', he went on, 'I was bound by the ties, not only of nature but also of gratitude, [they] being the distressed offspring of a very affectionate, loving brother to whom I was under many obligations and whose misfortunes . . . proceeded from a conviction of his doing his duty.'[3]

Given James Stewart's well-attested willingness to take on the task of bringing up the children – Ailean Breac and his siblings, for example – of people to whom he was related much more distantly than he was to the Ardshiel laird's family, James' account of why he rushed to this family's assistance is entirely plausible. The surviving evidence, however, suggests that James – while genuinely anxious to be of help to Isabel Stewart – had two further motives for acting as he did. The first, which would loom larger and larger as time passed, was James' deep and unshakeable conviction that he had a responsibility to defend and to preserve Clan Stewart's longstanding supremacy in Duror. The second (and this is to allow that James' 1752 prosecutors were not wholly wide of the mark) is to be found in the fact that James Stewart, who was no saint, succeeded in managing Ardshiel estate affairs, during the winter of 1746–47 and subsequently, in ways which, while they brought Isabel Stewart a reasonable income, also added substantially to the area of land he tenanted personally.

James was hampered when trying to secure those twin objectives by the Hanoverian government's unrelenting determination to subvert the social and cultural foundations on which clanship, especially Jacobite-inclined clanship, rested. Throughout 1746, and into 1747, the British parliament's legislative agenda was dominated by measures 'for the more effectual securing of the peace in the Highlands of Scotland'. Prominent among these measures was one which a leading politician, Henry Pelham, hoped would lead to the 'disarming and undressing of . . . [Highland] savages'. As Pelham indicated, this particular Act made it illegal for Highlanders to possess weapons or to wear tartan plaids, centuries-old badges of Highland distinctiveness. To enforce such measures, soldiers repeatedly raided Duror homes, James Stewart's included, searching for hidden guns the prohibition of the wearing of tartan accounts for the appearance in military records of an entry concerning Orinocco, the African-born slave kept by Dougal Stewart, the Appin Stewarts' chief. 'Orinocco, servant to Dougal Stewart of Appin Esquire,' this entry reads, 'was apprehended by Henry Paton, commanding officer of the forces stationed in the Rannoch district, for wearing the Highland garb or being dressed in tartan livery.'[4]

That episode demonstrates the extent to which the forces ranged against people like James Stewart were global in their reach. A man who had been born into an African tribe had been arrested in Scotland as a consequence of his wearing clothes of the kind worn traditionally by the inhabitants of the one corner of Europe, the Highlands, where tribalism had survived into the eighteenth century. The politicians presiding over a country capable of altering so dramatically the previously settled order of things were unlikely to tolerate much interference by James Stewart in their plans. And so, in the end, it proved.

This, however, is the wisdom of hindsight. James, in 1747, was definitely in no mind to concede the inevitability of his final failure. And if he took time to reflect on what the United Kingdom's parliament was then doing legislatively, the chances are that James – who, moments before his death in 1752, would describe himself as 'an unworthy member of the Episcopal Church of Scotland as established before the revolution [of 1688]' – was a good deal more outraged by the British government's religious enactments than by the measure which led to Orinocco's imprisonment.[5]

'His Royal Highness on coming to Aberdeen', it had been noted of the Duke of Cumberland's northward progress in 1746, 'immediately stopped all the non-jurant ministers [from preaching] and, soon after, ordered their meeting-houses to be destroyed, which was accordingly executed, both in town and country, as the army marched along.' By the summer, those Episcopal churches and chapels which had not been burned were reportedly 'shut up all over the kingdom'. None, it turned out, would be allowed to reopen until Episcopalian preachers swore oaths of loyalty to George II and promised that 'at some time during the exercise of divine service they [would] pray for the king, his heirs [and] successors by name' – this proviso being designed to put an end to the former Episcopalian practice of praying publicly for the king without making clear which monarch, Hanoverian or Jacobite, was being commended to God's care.[6]

At the point that James Stewart became involved in the management of the Ardshiel estate, then, Duror people were at an extremely low ebb – spiritually and psychologically as well as physically. They had suffered the death in battle of many of their menfolk; they had witnessed the destruction of their homes; they had seen their recognised leader, Ardshiel's laird, turned into a political refugee; they'd had to cope with the consequences of their faith being openly discriminated against, their age-old forms of dress being outlawed and their equally age-old practice of carrying swords, dirks and other armaments being declared a criminal offence. In such circumstances, it seems little short of miraculous that James Stewart – his success pointing to a preparedness to deploy coercive tactics of his own against backsliders – managed rapidly to collect the Ardshiel rents which had been due in 1746. He was to perform the same service in respect of the rents payable in 1747 and 1748 – making those rents over, in every instance, to Isabel Stewart. The resulting revenues, Isabel was to assert, had been devoted in their entirety to 'the maintenance of her family'. Perhaps so. But 'maintenance', in this context, was an elastic term chosen with a view to its covering the considerable expenditure incurred when, in the somewhat jaundiced phraseology of a Hanoverian observer, Isabel, 'about the end of the year 1748 . . . made her elopement and went off, bag and baggage, to her husband in France'.[7]

During the three or four years following the Battle of Culloden, James Stewart lived, with his wife, Margaret, and their family, in the Duror township of Achindarroch, part of the Ardshiel estate. In the medieval denominations still being used in eighteenth-century leases, Achindarroch's extent was reckoned in the 1740s – just as it had been in the charters of more than 250 years before – at five merk-lands. Of these, James had the tenancy of three, Achindarroch's other four tenants having half of one merk-land apiece. In respect of his share of Achindarroch, James paid, to Isabel Stewart, or Lady Ardshiel as she tends to be designated in contemporary documentation, a yearly money rent of £80 Scots – or £6 13s 4d sterling.[8] In addition to this cash sum, James, in his capacity as an Achindarroch tenant, was obliged to make over annually to Isabel, as he testified to British government representatives in the course of a 1748 inquiry into the overall situation on the Ardshiel estate, 'three stones weight of cheese and three quarts of butter, or £9 Scots as the converted price thereof, four calves, or 12 shillings money foresaid for each calf, and four one-year old wedder sheep, or £1 Scots for each sheep'.[9]

As those details show, the estate of Achindarroch, at this point, was not managed in like a modern estate. Not only was a proportion of its rents still due in kind instead of cash, its arable land, instead of being divided into a limited number of the systematically laid-out fields associated with twenty-first-century farming, consisted – as arable land consisted everywhere in the Highlands at this time – of a series of the plots and patches which Scots called *rigs*. James Stewart would have had the use of three-fifths of those rigs; his neighbours would have had the other two-fifths between them. And to make an already complex position more complicated, it is probable that James – who certainly did not work his Achindarroch landholdings unaided – sublet at least some of his rigs to men who, in return for the scraps of territory they thus obtained, would have been obliged to turn out when James was in need of labour to get the ground ploughed, sown or harvested.

Although centred on the eastern slopes of the Strath of Duror – to revert to eighteenth-century nomenclature – just north of the point where the Water of Duror exits from the glen of the same name, Achindarroch's lands spread across the floor of the strath and took in the hillside, on the Strath of Duror's western flank, where Duror Hotel stands today. Eastwards, those lands extended, as noted previously, for some distance up Glen Duror, terminating on the western bank of Allt nam Meirleach. Beyond this swiftly flowing burn, as also noted previously, lay the further Ardshiel holding of Glen Duror. Its three or four houses were located a little beyond Allt nam Meirleach. And like Achindarroch's more numerous homes, those houses had been set ablaze by Caroline Scott's troops in 1746. But Scott's activities notwithstanding, Glen Duror remained an attractive proposition agriculturally. Although documents of the period make clear that there was 'no sowing' of any consequence 'upon this farm', they make equally clear that much of its pasture was excellent – Glen Duror supporting, in summer, between two and three hundred head of cattle.[10]

James Stewart's nickname, Seumas a' Ghlinne, derived – to repeated a point made previously – from his connections with Glen Duror, which he had tenanted at some point in the past.[11] According to Alexander Stewart of Invernahyle, speaking in 1752, James' original tenancy of the glen, having begun 'a great many years' previously, had ended 'several years ago'. Why this happened is not known. What is known is that Glen Duror, immediately prior to the rebellion of 1745/46, was in the direct occupancy of Ardshiel's laird, Charles Stewart. This means that its cattle stock would have been managed on Charles' behalf by, among others, John MacColl, who, as mentioned already, described himself as 'herd to Charles Stewart of Ardshiel in the lands of Glen Duror'. Since this arrangement, assuming reasonably efficient management by John MacColl, would have secured a larger income for Charles Stewart than he would have got from renting out Glen Duror to his half-brother or to anyone else, the termination of James' pre-1745 tenancy of the glen was probably a consequence of Charles' need for more money – with James conceivably being compensated for the loss of Glen Duror by his being awarded the lion's share of Achindarroch.[12]

Although Seumas a' Ghlinne's departure from Glen Duror – which certainly caused no irreperable rupture with his half-brother, Tearlach Mor – doesn't seem to have rankled unduly with him, James, as a cattle-rearer and cattle-trader on a subtantial scale, may have continued to cast envious eyes at the rich summer grazings on the far side of Allt nam Meirleach. And in 1747 he was presented with a chance to reaquire them. Following the confiscation of the greater part of Charles Stewart's livestock by General John Campbell, and Charles' subsequent flight to France, the lands of Glen Duror – together with Lettermore and those parts of Ardshiel township which had also been in Charles' personal occupancy – were, as a document of 1748 puts it, 'waste'. To remedy this situation, it was said in 1752, '[Stewart of] Ardshiel's lady and [James Stewart] jointly introduced new tenants of their own into different parcels of the land which [Stewart of] Ardshiel . . . had himself occupied before the rebellion.' In the case of Glen Duror, the 'new tenant' in question was none other than James, who, as he stated in 1748, 'entered the possession there in terms of an agreement between [himself] and the Lady [Ardshiel]'.[13]

For much of 1746, James Stewart, as he acknowledged a couple of years later, had 'been from home'. Prior to April of that year, of course, he had been with the Appin Regiment; from May onwards, it is likely that he was in hiding from Caroline Scott and his men. James, then, must have warmly welcomed the Indemnity Act of June 1747 – a piece of legislation which, while not extending any forgiveness to Jacobite ringleaders, guaranteed that more minor players in Charles Edward Stuart's rebellion would face no punishments beyond those they had endured already. The Indemnity Act did nothing for Charles Stewart of Ardshiel – who was explicitly exempted from its provisions and who remained immovably on the British government's wanted list. But it did permit the Appin Regiment's more junior officers, such as James Stewart and Alexander Stewart of Invernahyle, to live fully in public gaze once more. James' reoccupation of Glen Duror – agreed in 1747 and made effective in the spring of 1748 – occurred, therefore, at a point when things were generally looking up for him. He was, for most practical purposes, in charge of the Ardshiel estate; his farming interests were expanding; his trading operations were being gradually resumed; and now, with the passing of the Indemnity Act, he could go about his business without fear of arrest or harassment. In fact, the only significant cloud on James Stewart's horizon, as 1747 drew to a close, derived from the threat posed to his new-found position by the government's decision to take over lands belonging to those Highlanders who were judged to have played especially prominent roles in Charles Edward Stuart's rising. Charles Stewart being very much in this latter category, the Ardshiel estate was among the properties destined to pass into public ownership in consequence of the 1747 Act giving effect to such expropriation. What would follow from this change of ownership? And who would the Hanoverian authorities appoint to the managerial post he had recently been occupying? Those questions are bound to have greatly exercised James Stewart in the months preceding his becoming, once again, the tenant of Glen Duror.

By politicians in London, the administration of Scotland's forfeited estates – as confiscated territories like Ardshiel became known – was entrusted to an Edinburgh-based organisation, the Court of Exchequer. An early example of those officially constituted bodies which a later age would christen 'quangos', the court was controlled by a five-man board whose members were entitled barons of exchequer and whose duty it had now become to run a whole set of landholdings in the Highlands.

The Court of Exchequer, like most bureaucracies, operated slowly. It operated particularly slowly in the case of Ardshiel, as a result of Isabel Stewart having mounted a legal action intended to show that her husband's property, on his departure for France, had passed automatically to his eldest son who, being still a boy, had taken no part in the events of 1745/46. This attempt to keep Ardshiel out of the Edinburgh barons' clutches was eventually – and inevitably – to fail. But it did delay for several months the formal commissioning by the barons of the man they had decided to appoint as factor, or manager, of the Ardshiel estate. This man was Colin Campbell of Glenure.

Known throughout the northern part of Argyll as *Cailean Ruadh*, Red Colin, because of his unusually fiery hair, the Ardshiel estate's new factor belonged to a family with whom the Stewarts of Appin had been semi-permanently at war since the family in question had ejected the Stewarts from Lorn some three centuries before. At the head of this family in the 1740s was John Campbell of Barcaldine – with whom the Appin Regiment's recruiters had tangled in August 1745. John, who had gone on from that encounter to play a prominent role in raising the Argyll Militia detachments responsible for inflicting so much damage on the Appin Regiment at Culloden, was Cailean Ruadh's half-brother – John being a son of his father, Patrick's, first marriage, Colin a product of his second. On Patrick Campbell's death, John had inherited the family's principal estates in and around Barcaldine. Colin, however, was not left unprovided for, having been established by Patrick in a property of his own. This was the Glenure estate, centred on a valley opening onto Glen Creran from the east and located, therefore, just beyond the boundary of one of the possessions constituting the lands of the Appin Stewarts. This possession, Fasnacloich, was not much more than a mile to the west of Colin Campbell's home, Glenure House.

The British army regiment in which Colin Campbell of Glenure had been serving at the time of the Jacobite rebellion – during which, of course, Colin came close to losing his commission as a result of his being absent from his Perthshire post on the night of Lord George Murray's attack on it – was disbanded in June 1748. The Glenure laird's appointment as the Court of Exchequer's Ardshiel factor – agreed by the barons of exchequer that month and, with Isabel Stewart's legal pleadings out of the way, confirmed by them in February 1749 – came along, therefore, at what must have seemed to Colin Campbell to be just the right moment. It was an appointment, however, which was fraught with difficulty and danger from the first.

To begin with, Cailean Ruadh's problems centred not so much on Ardshiel as on the two Lochaber estates for which the Court of Exchequer had also made him responsible. The first was an extensive area previously belonging to Donald Cameron of Lochiel in the vicinity of Fort William, and the second was a smaller property, situated on the north shore of Loch Leven, which had been taken by the government from one of Donald Cameron's kinsmen, Alan Cameron of Callart. Like their Ardshiel equivalents, tenants on those Cameron lands were expected, as of 1749, to pay their rents to Colin Campbell. But this, as Colin quickly discovered, they were most reluctant to do.

'I soon found in this country of Lochaber', Colin Campbell reported to the barons of exchequer from Fort William in the closing weeks of 1749, 'that [any] step to levy the king's rents is a matter of ridicule and [is] treated as such.' His rent demands having produced next to no money, Colin went on, he had 'set out amongst the tenants to seize and poind [or confiscate] their effects as the law directs'. However, both 'the law' and 'the crown's factor', Cailean Ruadh explained to his Edinburgh superiors, were 'no more regarded by those barbarians than if there were no law or government in Great Britain'. The men he had employed to poind goods to the value of the Cameron tenantry's unpaid rents were told in his presence, Colin Campbell wrote, 'that if they dared touch or seize any part of their [the tenantry's] effects for payment . . . they [the tenants] would beat out their brains'. In such circumstances, Colin observed, 'he could not levy . . . rents [in Lochaber] without the assistance of the military'. Indeed, if he were to be denied an escort of soldiers, the factor concluded, 'I shall never go to call for these [Lochaber] rents again, as I know it would be very idle as well as dangerous to do it.' That was why, in November 1749, the Court of Exchequer issued orders to the [commanding] officer at Fort William to give a party of the military to attend to Mr Campbell'.[14]

Ironically, in view of what was to happen to him there eventually, Colin Campbell's earliest Ardshiel dealings, compared to his Lochaber experiences, were almost trouble-free. This was mainly because, as was stated at James Stewart's trial, Colin began, in effect, by making James his Ardshiel sub-factor – entrusting to James 'the management of the whole estate of Ardshiel [including] power to put in and remove tenants and to raise the rents as he should think proper'.[15]

Given the longstanding enmity between the Barcaldine Campbells and the Appin Stewarts, to say nothing of the fact that James Stewart and Colin Campbell had served on opposite sides in the rebellion just three years previously, this arrangement, at first sight, appears extremely odd. It has to be kept in mind, however, that despite their belonging to mutually hostile clans, Cailean Ruadh and Seumas a' Ghlinne knew each other very well. By way of modern roads, Glen Duror is many miles from Glenure. By way of the hill paths that were the standard means of travel in the eighteenth-century Highlands, however, Glenure House was no more than a morning's walk from the home James Stewart would have occupied on first becoming Glen Duror's tenant. Colin and James, then, were neighbours; James implied, on occasion, that they may even have been distantly related; and over and over again, both at James' trial and previously, the two men were said to have been, until 1749 or 1750 at any rate, close friends.

This is implicit in the cordial nature of the contact between Colin Campbell and James Stewart during the opening year or so of the former's Ardshiel factorship. 'I think I can now, with some certainty, tell you', Colin writes to James in November 1748, 'that I am now appointed factor over the lands you possess [in Achindarroch and Glen Duror] and other lands that belonged to your brother, [Stewart of] Ardshiel; and as the term [meaning the rent-day] is now at hand, [I] will beg the favour [that] you desire the tenants and possessors to be preparing the rents.' This letter, as it happened, proved a little premature – the Court of Exchequer's confirmation that Colin Campbell was to be their Ardshiel representative did not reach Glenure for another four months. But it sets the tone of the exchanges that were to follow. He looks forward to meeting with him in Taigh na h-Insaig, Colin tells James in October 1749. He asks James, on this occasion, to get the Ardshiel estate's 1749 rent-collection underway. 'Your payments are very good for which I am obliged to you,' the factor informs James a month or two later.[16]

That summer Cailean Ruadh married Janet MacKay, the daughter of a Sutherland laird, who, when the pair wed in June, was less than half her husband's age – she being 17 or 18 and he being in his early forties. 'My wife . . . is your sincere well-wisher,' Colin writes to James in December 1749. 'My wife returns you her thanks for your good wishes,' he remarks in a letter of the following April. And while these are conventional enough sentiments, they suggest that James Stewart was, throughout this period, a regular visitor to Glenure House – now becoming a family home as a result of the first of Colin and Janet's three daughters being on the way within months of their wedding.[17]

So good were relations between Colin Campbell and James Stewart at this stage, in fact, that the former did absolutely nothing to curtail the latter's continuing activities on behalf of the Jacobite escapee, Charles Stewart of Ardshiel. From 1749 onwards, to be sure, James could no longer transfer Ardshiel estate rents directly to Charles' wife, Isabel, as he had been doing up to that point. Those rents now had to be remitted to the Court of Exchequer. Prior to determining how much rent they would extract from Ardshiel, however, the court's barons, being sticklers for the correct procedure, had insisted on the Ardshiel estate being valued, in the summer of 1748, by one of the surveyors, David Bruce, whom they employed for such purposes. The estate's total rent, Bruce reported to the barons, should be £47 sterling annually. And since the barons were perfectly happy as long as that sum reached them from Ardshiel at each year's end thereafter, this left James Stewart, whom Colin Campbell had asked to collect the estate's rents on his behalf, free to levy a higher figure than the official one – with the difference between the two amounts being promptly remitted to Charles and Isabel Stewart at their place of exile in Sens.

The exact amount of the additional or 'double' rent thus extracted from the Ardshiel estate tenantry by James Stewart is impossible to determine. Equally impossible to know is whether James, as seems likely, had to resort to threats to obtain the sums at stake. What is certain is that James always insisted that, in doing what he did, he was simply acting in the best interest of his nephews and nieces, the several children of Charles and Isabel Stewart – the oldest of whom was just 15 in 1749. 'The tenants generally allowed some gratuity to [Stewart of] Ardshiel's children,' James told Alexander Stewart of Invernahyle. 'Whatever was made of these [the Ardshiel] rents over what was paid into the exchequer', he remarked to Donald Campbell of Airds, 'was accounted for to the children of [Stewart of] Ardshiel.'[18]

But while Colin Campbell began by tolerating those arrangements, he gradually became aware – and should arguably have been aware much sooner – that implicit in them was much that was potentially disadvantageous to his employers, the barons of exchequer. James Stewart, for a start, had a clear vested interest in driving down as far as possible David Bruce's valuation of the Ardshiel estate. And this, naturally enough, James made every effort to do – ensuring, for example, that Ardshiel tenant after Ardshiel tenant, when appearing in front of Bruce, made the most of the damage inflicted on their homes and their holdings in 1746. Did this give Colin Campbell pause for thought? Perhaps. But what definitely led to a cooling of the factor's friendship with James Stewart was the latter's reaction to his efforts to give effect to the Court of Exchequer's instructions regarding those Ardshiel rents which had fallen due in the years preceding the commencement of his factorship – 1746, 1747 and 1748. Since Charles Stewart of Ardshiel had been outlawed in 1746 and his lands formally declared forfeit the following year, those rents, as far as Colin Campbell was concerned, were owing to him and the exchequer barons. 'I intend Monday next to be in Duror,' he informed James Stewart on 14 October, 1749, 'and [to] call for the bygone rents.'[19]

By the start of 1750, Colin Campbell had established to his own satisfaction exactly how much was owing in back rent on the Ardshiel estate. James Stewart himself was reckoned to be due £381 12s Scots in respect of his Achindarroch lands, £169 4s Scots in respect of Glen Duror. Other Achindarroch tenants, such as John MacColl, Duncan MacColl, Mildret MacColl and Ann MacLaren, the last two of whom may well have been Culloden widows, were judged to have proportionate debts. So were further tenants in the townships of Achara and Ardshiel.

James Stewart responded to this development by firing off a petition from the Ardshiel tenantry, himself included, to the Court of Exchequer in Edinburgh. Colin Campbell, the Ardshiel petitioners maintained, was 'greatly distressing' them by threatening to embark on the 'poinding', or confiscating, of goods equivalent to the value of rents which, James and his associates pointed out, they had already paid to Isabel Stewart. With a view to determining the facts, a legally constituted hearing was held, on the Court of Exchequer's orders, at Ballachulish on 5 March 1750. At this hearing, first James Stewart and then a parade of other Ardshiel estate tenants 'solemnly swore' that, while they would have been happy to pay their rents, from 1746 onwards, to the Edinburgh barons, they had unfortunately been forced to hand over those rents either to Charles Stewart (in 1746) or to Isabel Stewart (in subsequent years). 'He was so far compelled by [Stewart of] Ardshiel to pay [to Stewart] the rent of his possession', the Ballachulish hearing was told by one Achindarroch tenant, John MacColl, 'that he [MacColl] was threatened to have his horse removed out of his plough if he would not do it.'[20]

Although much of this was the most transparent fiction, it appears to have done the trick. No back rents were to be levied, it was agreed, on the Ardshiel estate. And if anyone was to be proceeded against in relation to those rents, it should not be the Ardshiel tenants but rather Isabel Stewart. 'I can't see the least chance of recovering a shilling off her,' Colin Campbell wrote disgustedly

– his irritation intensified, perhaps, by a growing suspicion on his part that he'd allowed James Stewart so much latitude as to enable James to make him look something of a fool.[21]

The consequent deterioration in relations between Colin and James accelerated in the course of the 1750s when Colin's management style began to be interpreted in high places as evidence of pro-Jacobite tendencies on his part. Colin Campbell, it was noted, had rented farmland on one of the Lochaber estates in his charge to John Cameron of Fassifern. John, though he had taken no active part in the 1745/46 rebellion, was strongly suspected by the British government (not least because he was Donald Cameron of Lochiel's brother) of being a Jacobite agent. His favouring of John Cameron resulted in Colin Campbell being 'severely reprimanded' by the barons of exchequer. It also had the effect of reminding more than one senior politician that Colin Campbell, whose mother had been a Lochaber Cameron, had family connections both with Cameron of Fassifern, whose interests he had apparently been promoting in Lochaber, and with Cameron of Lochiel, a man seen – correctly – in government circles as the key Highland contributor to such success as Charles Edward Stuart had managed to achieve in 1745.[22]

Although *his* mother had actually been a Campbell, not a Cameron, John Campbell of Barcaldine, Colin's half-brother, who'd also been given a factoring job by the Court of Exchequer, found himself caught up in the backwash of what had occurred in Lochaber. A letter written by a government minister, Henry Pelham, makes this clear: 'I find that Campbell of Glenure and Campbell of Barcaldine, who is Glenure's brother, are . . . related in some degree to the Camerons and other rebels, and there is good reason, from intelligence, to suspect the loyalty of both these factors themselves. If this is the case, as I believe it will be found to be, I am of [the] opinion proper persons should be appointed factors . . . in their rooms [places].' To Lord Glenorchy, afterwards Earl of Breadalbane and the man who headed the wider segment of Clan Campbell to which both John and Colin belonged, such charges seemed ludicrous. Since he had 'recommended' the brothers to the Court of Exchequer in the first instance, Glenorchy informed the Edinburgh barons, he thought it 'incumbent upon him to vindicate them' from the 'false aspersions' being so widely cast in their direction. This Lord Glenorchy proceeded to do over several closely written pages – with the result that the barons of exchequer pronounced themselves persuaded. 'As to the two Campbells [John and Colin],' they noted, 'we cannot, upon the strictest enquiry, find the least suspicion of their disloyalty.' Not everyone in London was convinced, however. And though both Colin and John were permitted to remain in post, the two men would have been well aware of how precarious their position had become, and of how much care they'd have to take in future to avoid stepping out of line.[23]

Colin Campbell, in particular, would have had no illusions as to the ease with which a case could be built against him. As a son of his father's second marriage, he was Donald Cameron of Lochiel's cousin. And while he'd served in the Hanoverian forces during Charles Edward Stuart's rebellion, he had not actually fought the Jacobites, having been absent without leave on the one occasion when he might have done. None of this was alterable. Nor was the fact of his having let land to his other Cameron cousin, John of Fassifern. That made it all the more urgent, Colin Campbell must surely have concluded, to mend his ways in respect of Ardshiel – where he had allowed a former Jacobite officer, James Stewart, to operate as his proxy and where he had turned a blind eye to the fact that James was supplying the family of a still more prominent Jacobite, Charles Stewart of Ardshiel, with cash raised on Charles' supposedly forfeited estate. Luckily for Cailean Ruadh, his methods of doing business on the Ardshiel estate – methods which were capable of having the worst possible construction placed upon them – seem not to have been drawn to the attention of anyone of consequence in the south. But it is clear that by the end of 1750, if not before, its factor had come to the conclusion that, in future, the Ardshiel estate would have to be managed very differently.

Colin Campbell was no Jacobite. But having tried and failed, right at the start of his factorship, to collect those Lochaber rents which he had finally been able to get in only with a detachment of heavily armed soldiers at his back, Colin had sought to make things easier for himself by striking deals, both in Lochaber and on the Ardshiel estate, with men of influence – Cameron of Fassifern on the one hand, James Stewart on the other – who thereafter minimised open and active opposition to the factor by exercising their substantial local clout on his behalf. Because he had had to make concessions to those men – renting a farm to John Cameron, doing nothing to stop James Stewart sending money to France – and because both of them continued to be Jacobite sympathisers, this strategy, always a hazardous one, had eventually backfired so spectacularly as to have jeopardised the factor's job, indeed his freedom. As a result Colin Campbell, conscious of his need to reingratiate himself with his superiors, was obliged to dispense with James Stewart's rent-collecting services. His doing so, not least because this action immediately cut off the flow of funds from Duror to Sens, was bound to have caused a rift between the former friends. Of itself, however, the termination of James' unofficial subfactorship would not have caused the two men to become, as they shortly became, the bitterest and most implacable of enemies. That development was due to something else entirely.

On 25 July 1751, the barons of exchequer, meeting in Edinburgh, agreed a detailed set of instructions as to how Colin Campbell of Glenure was to conduct the administration of the properties he factored on their behalf. One of those instructions was intended to ensure that suspect individuals such as John Cameron of Fassifern would never again be granted farms on forfeited estates. 'You are on no condition whatever', Colin Campbell was told, 'to let a farm to any of the friends of the forfeiting person.' As Colin well knew, this prohibition, though aimed more at 'friends' of Donald Cameron of Lochiel than at relatives of Charles Stewart of Ardshiel, debarred him from letting land to James Stewart, the former Ardshiel laird's half-brother. In anticipation of just such a command, which he was said subsequently to have expected for some time, the factor had already taken the required action; towards the end of 1750, he had ordered James Stewart to quit Glen Duror. Formally, James' eviction did not take effect until the following May – farm tenancies in Scotland traditionally starting and finishing at Whitsun. But possibly because he preferred to leave in his own time than wait for an eviction order to be served on him, James Stewart broke his links both with Glen Duror and with his Achindarroch landholdings – from which, it appears, Colin Campbell also ejected him – at some point in the winter of 1750–51.[24]

Although James, still trying to do what he could to keep Charles and Isabel Stewart in funds, continued to be involved – even at this late stage – in the collection of Ardshiel estate rents, relations between James and Colin Campbell had reached, by the start of 1751, a new low. They were to deteriorate further when Colin's plans for Glen Duror became apparent. The glen's new tenant, as everyone in Duror had learned before the close of 1750, was to be the Ardshiel factor's cousin and near neighbour, John Campbell of Baleveolan, whose home was situated at the head of Glen Creran and whose lands were immediately adjacent to Colin Campbell's own Glenure estate. From a Clan Stewart standpoint – given that the Stewarts of Appin had been fighting for centuries to keep the Campbells out of their territories – this was bad enough. But what caused still more outrage among the Appin Stewarts, now convinced that Cailean Ruadh was deploying his Court of Exchequer powers in ways calculated to advance his own interests, was the fact that, while Campbell of Baleveolan was entered in the Court of Exchequer's books as Glen Duror's tenant, half of the glen's cattle stock was in the ownership of none other than Colin Campbell himself.

Some time after his half-brother's murder, John Campbell of Barcaldine explained that this development was due to the virtual impossibility of persuading a more neutral figure to take on Glen Duror in the wake of James Stewart's removal from the place. This is not wholly implausible, especially if account is taken of a contemporary summary of 'If a clan or family have had immemorial possession of a country or glen, which possession they call duchus, they imagine that this constitutes a natural right thereto, and that they ought not, upon any account, to be dispossessed thereof.' What is referred to here is the very ancient notion – encapsulated, as this eighteenth-century author commented correctly, in the Gaelic term *duthchas* – that anyone who occupied a piece of ground established, by virtue of such occupation, an entitlement to occupy it indefinitely. No such thinking featured, of course, in the property law of Scotland – the concept of duthchas, as the Duke of Argyll was to observe condescendingly at James Stewart's trial, being confined to 'uncivilised parts of the Highlands'. In the localities – and Duror was definitely one – where the notion survived, however, any interference with its provisions was a serious matter. Hence the problem facing Colin Campbell in the case of Glen Duror. Because either they or their nominees had occupied Glen Duror since the fifteenth century, members of Clan Stewart considered themselves to have a well-established right of duthchas over it. In those circumstances, anyone taking the tenancy of Glen Duror in the aftermath of James Stewart's eviction would be seen as 'usurping' this right, as another eighteenth-century writer put it. And that is why, or so John Campbell of Barcaldine argued, '[Campbell of] Glenure found difficulty in getting people to take the grounds which [James] Stewart [had] occupied.' It was solely with a view to getting round this difficulty, Campbell of Barcaldine went on, that his brother had turned for help to their common cousin, who, his bargaining position being a strong one, had made his (the cousin's) tenancy of Glen Duror conditional on this tenancy being in effect a partnership between himself and Glenure's laird: 'He [Colin] at length prevailed with Mr Campbell of Baleveolan to take possession of Glen Duror, the principal grass-possession [James] Stewart had, with the proviso [insisted on by the prospective tenant] that the factor [Colin] would stock the one half; and, as he [Colin] could not get another tenant, he agreed to [Campbell of] Baleveolan's scheme.'[25]

Needless to say, this was not how the Glenure laird's behaviour was understood in Duror. By Duror people, as would be recalled long afterwards, 'the intentions of [Colin Campbell] were believed, rightly or wrongly, to be purely selfish'. Colin was held to be 'very covetous of managing matters in such a way as to conduce to his own profit'; indeed, it was insisted that the factor had been heard to remark: 'I will yet see that a clod of Appin shall not be possessed by a Stewart.' Perhaps Colin Campbell said this, perhaps he didn't. Either way, there is no doubt that his actions during 1751 and 1752 came close to ending – formally and legally at any rate – Clan Stewart's long domination of Duror.[26]

Following his installation of John Campbell of Baleveolan as tenant of Glen

Duror, in partnership with himself, Colin went on to acquire outright ownership of Lagnaha. This township – which, as mentioned earlier, lay between two of the several tracts of land constituting the Ardshiel estate – was one of the parts of Duror belonging to the Stewart chieftain, Dougal Stewart. Since Dougal had declined to turn out in support of Charles Edward Stuart in 1745, Lagnaha remained his property. But Dougal – whose lack of any very great passion for the Highlands has already been stressed – was in no way committed to hanging on to clan territory if, by disposing of it, he could improve his own financial situation. Hence the chief's pre-1745 sale of several Duror townships, notably Keil and Acharn, to Donald Campbell of Airds. Hence, too, Dougal Stewart's attempt, in the course of the winter of 1746/47, to interest a prominent political figure, Andrew Fletcher,[27] in the possibility of his buying all that remained of Dougal's lands both in Duror and in the rest of Appin. When this prospective deal fell through, Dougal Stewart was left with no alternative, as he saw it, but to go on adding to his indebtedness by organising loan after loan – loans invariably secured against various portions of his estate. Since Colin Campbell – to whom, by the early 1750s, Clan Stewart's chief owed some £2,000 – was a major source of the loans in question, it was a simple matter for Colin, in 1751 or thereby, to demand part-repayment in the shape of Lagnaha.

Colin Campbell's decision to put the squeeze on Dougal Stewart may have been a consequence of the Glenure laird's needing, at this point, some ready cash. In 1751, two years after his marriage and with his family growing rapidly, Colin embarked on extensive and costly building work at Glenure House. Contractors started putting up a new wing that June, and, by September, the building's former thatch had given way to slates. Like his stake in Glen Duror's cattle stock, the Glenure laird's acquisition of Lagnaha – its rents now coming to him instead of Dougal Stewart – would have helped generate the funds required to pay for those home improvements. But for all that Colin Campbell's income was boosted both by his taking a half-share in Glen Duror and by his seizure of Lagnaha, short-term gain of this type, while doubtless welcome, was less important than the wider strategy of which the Lagnaha and Glen Duror transactions were merely components. Colin Campbell was ultimately trying to engineer a situation in which he, not James Stewart nor any other representative of James' clan, would be the dominant influence – territorially and every other way – in Duror. As part of this strategy, having granted the tenancy of Glen Duror to John Campbell of Baleveolan in May 1751, Colin Campbell, now Lagnaha's laird as well as the Ardshiel estate's factor, went on to make clear that other Campbells, or Campbell nominees, were, in May 1752 or shortly thereafter, to have tenancies in Ardshiel, Lettermore and Achindarroch.

Patrick Campbell, one of the beneficiaries of this decision and a nephew of Colin Campbell of Glenure, afterwards presented this Campbell takeover of Duror as an unavoidable consequence of the barons of exchequer having ordered Colin 'to dispossess such of the [Ardshiel] tenants as were known to be disaffected to government and, in particular, the friends and retainers [for example, James Stewart] of the [Ardshiel estate's] forfeiting family'. 'In pursuance of these instructions,' Patrick maintained, 'the factor [his uncle] set about warning [i.e., issuing notices of eviction to] such of the old possessors as were notorious for their disaffection; but in the course of removing them he met with numberless, and almost insurmountable, obstacles.' Having begun by 'disputing inch by inch' his uncle's eviction orders, Patrick alleged, the recipients of those orders next 'had recourse to the less eligible plan of threatening the lives of any who should . . . attempt succeeding them in their possessions'. This tactic, according to Patrick, had the desired effect in that the only people whom Colin could persuade 'to take possession' were men 'who were by natural ties bound to support his interest'. If he was to get rid of Duror's Jacobite-inclined and Stewart-affiliated tenants, in other words, Colin Campbell had no option but to replace those tenants – as had already happened in the Glen Duror case – with his own relatives.[28]

Not least because no such policy was implemented on any other forfeited estate, it is doubtful if the barons of exchequer actually intended their Ardshiel factor to do what he did in 1751 and 1752. But that is neither here nor there. What matters is the fact that, by the end of 1751, Colin Campbell's intentions were known to – and had been received very badly by – everyone in Duror. Ardshiel township, together with its mill and the remains of Ardshiel House, the former residence of Charles and Isabel Stewart, was, from May 1752, to be tenanted by Patrick Campbell's brother, Alexander – with Patrick himself serving as Alexander's 'assistant'. Lettermore, for its part, was to be shared by two more Campbells – one of them the brother of Patrick and Alexander, the other a nephew of Glen Duror's principal tenant, John Campbell of Baleveolan. And though the part of Achindarroch which had previously been tenanted by James Stewart was not, for the time being, to have a Campbell occupant, its designated tenant was a man who would have been every bit as unacceptable as any Campbell to the folk of Duror.[29]

This man was John MacAulay. His principal claim to posthumous fame is to be found in the fact that he was the paternal grandfather of Thomas Babington Macaulay, nineteenth-century Britain's most renowned historian.[30] In his lifetime, however, John MacAulay, a Presbyterian clergyman, was best known for the persistent efforts he made, while Church of Scotland minister in South Uist, to hunt down Prince Charles Edward Stuart in the course of the prince's post-Culloden wanderings in the Hebrides. While failing to capture the prince, the island minister had amply demonstrated where his heart lay politically. That may be why the Duke of Argyll (who, because of the way such matters were customarily arranged in eighteenth-century Scotland, had a decisive say in the appointment in question) made it known to John MacAulay, during the winter of 1751/52, that he wanted him to move from South Uist to the parish of Lismore and Appin. This parish, of course, included Duror. Perhaps the duke thought that its stubbornly Jacobite and Episcopalian population might learn something from the sermonising of a staunchly pro-Hanoverian and anti-Episcopalian cleric like MacAulay.

The latter agreed to the proposed transfer. It is improbable, however, that many Duror people were persuaded to abandon Episcopacy for the Church of Scotland as a result. By the residents of his new parish, in fact, MacAulay seems to have been disliked intensely. He was, people said, '*duine rag, danarra, ceann-làidir, ceannsgalach*': an obstinate, opinionated, dogmatic, domineering man. He was also – and this would not have enhanced his reputation locally – more than happy to accept the tenancy of half of Achindarroch from Colin Campbell. It was 'a difficult matter to support a family and have the necessaries of life' on a minister's stipend, John MacAulay wrote in March 1752. He was anxious, therefore, to arrange some additional source of income prior to leaving South Uist for Lismore and Appin. His share of Achindarroch, MacAulay made clear, would help greatly in this regard.[31]

During the early 1750s, then, a new division of territory began to be put in place in the northern part of Argyll. Directing this development was a close-knit group, centred on the families of Colin Campbell of Glenure and John Campbell of Baleveolan, whose leading figures hoped, as a result of their efforts, greatly to add to landholdings which had previously been confined to Glen Creran. The first such addition, secured in 1751, was Glen Duror – which connected with Glen Creran's upper reaches by means of well-used hill tracks and passes. Beyond Glen Duror, but also starting to be incorporated into the Campbell domain, were Achindarroch (where John MacAulay had been invited to take charge) and Lagnaha (which Colin Campbell had obtained from Dougal Stewart). Since the townships of Ardshiel and Lettermore were also scheduled to pass into Campbell hands during 1752, it followed that a wedge of Campbell tenancies and possessions was being driven right through an area which the Stewarts of Appin had occupied for the better part of three centuries – separating, in the process, lands belonging to Alexander Stewart of Ballachulish from lands held by the Ballachulish laird's kinsmen, the Stewarts of Achnacone, Invernahyle and Fasnacloich. This, from a Stewart standpoint, was menacing enough. But even more alarming was the fact that this rapidly growing area of Campbell supremacy adjoined other formerly Stewart lands – the townships of Acharn, Keil, Achabhlar and Bealach – bought from the Appin chief, Dougal Stewart, a few years before, by Donald Campbell of Airds. Nor was there any obvious reason, at the close of 1751, as to why the Stewart position should not deteriorate further. Given the extent to which Dougal Stewart, the clan's hopelessly ineffectual chief, continued to be in hock to Colin Campbell of Glenure, key instigator of the machinations which had brought Glen Duror, Achindarroch, Lagnaha, Ardshiel and Lettermore under Campbell control, much more Stewart territory was clearly in danger of falling into the Glenure laird's clutches.

As both he and his contemporaries would have been aware, the methods which Colin Campbell employed to bring Duror under his personal dominance were those which had been fundamental to Clan Campbell expansionism for hundreds of years. Those methods involved, first establishing a legal claim to some particular piece of land and, second, making Campbells or their close allies the principal occupiers of the land in question. Tactics of this sort had made Colin Campbell's ancestors the masters of Lorn in the fifteenth century. In the course of the sixteenth and seventeenth centuries, ruthless use of the same tactics – backed, where necessary, by force of arms – had enabled other Campbells to take, for example, Kintyre and Islay from the MacDonalds, and Mull from the MacLeans. In 1737, reporting to the Duke of Argyll from the latter island, Archibald Campbell of Stonefield – in a classic summary of how his clan went about the task of colonising successive tracts of territory – noted that much of Mull had been parcelled out among 'gentlemen of the name of Campbell who have gone a good length to plant their several districts with people of the same name or their friends'.

Although Campbell of Stonefield – who was destined, incidentally, to spend a lot of time in Duror in 1752 – did not dwell on the point, incoming Campbells naturally expected to encounter resistance. Mostly, this resistance was fairly limited in its impact. Occasionally, however, it could scare Campbell colonists so badly as to persuade them to abandon particular colonisation projects. This happened, for instance, in Morvern, which had been annexed by Clan Campbell at much the same time as Mull and which, like Mull, experienced extensive Campbell settlement. So miserable was life made for Morvern's new arrivals by its original inhabitants – who, having begun by maiming and killing Campbell cattle, went on to threaten Campbell families with the same fate – that, by the 1720s and 1730s, it had become practically impossible to persuade any member of Clan Campbell to rent land in the locality. Might what had been encountered by Campbells in Morvern not also be encountered by other Campbells, just across Loch Linnhe, in Duror? Patrick

Campbell, for one, thought so. On first reconnoitring the Duror townships he was jointly to occupy with his brother, Alexander, Patrick was not greatly surprised, therefore, to meet with 'lawless schemes of opposition'. Those schemes, Patrick added darkly, 'were strongly supported by a certain party, at that time very powerful, whose resentment was much dreaded in the country'. The 'party' Patrick talked of was James Stewart.[32]

Although preceding paragraphs may well have given a contrary impression, Clan Campbell was by no means completely united and homogenous. It contained rival camps; it experienced internecine quarrels; sometimes it split. This was much to the advantage of Seumas a' Ghlinne, for, when James was obliged to pull out of Glen Duror and Achindarroch, tensions between the two Campbell factions then operating in Duror – one led by Colin Campbell of Glenure, the other headed by Donald Campbell of Airds – enabled him to secure an alternative home.

It is a little hard to understand why the Airds' laird – who, just four or five years before, had been pouring musket fire into James Stewart's Appin Regiment unit at Culloden – should have come so readily to James' assistance. Perhaps Donald Campbell hoped to be the sole beneficiary of the steady disintegration of Dougal Stewart's landholdings and was resentful, therefore, of Colin Campbell's takeover ambitions. Possibly he disliked both Colin and the devious way the Glenure laird was establishing himself and his relatives in Duror; or maybe Donald Campbell was the sort of man – common enough in the eighteenth-century Highlands – who did not allow his pro-Hanoverian politics to debar him from forming friendships with men who were Jacobites. All that is certain is that, by the close of 1750, James Stewart was being described in correspondence as 'tacksman [or principal tenant] of Acharn', one of the Duror townships under Campbell of Airds' control.[33]

Acharn, where James was to live for what remained of his life, is less than half a mile from Achindarroch. And like Achindarroch, Acharn, in the mid-eighteenth century, was a well-populated township, not a single farm. As this township's leading man, James occupied – along with his wife, his children and an indeterminate number of the servants and labourers then invariably employed by someone of his status – a home which remained more or less intact until the 1960s.[34] This home – a surviving, though much modernised, equivalent of which can be seen at nearby Achara – was a cut above houses of the sort occupied by the majority of Duror's eighteenth-century residents. Its walls were mortared, rather than consisting simply, as was standard in Duror at that time, of stone and rubble. And though this house, in the manner of practically every other Highland home of its era, was thatched, not slated, it contained several spacious apartments. On quitting Achindarroch and Glen

Duror for Acharn, then, James Stewart, Margaret Stewart and their family did not experience any reduction in living standards. Indeed, it is possible that in purely material terms James and Margaret gained, rather than lost, from their enforced move.

Nor were James' connections with Glen Duror severed completely as a result of his becoming one of Donald Campbell's tenants. Acharn is Achindarroch's counterpart in that, while on the opposite bank of Duror's river, it is located, like Achindarroch, at the point where Glen Duror meets the north-south strath which has always contained most of Duror's settlements. From Acharn, then, just as from Achindarroch, there is easy access to Glen Duror – the difference being that anyone heading into the glen from Acharn, as opposed to Achindarroch, traverses the lower slopes of Fraochaidh, not those of Beinn a' Bheithir. As a result, eighteenth-century Acharn's hill grazings included the part of Glen Duror lying to the south of the glen's river. And though those north-facing pastures were not so attractive agriculturally as the sunny slopes where he had pastured his cattle when a tenant on the Ardshiel estate, James Stewart must have thought himself lucky to be conducting, from his new base at Acharn, a farming operation of the sort his eviction might easily have ended.

This may explain why James, on his arrival to Acharn, told his new laird, Donald Campbell of Airds, that he was 'easy' as to his removal from Glen Duror. At this stage, too, James appears to have imagined – presumably as a result of what had been said to him, prior to his eviction, by Colin Campbell of Glenure – that his departure from Glen Duror and Achindarroch, though made unavoidable by the decision of the exchequer barons to move against the close relatives of prominent Jacobite exiles, would not automatically result in his being excluded from the management of the Ardshiel estate. He hoped, James remarked to Campbell of Airds, to ensure that what the latter called the 'excrescence' of Ardshiel estate rents – meaning the difference between the estate's officially fixed rental and the amount James had actually been collecting from Ardshiel's tenants – would continue to find its way to Charles and Isabel Stewart in France. In this respect, however, James was wildly over-optimistic as to what Campbell of Glenure – in the aftermath of the trouble in which the factor found himself as result of his dealings with Cameron of Fassifern – might be prepared to tolerate. In truth, Colin was moving rapidly to terminate James Stewart's subfactorship. He was moving just as rapidly both to consolidate his grip on Lagnaha and to establish his relatives or nominees in Ardshiel township, Achindarroch and Lettermore. This was soon to become clear to all concerned, James Stewart included. Hence the very obvious tendency on James' part, as 1751 advanced, to indulge in more and more outspoken denunciations of Colin Campbell, Colin's collaborators and all their works.[35]

On hearing that Ewan MacIntyre, a Duror man in his early twenties, had taken a job as a herdsman with Glen Duror's incoming tenant, John Campbell of Baleveolan, James sought out MacIntyre and – or so the young man afterwards alleged – threatened him with violence. However 'easy' he might originally have been about leaving Glen Duror, James Stewart, this episode demonstrates, was easy no longer. And there were other indications of James' ever blacker mood. In the course of his regular encounters with Alexander Stewart of Invernahyle, for example, James was increasingly inclined to express himself 'much dissatisfied' with what was being done with his half-brother's former lands. Something of the nature of this dissatisfaction, which quickly communicated itself to James' elder son, Alan, can be discerned in a letter which Alan wrote, in the spring of 1751, to David Stewart of Glenbuckie, a Balquhidder and Strathgartney landowner to whom James and his family were related. 'Now I am sorry to acquaint you [that] affairs are going quite wrong upon [the Ardshiel] estate,' Alan Stewart observed. '[Campbell of] Glenure wants [the townships of] Ardshiel and Lettermore in his own hands ... How far these things will take place, God knows.' Already, Alan went on, Campbell of Baleveolan and his people were installing themselves in Glen Duror. 'However,' he added, 'it shall be a dear glen to them or [ere?] they shall have it.'[36]

After Colin Campbell's murder, this last remark would be seized on by James Stewart's accusers as evidence of his and his family's 'hatred' of the men who had displaced them from Glen Duror. So would a tale to the effect that, on hearing of Colin Campbell's intention 'to take ... the management of the estate of Ardshiel' fully into his own hands, James responded by saying that 'he would be willing to spend a shot upon [Campbell of] Glenure, tho' he went upon his knees to his window to fire it'.[37]

Decades after James' death, outbursts of this sort were linked in Duror with James' growing tendency, following his departure from the Ardshiel estate, to drunkenness. 'He became much addicted to drink thenceforth,' it was said of Seumas a' Ghlinne in Victorian times, 'and when he would be drunk, as often he was, he reviled Colin of Glenure, spoke of his ill-will to him, threatened that he should do as much harm to Colin of Glenure as Colin had done to him, and he did not conceal his resentment.' In fact, James Stewart's consumption of alcohol does not seem to have greatly exceeded the eighteenth-century average. But the spirits he did consume had the potentially fatal effect of loosening his tongue – as appears to have happened, for example, in his Acharn brew-house at the start of the Yule, or Christmas, season of 1751.[38]

In James' company on this occasion were three men whom he employed, Dugald MacColl, John MacColl and a second John MacColl – the two John MacColls being differentiated by their Gaelic nicknames, *Iain Mòr* (Big John) and *Iain Beag* (Little John). It being a December morning and consequently very dark, Iain Mòr recalled, he, Dugald and Iain Beag were at work 'before daylight', assisting James 'in distilling the second draught of a brewing of aqua vitae'. They were, in other words, making whisky – then commonly produced domestically in buildings which were also used, as was the case at Acharn, for brewing beer of the sort that, prior to the widespread use of beverages like tea or coffee, was generally drunk with every meal. James, Iain Mòr recollected, 'ordered' him 'to give ... the people present a dram'. This was done. And as the four men – James, the two Iains and Dugald – drank companionably in the slowly growing light of this pre-Yule dawn, their conversation turned, predictably enough, to the latest doings of Colin Campbell of Glenure.[39]

When 1751's rents had fallen due some three or four weeks before, Colin, it seems, had become caught up in a dispute with the tenants of Achara, the Ardshiel estate township just to the south of Acharn.[40] Part of Achara's rent was payable, like most rents of the time, in grain or meal. But 1751 being what Iain Mòr called 'a scarce year', the township's tenants had offered Cailean Ruadh cash in lieu of this payment in kind, preferring to hold on to such scanty food supplies as were in their possession. Possibly because shortages had pushed prices so high as to make the Achara men's grain worth more than the money they were offering, Colin had responded by rejecting all talk of cash and insisting that Achara's tenants hand over the grain and meal they had hoped to retain for the use of their families. By everyone in Duror, certainly by the four men drinking together in the Acharn brew-house, the factor's conduct – naturally enough – was bitterly resented. And at Acharn that December morning, talk of this conduct led – equally naturally – to Seumas a' Ghlinne reflecting more generally on Colin Campbell's plans. 'If [Campbell of] Glenure went on in the way he then did,' Iain Mòr remembered James saying, 'it was likely he would be laird of Appin in a very short time.' By this, of course, James meant that the financial leverage which Colin had obtained over the Appin chief, Dougal Stewart, was such as to enable the Glenure laird, if he so chose, to foreclose on all of Dougal's remaining lands – as he had already foreclosed on Lagnaha. To James, and to anyone else with even the slightest sense of the extent to which Clan Stewart's destinies had traditionally been bound up both with Duror and with Appin at large, that was a deeply depressing prospect. And it was one which James, as Dugald MacColl recalled, believed would be especially to the disadvantage of Clan Stewart's 'commoners or followers' – terms which, in the English record of what was said originally in Gaelic, probably stand for *tuath*, meaning tenantry or clansfolk. 'However he [James], or people in circumstances like him, would shift for themselves,' James told his hearers, 'they, the commoners, would be very badly off.' 'He knew commoners once in Appin,' James went on meaningfully, 'who would not allow [Campbell of] Glenure to go on at such a rate.'[41]

James was subsequently to maintain that he had no recollection of making any such remark. However, there was no denying his involvement in a slightly later episode which, since it involved both James Stewart and Colin Campbell in a very public quarrel, would instantly have become the talk of Duror.

The quarrel occurred not much more than a week after the Yuletide gathering in Acharn's brew-house and took place at Kentallen Inn. This establishment – which, despite its somewhat more pretentious name, would have been similar, both in function and appearance, to Taigh na h-Insaig – was located near the spot, towards the head of Kentallen Bay, where, if heading for the modern Ardshiel, you would turn off the Oban–Fort William road. Being more or less equidistant from James Stewart's Acharn home and from Ballachulish House, residence of Ballachulish's laird, Alexander Stewart, Kentallen Inn was a convenient meeting point for James and John Stewart, Alexander's elder son, and both of them had arranged to get together there on the evening of 31 December 1751 – Hogmanay. John and James – accompanied to Kentallen by a further James Stewart who had travelled there from Ardnamurchan and who was an uncle both of Seumas a' Ghlinne and of Seumas' exiled half-brother, Tearlach Mòr – would doubtless have had a convivial enough time had their party not encountered, at the inn, a second group headed by Colin Campbell of Glenure and Colin's cousin, John Campbell of Baleveolan. Since much now divided Cailean Ruadh from Seumas a' Ghlinne, and since John Campbell was the man who had taken over from James as tenant of Glen Duror, the atmosphere in Kentallen Inn must have been tense from the outset. It is hardly surprising, therefore, that before the evening was through, matters took a vicious turn.

Some hours after dark, Margaret Stewart, James' wife, suspecting that her husband might need help to get home after his Hogmanay celebrations, sent Dugald MacColl – one of the participants in the brew-house gathering – to escort James back to Acharn. But James was not to be budged. In a room which seems to have been set aside for the inn's more prestigious customers, he, his Stewart kin and the two Campbells 'drank', as Dugald MacColl reported, 'till it was late at night'. He'd 'heard them speaking together', Dugald replied when asked how the Campbells and Stewarts had been getting on together, 'but, as it was in English, he did not understand what they said'. There was no mistaking, however, the meaning of what next transpired. 'They began to speak very loud,' Dugald remarked of the men he had overheard, 'and got up upon their feet.' He and 'several other commoners who happened to be in the house at the time', Dugald went on, 'apprehending they [the Campbells and Stewarts] were going to quarrel, went into the room in order to prevent it'. There Dugald and his friends – two MacCombies from Ardshiel and a man by the name of MacCorquodale from Lettermore – were asked by John Stewart, the Ballachulish laird's son, to get Seumas a' Ghlinne and Seumas' uncle into the fresh air. He and his friends complied at once, Dugald said, and, seizing the two James Stewarts, who still 'spoke loud and in English', 'carried [them] out of the room'.[42]

This account was confirmed by John Stewart who quickly joined his fellow clansmen outside: 'After the company had drunk very hard and were all drunk,' John stated, 'some high words arose between [Campbell of] Glenure and Ardshiel's uncle [meaning James Stewart from Ardnamurchan], and they were like to come to blows which both of them attempted.' Hence John's decision to have James and his uncle taken bodily from the inn.[43]

But no sooner had Seumas a' Ghlinne been removed from Kentallen Inn, John continued, than he became drunkenly insistent that he should be allowed to return. This, John explained, was because James 'had invited [Campbell of] Glenure next day to his house [at Acharn], which Glenure had accepted of, and therefore [James] pressed to come in again to the [inn] to renew the invitation, and to take his leave of Glenure'. Knowing exactly where such a further encounter was likely to lead, John Stewart, having told Dugald MacColl and his associates to keep James where he was, returned to the inn himself. There he found Colin Campbell 'standing with a drawn hanger [sword] in his hand'. Hearing the commotion outside and knowing himself to be in a place thick with Stewarts and their clansfolk, Cailean Ruadh, it seems, had concluded – understandably enough – that he was about to be mobbed. On being firmly assured by John Stewart 'that he [John] should not allow him [Colin] to be mobbed', the befuddled, but obviously alarmed, factor 'threw [his sword] upon [a] bed'.[44]

Re-emerging into the night, John Stewart was able to tell James that both Colin Campbell and Colin's cousin, Campbell of Baleveolan, would be pleased to eat with him at Acharn on New Year's Day. James, however, remained as bellicose as ever – taking out his bad temper, it seems, on Dugald MacColl, whose unenviable job it was to get his hopelessly intoxicated employer safely home. James had to be 'carried over a burn adjoining to the [inn] of Kentallen' – this stream, incidentally, being the one which, nearer its source, flows in front of the Lagnaha cave where Charles Stewart of Ardshiel had sheltered back in 1746. Only dimly aware of where he was, but seeing Dugald MacColl and various other Duror men around him, James, according to Dugald, 'asked the tenants then present what kept them there so late, and why they did not go home in proper time of night'. 'And they answering that they were waiting upon him,' Dugald continued, '[James] replied that it was not waiting upon him they were, but upon [Campbell of] Glenure, to see what they could get by [meaning from] him.'[45]

James, Dugald recalled, 'continued at such conversation as this till they came to the fields of Achindarroch, hard by Acharn', at which point James happened to hear one of Dugald's companions remark 'that he was told that [Campbell of] Glenure had a drawn hanger in the room where they [James and his party] had been drinking'. 'Upon which,' Dugald went on, '[James] asked them why they did not tell him [this] before he came away from the [inn], that he might see if it was true, and what Glenure meant by it, and insisted then on going back to know the truth of it.' Doubtless anxious to be at home with their families or in their own beds, James' escorts were in no mood to contemplate a return trip to Kentallen. On their duly 'declaring that they would not allow him [James] to go back', Dugald concluded, 'he [James] bid them go about their business and leave him, which they accordingly did'.[46]

Somehow James Stewart got home to Acharn in the early hours of New Year's Day, 1752. And there, the following morning, he was up and about in time to play host to Colin and John Campbell – who, as they had promised they would, called at Acharn for their midday meal.

The fact that Colin and his cousin sat down with James at James' table on 1 January would, at James' trial, be taken as evidence of his still being on speaking terms with Colin just four or five months prior to the latter's murder. This, from a defence counsel's standpoint, was a fair enough argument to advance – in that, at Acharn, the appropriate civilities were doubtless observed. But no amount of New Year's Day dinner-table chat could conceal the growing tension between the two men; tension evident in Colin having felt the need, at the height of the Kentallen Inn fracas, to reach for his sword; tension equally apparent in the tenor of James Stewart's drunken comments to the men who had brought him home. While there was, in reality, little risk of the Ardshiel estate's tenants – all of whom stood to gain as little as their Stewart superiors from a Campbell colonisation of Duror – switching their allegiance from James and his kin to Cailean Ruadh, it is indicative of James' state of mind that, when deep in whisky-induced paranoia, he accused Dugald MacColl and his associates of having come to Kentallen Inn solely in the hope of currying favour with Campbell of Glenure. At the start of 1752, then, James Stewart was a man tormented by the thought that Duror, if he could find no way of stopping Colin Campbell in his tracks, was about to slip completely from Clan Stewart's grasp. And that James was right to be deeply worried about this became apparent when, as the days began to lengthen, it was made known who was to be evicted from the Ardshiel estate, on the term-day of 15 May 1752 to make way for Colin's relatives.

Among the twenty or so individuals whose Ardshiel estate tenancies were to be terminated on that date was James Stewart himself – his name featuring on Colin Campbell's blacklist as a result of his having managed to retain, even after the loss of his Glen Duror and Achindarroch landholdings, a share in some hill pasture at Lettermore. Also due to lose their stake in Lettermore were John MacCorquodale (one of the men who had been in Dugald MacColl's company at Kentallen Inn on Hogmanay) and Sarah Cameron, a widow. Kentallen Inn's keeper, MacCombie or Colquhoun by name, was to be deprived of lands he occupied in Ardshiel township. So were John Colquhoun senior, John Colquhoun junior, Dugald Colquhoun and one of the locality's many Dugald MacColls – all tenants, like the Kentallen innkeeper, of Ardshiel township. A further John Colquhoun, the miller at Ardshiel, was to be ejected from his mill. John MacColl, John Stewart and Catherine Colquhoun, a widow, were to be evicted from Achara. Four more widows – Margaret Campbell (no relative, presumably, of the Glenure laird), Mary MacKenzie, Ann MacLaren and Mildret MacColl – were to be turned out of lands in Achindarroch. Also scheduled for eviction from Achindarroch were Duncan MacColl senior, Duncan MacColl junior, John MacColl senior and John MacColl junior – the last two being possibly connected with, maybe even identical to, those other MacColls, Iain Mòr and Iain Beag, with whom James Stewart had shared a Yuletide dram in Acharn's brew-house.[47]

While some of the Achindarroch people whose tenancies were in Colin Campbell's sights may have acquired those tenancies no more than a year previously, when James Stewart was deprived of his landholdings in the township, others of the Achindarroch residents now waiting anxiously for their formal notices of eviction were folk whose families were said to 'have been possessors of the farm of Achindarroch for several generations'. Much the same, it is likely, could have been claimed of some at least of the Lettermore, Ardshiel and Achara folk whose names were among those the Ardshiel estate factor had supplied to the Inveraray-based functionaries he had asked to provide him with the legal documentation needed to give effect to his planned evictions. And since each one of Colin Campbell's intended victims – irrespective of how long they had held their tenancies – would have had many friends and relations among the wider population of Duror, it is certain that, as winter began to give way to the spring of 1752, Duror was a community in turmoil. Into this turmoil, as luck would have it, there was now injected a further, highly destabilising, ingredient in the shape of James Stewart's foster-son, Ailean Breac.

At the end of the period the pair had spent dodging the troops who had vainly scoured the Duror and Appin hills in search of them, Ailean appears to have accompanied Charles Stewart of Ardshiel to France in 1747. There Ailean is known to have enlisted in the French military, joining, in January 1749, Ogilvy's Regiment, which, though in the King of France's service, consisted mostly of exiled Scots Jacobites. From records kept by the French army, the third in which Ailean had served in not much more than three years, it is possible to derive a reasonably detailed impression of how this young man – 26 in 1752 – looked to his contemporaries. He was five feet ten inches tall, well above the eighteenth-century average. His hair was 'black' and 'curly'. His face was 'extremely marked by smallpox scars'. His nose was 'long', his mouth 'ordinary'. And by his regimental superiors, it appears, Ailean was known officially as Allan Stuart, a 'native of Argile in Scotland'.[48]

Ailean Breac, however, was no common soldier, being released from his unit for months at a time, almost from the moment he enlisted, to enable him to make regular return trips to Scotland. According to Donald Campbell of Airds, speaking in 1752, Alan 'was in use of coming every year to the country [by which Campbell meant Duror and Appin] since [Stewart of] Ardshiel went to France'. This can be substantiated from other sources which, as well as confirming that Ailean was in Scotland between 1749 and 1751, suggest that his visits home served several distinct, if overlapping, functions. One of his tasks was to act as a recruiting agent for the French military in the Highlands. Another, it is virtually certain, was to keep Jacobite exiles, such as Charles Stewart of Ardshiel, in contact with their relatives, friends and allies back in Scotland. And a third, it's reasonable to suppose, was to act as a courier in respect of the cash which Ailean's foster-father, James Stewart, was then raising in Duror for the benefit of the Sens-based Stewart of Ardshiel and his family.[49]

'When he came up to . . . Appin, among his relations,' it was said of Ailean Breac in 1752, 'he used to stroll about without any settled residence and, whenever he came, he generally threw off his French clothes, as they were remarkable [meaning conspicuous] and improper for that hilly country, and borrowed from any acquaintace wherever he happened to be at the time. Among others, he used to visit at [James Stewart's] house, though he came seldomer there than to other places in the neighbourhood, as [James] used to take a good deal of freedom in blaming his conduct and extravagance.' While willing to provide a bed for his foster-son – at Achindarroch, in the first instance, then at Acharn – and while obliged to use Ailean's services when trying to keep Charles and Isabel Stewart in funds, Seamus a' Ghlinne evidently continued to regard his foster-son as something of a waster. This opinion was not one that James would have cause to alter in the course of Ailean Breac's 1752 sojourn in Scotland.[50]

That sojourn, like others before it, began in Scotland's capital, where Ailean, having disembarked from one of the many ships then trading between the continent and Edinburgh's port of Leith, lodged at the start of each of his Scottish trips, with Hugh Stewart – yet another member of the enormously extended family to which Ailean and James belonged – whose home was located in the vicinity of the Fountain Well in Edinburgh's High Street. Because most of the various activities – all of them pro-Jacobite in purpose – which brought Ailean to Scotland were indictable offences, and because he was still wanted in Scotland as a deserter from the British army, when in Edinburgh Ailean tended to keep a low profile. 'He seldom went out but in the night,' it was reported of him, 'and more than once narrowly escaped being apprehended.'[51]

However, once in the Highlands, where, for the most part, he was surrounded by friends and where he repeatedly demonstrated an unrivalled ability to fade into the landscape at the first hint of danger, Ailean Breac felt free to go about his business more openly. From Edinburgh, which he reached at the end of February or the beginning of March 1752, Ailean accordingly struck out after just two or three days for the north – spending a night, or a couple of nights, in each of the several houses at which he called on the way. Most of these houses belonged either to prominent Jacobite sympathisers or, and the two categories were by no means mutually exclusive, to folk possessing kinship links of some kind with the Stewarts of Appin. One of Ailean's initial destinations was the residence of David Stewart of Glenbuckie, the Balquhidder and Strathgartney laird with whom Ailean's foster-brother, also called Alan Stewart, had corresponded with from Acharn the year before. From Stewart of Glenbuckie's home, located at Brenachoile on the north shore of Loch Katrine, Ailean next headed for Rannoch, where his parents had lived and where he was assured of a welcome from relatives who had known him since he was a child. Next, probably by way of hill tracks he had followed in the company of James Stewart and other Duror men in Culloden's immediate aftermath, Ailean Breac made his way to Acharn. 'In the beginning of April [1752],' it was said of his getting there, '[Ailean] came to [James'] house . . . and, staying a day or two, went off . . . and continued strolling about the country . . . until the latter end of April.'[52]

From James, of course, Ailean would at once have heard of Colin Campbell's planned evictions – evictions now no more than five or six weeks away. And in the course of his various 'strollings' from one Duror or Appin household to the next, Ailean Breac was to take every possible opportunity, first, to condemn Colin in the strongest possible terms and, second, to make it clear that the Ardshiel estate's factor deserved, in his opinion, to come to a quick and bloody end.

At Acharn, falling in with Iain Mòr MacColl and Dugald MacColl, both of them in his foster-father's employment, as they were 'yoking the horses' prior to starting a day's ploughing, Ailean declared that if 'the people of Appin . . . were worth . . . they could keep out [Campbell of] Glenure and hinder him from oppressing them'.[53]

This was relatively mild. But soon – according at least to Robert Stewart, whose father, a man of the same name, was miller in the Duror township of Cuil – Ailean Breac had acquired his own personal grievance against Cailean Ruadh. The factor, Ailean claimed in Robert's presence, 'had sent notice' to the garrison commander at Fort William 'that he [Ailean] was in the country, that he might be apprehended'. But unlike the Ardshiel estate tenantry, Ailean Breac went on to declare, 'he [Ailean] was not in his [Colin's] reverence [was not in awe of him, in other words], as he had the King of France's commission in his pocket; and . . . he would be evens with him [the factor]; and . . . he would take the opportunity to dispatch or murder either [Campbell of] Glenure or [Campbell of] Baleveolan before he left the country'.[54]

In the various Duror and Appin dramshops where Ailean often spent his evenings, he would do a lot more boasting to the same effect. Should any Duror people dare to assist Colin Campbell with his forthcoming evictions, Ailean announced, 'he would make blackcocks out of them' – an expression which, 'it being a common phrase in the country', his hearers interpreted to mean that, if they were to have dealings with Cailean Ruadh, they would run the risk of being shot by Ailean Breac. 'He hated all [by] the name of Campbell,' Ailean proclaimed one night. He would 'take his opportunity to attack . . . Campbell of Glenure,' he said on another occasion. 'If you will bring me the red fox's skin, I will give you more,' he told a beggar to whom he had handed a few coppers.[55] Since Cailean Ruadh was so named because of his red hair, it was remarked by a witness to this particular exchange, he had 'at the time suspected that under the words red fox was meant Mr Campbell of Glenure'.[56]

Most of this, of course, was idle boasting, pub talk which acquired significance only in retrospect. In late April, however, there occurred an event which seems to have involved Ailean Breac, among others, and which, in contrast to the bombast in which Alan had been engaging up to that point, was heavy with genuine menace. This event's importance is underlined, a little paradoxically, by the difficulty which people had, both then and subsequently, in pinning down its precise nature – let alone the identities of the several men who were party to it. In eighteenth-century Duror, the sort of place where virtually nothing stayed secret for more than five minutes, keeping something confidential was, to put it mildly, very, very hard. That is why the shooting match in which Ailean Breac apparently participated towards the end of April

1752 can justifiably be called conspiratorial. This shooting match's organisers took immense care to keep every detail of it out of public view.

In 1865, probably by Archibald Colquhoun who was then 83 and living in the Airds district of Appin, a collector of Gaelic folklore learned that just weeks before the killing of Colin Campbell in the Wood of Lettermore, a number of the 'principal men' both of Duror and of Appin more generally – each of them carrying a gun – met in the vicinity of Lochan Blar nan Lochan, a little body of water deep in the hills a mile or two to the south of Bealach. They were there to establish which of them was the best shot. The place they'd selected as their rendevous, Lochan Blar nan Lochan, isn't much visited today. It wasn't much visited in the eighteenth century either. That, commented Archibald Colquhoun, was why the shooting match he described took place on the lochan's banks: 'The sound of the guns fired there would not be heard.'[57]

Testimony gathered more than a hundred years after the event to which it relates is by no means to be relied on. However, Archibald Colquhoun, having been born in 1782 and having spent his entire life in Appin or Duror, would have heard the story first hand from folk who had lived through the 1740s and 1750s. His account of the Lochan Blar nan Lochan shooting match should not be automatically discounted, therefore; still less when cognisance is taken of the fact that, as is clear from their correspondence, the men who investigated Colin Campbell's killing became aware, during the summer of 1752, that some such shooting match had taken place. This, to be sure, was all that could then be established, Duror's residents refusing absolutely to disclose, in the course of the 1752 murder investigation, any knowledge of a rumoured April gathering of prominent, and armed, men. It is impossible, then, to be conclusive about what transpired at Lochan Blar nan Lochan, but it is reasonable, on the basis of later tradition and contemporary allusions, to state the following: a number of men met at Lochan Blar nan Lochan prior to the assassination of Colin Campbell; among them, probably, was Ailean Breac; also there, it is likely, was Alan Stewart, Seumas a' Ghlinne's son, together with several other Stewarts, all of them close friends of the two Alans and most of them drawn from the younger generation of those gentry families, including the Stewarts of Ballachulish and the Stewarts of Fasnacloich, in whose homes Ailean Breac spent so much of his time that spring.

Years before, Edmund Burt, whose Highland writings have already been quoted, had watched Highlanders engage in target practice. What Burt saw then would not have been dissimilar to the Lochan Blar nan Lochan shooting match. And given the background to that shooting match, especially the growing feeling among the Appin Stewarts that Colin Campbell's assault on their landholdings and their tenants had somehow to be countered, there is much that is appropriate, in the Lochan Blar nan Lochan context, about Burt's choice of words: 'To shoot at a mark, they [Highlanders] lay themselves all along behind some stone or hillock on which they rest their piece [or firearm], and are a long while taking their aim; by which means they can destroy anyone unseen, on whom they would wreak their malice or revenge.' It was, as it happened, exactly in this manner that Colin Campbell of Glenure was shot.[58]

CHAPTER SIX

First, James of the Glens rode to Edinburgh and got some lawyer (a Stewart, nae doubt — they all hing together like bats in a steeple) and had the proceedings stayed. And then Colin Campbell cam' in again, and had the upper hand before the Barons of Exchequer. And now they tell me the first of the tenants are to flit tomorrow. It's to begin at Duror under James' very windows, which doesnae seem wise by my humble way of it.

Robert Louis Stevenson, *Kidnapped*

Duror, in April 1752, was full of gossip and speculation as to what might happen when Colin Campbell attempted to carry out his planned evictions. If, at Lochan Blar nan Lochan or elsewhere, a conspiracy to kill Cailean Ruadh had indeed begun to take shape, its existence at this stage was known only to those involved. But violence of some sort was widely anticipated, not least by the Fasnacloich laird, John Stewart, who commented that 'he . . . was apprehensive, if the tenants were removed, that some squabble might happen'. Talk to the same effect was to be heard in *taighean*, or dramshops, both in Appin and in neighbouring localities. 'It was the common rumour of the country', according to the operator of one hostelry, 'that they [the Duror folk] would do harm to any [Campbell tenant] that came into the lands of Ardshiel.' In another such establishment – this one at Bunree near Onich – it was thought 'that the whole people of the Strath of Duror were to be gathered in a body at Ardshiel upon the day that they were to be charged to remove in order to keep out the people with their cattle whom [Campbell of] Glenure intended to introduce to the possession of the lands of Ardshiel, and were to kindle a bonfire upon an adjacent hill in order that their neighbours of Lochaber [including Onich] would come to their assistance in case of difficulty'.[1]

Following Colin Campbell's death, James Stewart was to be accused of fomenting this unrest. Maybe he did. But much of James' energy was invested, during the spring of 1752, in an attempt to enlist the law on the side of those Duror tenants whose dispossession was now imminent. It was with this aim in view that James left Acharn, on Friday, 3 April, bound for Edinburgh.

His prosecutors were afterwards to allege that Seumas a' Ghlinne made his Edinburgh trip 'without any warrant or authority' from the families who were due to be evicted. James disagreed. 'I do declare,' he said of the tenants on whose behalf he claimed to be acting, 'that it was their desire that all lawful ways should be taken to keep them in possession.' This is entirely plausible. Some of the Duror men whose leases were to be terminated are known to have offered to 'refund [James'] expense for representing their case'. And given that the Ardshiel estate tenantry's only alternatives to falling in with James' plans were to go quietly or engage in a violent confrontation which they were unlikely to win, it is probable that when James rode out of Duror on 3 April, practically everyone in the place wished him well.[2]

That Friday, James travelled no further than Carnoch, where Glencoe opens onto Loch Leven. There he lodged overnight with his half-sister, Isabel, widow of the Glencoe chief and Culloden veteran, Alexander MacDonald, who had died a couple of years previously. From Carnoch the next day James rode, by way of Bridge of Orchy, to Tyndrum, Sunday morning finding him pressing on through Glen Dochart, where, in the township of Luib, he called at a roadside dramshop 'to have his horse corned'. While the horse fed, James entered the dramshop in search of breakfast. There he fell in with a Stirling merchant, Colin MacLaren, who had been staying at the Luib dramshop overnight. Since MacLaren was a common name both in the Appin country itself and in those Balquhidder communities to which the Stewarts of Appin had long looked for support in times of trouble, James may have taken it for granted that his new acquaintance was a man with whom it was safe to share a drink. If so, he was mistaken. In fact, Colin MacLaren's business partner in Stirling was none other than Robert Campbell, a younger brother of Colin Campbell of Glenure. And in the aftermath of Colin's murder, MacLaren was to state repeatedly that James' talk in Luib's dramshop had been such as to show him eaten up with hatred for Colin Campbell of Glenure.[3]

'The removing [of the Duror tenants] was much at [James'] heart,' the Stirling merchant said. '[James] told him that, if he failed [to win his case] at Edinburgh, he would carry it to the British parliament; and, if he failed there, [James] told him, after a little pause and with an emphasis, that he behoved to take the only other remedy that remained.' Colin MacLaren's testimony was hardly unbiased. But there is no doubt that the issue of how he might most effectively put the case of the Ardshiel estate tenants to Edinburgh's courts was very much on James Stewart's mind as, leaving Luib, he headed for Glen Ogle,

Lochearnhead and Callander. What James wanted to obtain prior to getting to Edinburgh, it appears, was advice as to how he might best go about securing his legal objectives in the city. This advice, it seems, James got from people he lodged with, or visited, in the course of the first half of the week that began with his encounter with Colin MacLaren in Luib. Those people, all living in the vicinity of Callander, Doune and Stirling, included the Haldanes of Lanrick, David Stewart of Annat, Patrick Edmonstone of Newton, John Wordie of Cambusbarron and Hugh Seton of Touch. The Haldanes, of course, were the in-laws of James' exiled half-brother and Ardshiel's former laird, Charles Stewart. And their household – like the several other Stirlingshire households where James was hospitably received at this point – was staunchly Jacobite. Quite how far the Haldanes and their Jacobite friends were prepared to go in order to aid James Stewart and the Ardshiel tenants is unclear. But it is evident that, from one or more of the folk he visited, James got letters of introduction to lawyers and others who, it was felt, might be of assistance to him when he got to Edinburgh – which James finally reached, nearly a week after he left Duror, on Thursday, 9 April.[4]

Scotland's capital, in 1752 as for centuries previously, was confined to the narrow ridge which connects Edinburgh Castle with the Palace of Holyroodhouse. Along the spine of this ridge ran the city's High Street, 'thronged', as an eighteenth-century visitor observed, with 'buildings from seven to ten or twelve storeys high'. That summer there were to be published proposals which would lead, over the next fifty years, to the construction of Edinburgh's New Town on what had previously been meadowland to the north of the castle. But, for the moment, the place remained a hopelessly congested urban jungle of towering tenements separated by narrow closes or alleys – the latter, it was remarked in 1752, being noted principally for their 'steepness, narrowness and dirtiness'. 'In the closes or alleys,' one of eighteenth-century Edinburgh's visitors commented disgustedly, 'the inhabitants are very apt to fling out their filth without regarding who passes.'[5]

James Stewart was already familiar with Edinburgh. In the autumn of 1746, when a soldier in Charles Edward Stuart's army, he had spent several weeks there, and his trading activities had probably taken him back more than once in the interim. Where James found accommodation for the duration of what would turn into an eleven-day stay on this occasion is not known, though it may well have been with Hugh Stewart whose city home had regularly provided Ailean Breac with sanctuary. But there is no doubt as to how James spent his time. Although he succeeded in 'buying a bargain of meal' in the course of his visit, business of this type definitely took second place to James' drawn-out, but eventually productive, dealings with Edinburgh's extensive legal establishment.[6]

Unfortunately for James Stewart, the barons of exchequer, who were ultimately in charge of matters both on the Ardshiel estate and other forfeited properties of the same type, had met on 9 April, the day of James' arrival in the city and would not meet again until 3 June – some three weeks after Colin Campbell's planned evictions. However, James was able, perhaps with the help of the introductory letters he had been given in Stirlingshire, to get an hour or two with Thomas Kennedy, one of the barons and himself a senior Edinburgh lawyer. To Kennedy, as to other men of influence he met at this time, James made clear what those men would have been unaware of hitherto – that Colin Campbell was intent on turning the Ardshiel estate over to 'his own friends and relations'. James maintained that in so doing the factor was exceeding his authority. This was by no means wide of the mark, and the Duror people's case began as a result to attract some sympathy in high places. The 'conversation [he] had with Baron Kennedy' had gone reasonably well, James believed. Kennedy, James thought, had undertaken 'to represent the case to the whole barons' and had added 'that he made no doubt but they [the barons] would [at their meeting on 3 June] give . . . an order to the factor to continue the tenants in possession'.[7]

But if the promised order was to be of any practical value to those of James Stewart's Duror neighbours whom Colin Campbell intended to evict, some way had to be found of nullifying the factor's eviction notices for a period long enough to bridge the gap between 15 May, when these notices would otherwise come into force, and 3 June, when the barons of exchequer would next meet. Hence James' decision (taken, no doubt, on the advice of Edinburgh lawyers such as John MacFarlane, whose signature appears on one of the legal documents now drawn up on James' instructions) to have recourse to the Court of Session – whose judges were, with regard to civil proceedings like evictions, Scotland's highest legal authorities. To this court, on 18 April, James and his legal team duly presented a bill of suspension or sist which, if granted, would confer absolute protection, for as long as it remained in force, on the Ardshiel tenantry.

James' submission to the Court of Session took the form of a petition in the name of the Ardshiel estate's occupiers. They had been given reason to believe, the court's petitioners explained, that the barons of exchequer would shortly take steps to confirm them in their tenancies. But until such time as the barons were in a position 'to give [the necessary] instructions or directions to their factor', the Ardshiel petitioners looked to the court 'to prevent [their] ejectment'. They also asked the Court of Session to stop Colin Campbell reopening, as it was thought in Duror he was set on doing, the matter of the rents which had been paid in 1746, 1747 and 1748, to Charles or Isabel Stewart. Their cattle and other possessions, the tenants suspected, were about to be seized by Cailean Ruadh in lieu of these rents – which meant that on 15 May, they would be left impoverished as well as landless.[8]

'We have all the reason in the world to believe we shall be treated by the factor with the greatest severity,' the Court of Session's petitioners argued, 'not only by having our families ejected but by having our cattle poinded . . . Upon a poinding, they [the confiscated cattle] will be valued at a small rate at this time of year when cattle are in the worst condition. But indeed it will import us little, if we shall be removed from our possessions, what shall become of our cattle, since we have no place upon earth to remove to, and therefore must become beggars and be a burden upon our friends.'[9]

There were no political or financial grounds for their eviction, the Ardshiel tenants maintained. 'As to our personal capacity,' they stated, 'we are willing to qualify ourselves [politically] by taking oaths to the government which we hope will be deemed good security for our affection.' Nor would the barons of exchequer suffer any loss of revenue, the threatened tenants concluded, if they, the Ardshiel estate's existing occupants, were permitted to retain their landholdings. They were 'willing to give more' in rent for those landlholdings, the Ardshiel people stressed, than Colin Campbell would obtain from the men he proposed to install in their place.[10]

It was greatly to James Stewart's advantage that the Court of Session judge to whom those points were made was David Erskine, Lord Dun, an elderly man – then into his eighties – whose politics were said to have 'approached very near to Jacobitism' and whose habit it was, in cases involving the British government or its agencies, to take the anti-government side. To Erskine, it seemed clear, on the basis of what he heard from James and from James' lawyers, that the Ardshiel tenantry deserved the Court of Session's protection. A bill of suspension was accordingly issued, and, his mission accomplished, James headed north – reaching Duror on Monday, 27 April.[11]

On his return, James at once convened a gathering of the folk in whose names he had appeared before the Court of Session, telling them 'he had procured a sist' and going on to tell them he'd been advised that as many Ardshiel estate tenants as possible should go personally to Glenure in order to make Colin Campbell aware of this development. He had also been informed, James went on, that it would be a wise precaution to have a lawyer present if, or when, the suggested meeting with Cailean Ruadh took place. 'If they pleased,' James told his Duror audience, 'he would send for a notary [lawyer].' This was agreed and James duly made contact with Charles Stewart, who practised law in Maryburgh, the name then given, as mentioned earlier, to the civilian settlement which had sprung up outside Fort William's walls.[12]

A cousin of James and possibly a brother of James' wife Margaret, Charles Stewart had been one of the Jacobite army's clerks or paymasters. By the evening of Thursday, 30 April, he was with James at Acharn. 'Next morning,' the Maryburgh lawyer was afterwards to comment, 'the tenants came there [to Acharn], and he then went along with the tenants to [Campbell of] Glenure's house.'[13] This was on Friday, 1 May, and James, Charles Stewart said, took care to tell the Ardshiel tenants who assembled that morning at Acharn 'that he did not desire them to go [to Glenure] unless they had a mind [to do so] themselves'. Perhaps suspecting that his presence at Glenure House might make things worse rather than better, James himself remained at home. But accompanying Charles Stewart and the dozen or more tenants who made the trek from their Duror homes to Glenure were one or two uninvolved individuals – there, very possibly, to serve as witnesses should anything of consequence transpire. In this category, for example, was Alexander Stewart, whose father, Duncan Stewart, had succeeded the dead Donald Carmichael as the man in charge of Taigh na h-Insaig. Alexander was closely related to the Stewart lairds of Achnacone and Fasnacloich. And he would, of course, have been well known to Seumas a' Ghlinne, who, judging by his overall behaviour pattern, was probably one of Taigh na h-Insaig's regular customers.[14]

The fact that men like Charles Stewart and Alexander Stewart offered immediate aid to the Ardshiel estate's tenants, like the assistance which James Stewart had received from socially prominent Stewart and Stewart-connected families when en route for Edinburgh, is indicative of the nature of the protest movement in which those tenants now found themselves engaged. This movement was no spontaneous outburst. Nor were James Stewart and its other organisers acting solely, or even primarily, in the hope of mitigating the plight of the many Duror people at risk of losing homes and livelihoods. What really motivated James, his allies and his backers was what also motivated those involved in the Lochan Blar nan Lochan shooting match: the growing likelihood that unless he was stopped, and stopped quickly, Colin Campbell of Glenure would shortly be in control of much of what had long constituted Clan Stewart's heartland. And since Colin, for his part, was no less clear than his opponents as to the magnitude of what was at stake, there was never much chance of him responding positively to the Duror folk who turned up at his home in Glenure on Friday, 1 May 1752.

'They were willing and ready to continue in their respective possessions,' those folk told Colin Campbell, 'and to pay . . . as much as any other person would pay for them.' To show their affection to this present [political] establishment, [they] were likewise willing and ready to qualify themselves by taking the oaths to the government prescribed by law.'[15]

'All which offers,' Charles Stewart noted later the same day, 'were refused by ... Colin Campbell.' Whereupon, the lawyer continued, the factor was notified formally that the Court of Session had agreed to suspend his proceedings of eviction. 'To which,' Charles Stewart concluded, 'Colin Campbell . . . made answer that, notwithstanding the said sist, he would proceed to the removings.'[16]

'The day was bad,' an Ardshiel township tenant, John MacCombie, said of his journey on 1 May to Glenure House. And though MacCombie provided no further details, it is reasonable to suppose that a wet and miserable hike awaited him and his neighbours when, leaving Glenure House, they headed up Glen Creran prior to turning westwards for Glen Duror and their homes. Nor would John MacCombie's morale have been improved by what happened next. Saddling his horse almost before his Duror visitors were out of sight, Colin Campbell 'went directly to Edinburgh by great journeys'. There Colin sought out a Court of Session judge who – being of a very different political bent from his colleague, Lord Dun – was persuaded to rule James Stewart's hard-won bill of suspension out of order on the grounds that 'the king's factor [meaning Colin], who is answerable to the Court of Exchequer for his conduct, would not wantonly and without a just cause have pursued a removing against the [Ardshiel] tenants'. This was on Tuesday, 5 May. Pausing only to recruit his nephew, Mungo Campbell, an Edinburgh-based lawyer whom Colin felt it would be useful to have on hand for the next week or so, the factor left Edinburgh on 7 May. The two men, it was reported, rode 'with expedition'. That was certainly the case, for just 48 hours later, on Saturday, 9 May, Colin Campbell was back at Glenure House. There, with a view to charging the sum in question to the barons of exchequer, he made careful note of the fact that his Edinburgh jaunt had cost him just over £10. And there the factor, it may be assumed, spent at least a part of Sunday, 10 May, discussing with his nephew, Mungo, the most appropriate way to handle, on the Friday following, evictions to which there was now no legal barrier.[17]

In late April, not long after his probable participation in the Lochan Blar nan Lochan shooting match which appears to have taken place during James Stewart's absence in Edinburgh, Ailean Breac took himself off to Rannoch. On Thursday, 30 April, he returned – installing himself once more in James' home at Acharn. Other than to watch from the sidelines as its participants gathered there on 1 May, Ailean seems to have played no part in the Ardshiel tenantry's Glenure expedition, setting off instead on a further round of visits to Duror and Appin households. Among his destinations this time were Cuil and

Achnacone. And by Friday, 8 May, Ailean had got as far as Glen Creran, where he intended to spend the weekend at the home of John Stewart of Fasnacloich.

There was nothing unusual about this. James Stewart, the Fasnacloich laird's 28-year-old son and heir, had served, like Ailean, in Charles Edward Stuart's army and had long been one of Ailean Breac's particular friends. But a good deal would be made subsequently – and with some justification – of the circumstance that, as noted previously, Fasnacloich House, the residence of John and James Stewart, was, by West Highland standards, practically next door to Colin Campbell's Glenure home. Almost as soon as Colin and Murdo Campbell returned home to Glenure House on Saturday, 9 May, therefore, Ailean Breac discovered, as John Stewart later confirmed, that the factor 'was come from Edinburgh with a warrant to remove the [Ardshiel] tenants'. By the Sunday, John Stewart said, Ailean was also aware that Colin would be going to Fort William, by way of Ballachulish Ferry, the following morning. Before long, Ailean was also to discover that Colin meant to return from Fort William, again by way of Ballachulish Ferry, on Thursday, 14 May; that he proposed to spend that night at Kentallen Inn; and that he planned, on Friday, 15 May, to carry out the Duror evictions for which he had managed to obtain the Court of Session's blessing.[18]

On the morning of Monday, 11 May, at about nine o'clock, Ailean Breac left Fasnacloich House for Acharn, getting there – in a time which testifies, incidentally, to the rate at which he could cross rough country on foot – by 1 p.m. There Ailean found James – assisted by Alan, his son, and Iain Mòr MacColl – planting potatoes in one of Acharn's fields. Ailean volunteered his services and joined the potato-planting party. But such conversation as there was between him and James was cut short on James receiving a message from his landlord, Donald Campbell of Airds, 'desiring him to come to Keil' – where, that Monday afternoon, the Airds laird was arranging who exactly should have tenancies in Keil township during the year commencing in mid-May.[19]

At Keil it was settled that James should have 'a part' of the township himself. This development suggests that Seumas a' Ghlinne, with Acharn already in his occupancy and with a piece of Keil about to come his way, was rapidly becoming as dominant a figure on Donald Campbell's Duror landholdings as he had formerly been on the Ardshiel estate. But this, it is clear, did not in any way bother the Airds laird. It is impossible to say why the latter, at this moment of crisis in Duror, was perfectly happy to befriend a man who was putting so much time and effort into wrecking the plans of those – Colin Campbell specifically – who shared both Donald Campbell's name and politics. All that is certain is that the Airds laird and James Stewart were on the best of terms at that time. When they had finished their day of discussion at Keil,

James accordingly accompanied Donald Campbell south through Dalnatrat and, on parting, the two of them – Campbell bound for his Airds home and James turning back towards Acharn – arranged to meet again the next morning.[20]

Having spent most of what remained of that evening in the home of Keil township's miller, where he drank a good deal and heard a couple of Duror's pipers playing, James didn't get back to Acharn until late. Next morning, James, hangover notwithstanding, was up and off to keep his appointment with Donald Campbell before Ailean Breac – who, as was usual in Highland households of the time, had been sharing a bed with Charles Stewart, James' younger son – put in an appearance. This meant, as things turned out, that Ailean and James missed, by just a few minutes, the last opportunity they were to have to be in one another's company.

While staying at Fasnacloich a day or two before, Ailean Breac, according to his host, John Stewart, had been 'dressed in a long blue coat, red waistcoat, black breeches and a feathered hat'. Those, of course, were the French clothes in which Ailean had turned up in Scotland that March and which, after a spell in more mundane garb, he must have donned at Acharn prior to making his visit to John Stewart's household. On returning to Acharn on Monday, 11 May, Ailean shed his French outfit once again – replacing this outfit with plainer and darker-coloured garments borrowed, as on many previous occasions, from his foster-father.[21]

Still dressed in James' clothes, Ailean Breac left Acharn, on the morning of Tuesday, 11 May, in the company of his foster-brother, Charles. They 'passed through Achindarroch and Lagnaha and spoke with some people as they went along', Charles later recalled. At the head of Kentallen Bay, Charles added, he and Ailean parted, Ailean afterwards calling briefly on Alexander Stewart of Ballachulish at Ballachulish House prior to pressing on for Carnoch, long the home of Glencoe's MacDonald chiefs.[22]

Heading the Carnoch household at this time was Isabel MacDonald who, as mentioned already, was James Stewart's half-sister – Isabel being a full sister of the exiled Ardshiel laird, and James' half-brother, Charles Stewart. Like her brother Charles, Isabel's dead husband, Alexander MacDonald, had played a leading part in the Jacobite rebellion of 1745–46. Also prominent in the rebellion had been Alan Cameron of Callart, whose wife, Helen, was another of Charles Stewart's sisters. The Ardshiel, Glencoe and Callart families were thus linked by marriage as well as by their Jacobite convictions. Around 1750, Alan Cameron, who had followed Charles Stewart of Ardshiel abroad in Culloden's aftermath, had died in Dunkirk. Like her sister Isabel, then, Helen was a widow. And though she continued to reside at Callart House, more or less opposite Carnoch on the north shore of Loch Leven, Helen had no jurisdiction over her deceased husband's estate – which, like the Ardshiel property, had been confiscated by the British government and which, also like Ardshiel, was administered from 1748 onwards by Colin Campbell of Glenure. Helen Cameron's Callart household, for which Ailean Breac headed on leaving Carnoch and where he spent the night of Tuesday, 12 May, was not one, therefore, where he would have been discouraged from speaking ill – as had become his custom – of Cailean Ruadh.

While Ailean socialised with Isabel MacDonald and Helen Cameron, James Stewart, Isabel and Helen's half-brother and Ailean's foster-father, was still casting about for some means of keeping Ardshiel, where both Helen and Isabel had grown up, in the occupation of its existing tenants. On Wednesday, 13 May, James met with Alexander Stewart of Ballachulish to explore the available options. Alexander, or so James said subsequently, was of the opinion that the Ardshiel estate's occupants, though they should 'use no force in keeping their possessions', should refuse to quit their homes and landholdings 'unless they were forced out'. If successful, such an approach, it was hoped, would enable the Ardshiel tenants to hold out for a further two or three weeks – by which point the barons of exchequer, at their June meeting, might have rescinded Colin Campbell's eviction orders.[23]

This approach to Friday's evictions having been agreed, it was next concluded that it might be helpful for the elder sons of the Ballachulish and Fasnacloich lairds to be present in Duror that day. Those 'gentlemen of character', as they were afterwards described, were John and James Stewart, the first being the man who had come to Seamus a' Ghlinne's assistance when he tangled with Colin Campbell at Kentallen Inn on Hogmanay, and the second being the friend with whom Ailean Breac had been staying at Fasnacloich House prior to his 11 May return to Acharn.[24]

It is not clear why James Stewart, still playing the lead in Duror's developing drama, thought the Fasnacloich and Ballachulish heirs ought to be in Duror on 15 May. Perhaps their role was to be merely that of witnesses to proceedings which were bound to be contentious. More probably – John of Ballachulish and James of Fasnacloich personifying, as it were, the next generation of Clan Stewart – their presence was intended to demonstrate a continuing, and powerful, Stewart interest in lands which, on the day in question, Colin Campbell would be endeavouring to place in the occupancy of his close relatives. But for all that symbolism of this type obviously meant a good deal to James Stewart, too much should not be made of it. Gestures, however meaningful, took second place, as far as James was concerned, to the more down-to-earth possibilities that might present themselves on Friday, 15 May.

And because those possibilities, if they materialised, were likely to be legal in character, James was anxious to have a friendly lawyer that day in Duror.

The obvious choice was James' Maryburgh cousin, Charles Stewart, who had last been called upon a fortnight previously, when the Ardshiel tenants had made their fruitless trip to Glenure House. Charles, however, was absent from Maryburgh at the start of the week ending on Friday, 15 May. Attempts were accordingly made by James to find a substitute. It was only on those attempts failing and on his learning late on Wednesday of his cousin's return home that James, at the very last moment, appealed to Charles Stewart for help.

Rising before dawn on Thursday, 14 May, James penned an urgent letter to Charles, urging the lawyer to 'be here [at James' Acharn home] without fail this night'. If it was necessary for him to 'hire a horse', James told Charles, he should do so. 'Everything must go wrong,' James went on, 'without a person [that] can act and that I can trust. This is such a tie upon all the members of our family that I'll press you no further, but [I] do depend on seeing you . . . this night.'[25]

Rousing two of his MacColl employees, Iain Mòr and Iain Beag, James now set off in their company for Kentallen Inn. On getting there at about seven o'clock in the morning, as the innkeeper, John MacCombie, afterwards recalled, James requested MacCombie to get out a boat and, with Iain Mòr's help, row Iain Beag across Loch Linnhe to Onich – 'that being the shortest road,' Kentallen's innkeeper explained subsequently, 'from Acharn to Fort William'. MacCombie 'at the first declined' to oblige, but, when James persevered, he was eventually persuaded to do as he was asked. As a result, Iain Beag, with his employer's letter to Charles Stewart in his pocket, was soon ashore in Onich and heading as fast as he could for Charles' Maryburgh home. There, however, matters went badly awry. Charles Stewart was nowhere to be found and, when contact was eventually made with him, Charles' attitude, from his cousin's standpoint, was desperately disappointing. Already suspect politically because of his Jacobite involvements and because of the fact that he was a business partner of John Cameron of Fassifern, the man who had been at the centre of the farm-letting furore which had so nearly caused Colin Campbell's downfall just a year or two previously, Charles Stewart decided that, on Friday, 15 May, he would do well to keep his distance from Duror. 'He received a . . . letter from [James Stewart] of date the 14th of May, desiring him to attend next day at the ejection,' Charles declared, 'but . . . he declined the same because he did not care to disoblige [Campbell of] Glenure.'[26]

While bound for Maryburgh, Iain Beag MacColl – described as 'a little short man' – had encountered Colin Campbell in the company of the three men the factor intended to have with him in Duror the following day. Those men were Mungo Campbell, Colin's lawyer nephew, John MacKenzie, Colin's personal servant, and Donald Kennedy, an Inveraray-based sheriff-officer who had joined Colin in Fort William on 13 May. With him Kennedy had 'a warrant for ejecting certain possessors of the lands of Ardshiel' and it was this warrant Cailean Ruadh was now intent on enforcing. First, however, he had some business to transact with tenants on what, prior to Charles Edward Stuart's rebellion, had been Alan Cameron of Callart's estate. Hence Colin's slow progress – although Iain Beag met with the factor and his colleagues well to the south of Fort William at about eleven o'clock in the morning, it was not until four or five in the afternoon that Colin and his party crossed Ballachulish Ferry.[27]

In the eighteenth century, ferries of the Ballachulish type were managed by two boatmen, one living on one side of the water, the other living on the opposite side. At Ballachulish in 1752, the ferryman resident on the southern shore was Archibald MacInnes. Possibly because he had only one eye, Archibald was reputed to possess 'the gift of second-sight' and was thought capable, as a result, of predicting disaster. Perhaps he did have this power, perhaps he didn't; but the Ballachulish ferryman, at all events, was long believed in North Argyll to have urged Colin Campbell, on the fateful afternoon of Thursday, 14 May, to head home that evening by way of Gleann an Fiodh – a valley running eastwards into the hills from the modern village of Ballachulish and offering, in 1752, much the most direct route from Ballachulish Ferry to Glenure. Cailean Ruadh, it was said afterwards, ignored Archibald MacInnes' urgings. Other things being equal, he would have been pleased to make haste, as he had often done before, for Gleann an Fiodh. But because he had business on Friday morning in Duror and accommodation arranged for Thursday night in Kentallen Inn, this would be impossible. So saying, Colin Campbell mounted his horse and, turning his back on Archibald MacInnes and on Gleann an Fiodh, took the road which, from Ballachulish Ferry, led towards Kentallen and Duror by way of the Wood of Lettermore.[28]

If this tale has any basis in fact, then such apprehensions as Archibald MacInnes may have expressed to Cailean Ruadh on the afternoon of 14 May probably had less to do with supernatural promptings than with the nature of the approaches made to Archibald earlier that same afternoon by Ailean Breac. On Wednesday, 13 May, Ailean had left Callart House and, after calling again on Isabel MacDonald at Carnoch, had turned up that evening – at 'about seven or eight', his host recalled – at Ballachulish House, the home of Alexander Stewart. Ailean, Alexander said, 'lodged with him all night' and, on Thursday morning, 'stayed . . . till eleven or twelve when he went out with a fishing-rod in his hand'.[29]

Ballachulish House stood, as it still does, about a quarter-mile to the south-east of the spot where Archibald MacInnes would have kept his ferryboat. Around the house are the fields (worked, in 1752, by the tenants of Ballachulish township) which constitute the northward-opening mouth of Gleann a' Chaolais. This steep-sided valley owes its distinctive configuration to the horseshoe-shaped Beinn a' Bheithir – Gleann a' Chaolais lying inside the horseshoe, Glen Duror and Gleann an Fiodh being on its outer edges. Out of Gleann a' Chaolais there flows Abhainn Greadhain, a hill burn which, prior to emptying itself into the sea a little to the west of the modern Ballachulish Bridge, passes close to Ballachulish House. It was on this burn that Donald Rankin, an eighteen-year-old 'herd to [Stewart of] Ballachulish' saw Ailean Breac fishing with his borrowed rod at about noon on Thursday, 14 May – the Thursday which, for Ailean, had begun in Ballachulish House and which, for Colin Campbell, had commenced with his riding out of Fort William in the direction of Ballachulish Ferry.[30]

That Colin Campbell would be crossing Ballachulish Ferry this Thursday was common knowledge. On the previous Tuesday, the Glenure laird had sent word to John MacCombie of Kentallen Inn that, as MacCombie put it, 'he [Colin] and some other company was to be at his [inn] upon Thursday [14 May]'. Not least because MacCombie – who, as well as operating his hostelry, worked land in Ardshiel township – was among the Ardshiel estate tenants scheduled to have his lease terminated on Friday, 15 May, the innkeeper saw no reason to keep those arrangements to himself. In the run-up to the Ardshiel evictions, after all, the factor's movements were of pressing interest to everyone in Duror; everyone in North Argyll, in fact. 'The whole neighbourhood knew of it,' John MacCombie said of Colin Campbell's projected stay in his establishment.[31]

Because Ailean Breac spent Wednesday evening in Alexander Stewart's company, and because Alexander, hours previously, had discussed the forthcoming evictions with James Stewart, Ailean's foster-father, it can be taken for granted – since James and Alexander are bound to have touched on the factor's message to John MacCombie – that Cailean Ruadh's travel plans for Thursday, 14 May, were as clear to Ailean Breac as to Colin himself. Having crossed Ballachulish Ferry, the factor and his associates would turn south and, having forded Abhainn Greadhain, would make for Kentallen Inn on the road which, a mile or so from the ferry, entered the Wood of Lettermore – this wood clinging to the craggy ridge forming the westerly end of the Beinn a' Bheithir horseshoe.

What could not have been known in advance to Ailean Breac or anyone else, of course, was the precise time at which Colin Campbell would cross the ferry. Hence the possible significance, in retrospect, of Ailean's fishing trip which quickly took him, as would afterwards be pointed out, to 'higher grounds from whence he had a prospect of the high road from Fort William'. This road, clearly visible from the slopes above Abhainn Greadhain, was the one which Colin Campbell and his companions would be obliged to follow as they passed through Onich en route for Ballachulish Ferry's northern terminus.[32]

Whether or not Ailean Breac was keeping a close eye on the Onich road that Thursday cannot be proved one way or the other. What is certain, however, is that in the early part of the afternoon, Ailean sought out Archibald MacInnes, who, seated close to his ferryboat, was deep in conversation with a friend. 'Alan Breck came behind . . . and hoasted,' the ferryman said, meaning that Ailean, to attract attention, had coughed and spat on the ground. Ailean indicated that he wanted to speak privately with MacInnes, who got up, a little stiffly perhaps (he was well into his sixties), and walked towards the young man. 'Alan inquired of him', Archibald MacInnes stated, 'if [Campbell of] Glenure had crossed the ferry from Lochaber to Appin.' On the ferryman replying that 'he was sure he did not', Ailean 'went away towards the high road' – and, MacInnes was to emphasise some months later, he had 'not seen him since'.[33]

Less than half-an-hour's walk from the point where Archibald MacInnes last glimpsed Ailean Breac, the eighteenth-century track heading for Kentallen and Duror plunged into the Wood of Lettermore. The modern Ballachulish–Oban road keeps much closer to Loch Linnhe, at this point, than its predecessor of 250 years ago. And Forestry Commission spruces have taken the place, in recent times, of the earlier wood's scattered cover of alder and birch. But although it has been planted over, the line of the eighteenth-century track, a couple of hundred feet higher than today's road, is clearly visible. Above it, the ground rises sharply in what was described in 1752 as 'a hanging brae . . . interspersed with rocks and stones'.[34]

Across that brae, on the afternoon of Thursday, 14 May, there walked a man carrying a musket. Painstakingly, for there was much at stake, this man looked for a boulder which would both conceal him from passers-by and provide him with the arm-steadying support he would need when levelling his musket at the rider he had come here to kill. Finding a rock which suited him, the gunman crouched down behind it and set about charging his muzzle-loading firearm. Into its barrel he first poured, from a powder horn, a measure of gunpowder. Next came a piece of wadding, tamped home with a ram-rod. Then followed a lead bullet, more wadding and a second bullet. This was a Highland deer-stalker's trick which had evolved to enable a hunter to deliver an especially disabling wound to his quarry. When a musket loaded in this way was fired, the second bullet – known in Gaelic as *an ruagaire*, the chaser – would, in flight, diverge slightly from the first. Entering the body of an animal or human some small distance apart, the two bullets effectively doubled the damage that could be effected by a single discharge. The tactic, admittedly, reduced a musket's range. But this would not have worried the man taking up position that Thursday in the Wood of Lettermore. From the spot he had chosen, he would be within a few feet of his intended target.

While the Lettermore gunman was finalising his preparations, Colin Campbell and his companions were disembarking from Archibald MacInnes's ferryboat and setting off for Kentallen. Donald Kennedy, the Inveraray sheriff-officer, was on foot. Colin, Colin's nephew, Mungo Campbell, and Colin's servant, John MacKenzie, were on horseback. To begin with, all four men would have been bunched together. But not far from Ballachulish House, they fell in with Alexander Stewart, Ballachulish's laird, and Colin – any such meeting then demanding this response – dismounted in order to talk with him. 'They [Colin and Alexander] travelled together on foot about the space of half a mile,' Mungo said afterwards, 'till they came to the [out]skirts of the Wood of Lettermore.' There, on what was the boundary between his own property and the Ardshiel estate, the Ballachulish laird bade farewell to Colin, who at once remounted and rode on into the wood.[35]

By the men who were shortly to investigate Colin Campbell's murder, it appears to have been assumed – as it has also been assumed by most later commentators – that Colin's meeting with Alexander Stewart was purely a chance encounter. Maybe it was. But it is worth remembering that Alexander Stewart – who had taken part in more than one Jacobite rising, who'd served with the Appin Regiment at Culloden, who had seen his second son killed there and who, like practically every other senior member of Clan Stewart, was committed to doing everything he could to keep his clan's landholdings intact – was no friend either of Colin Campbell or of the government Colin served. Bearing this in mind, it is also worth taking into account that Alexander Stewart, by engaging Cailean Ruadh in conversation, both delayed the factor, which may have helped the waiting gunman, and split up Colin's party, which, from the concealed marksman's point of view, was definitely of real assistance.

With Donald Kennedy now well ahead of them and John MacKenzie lagging behind, Colin and Mungo entered the Wood of Lettermore side by side. But 'coming to a part of the road that was rough and narrow, so as they could not ride conveniently two horses abreast', Mungo recalled, '[he] and [his uncle] separated' – Mungo taking the lead and Colin falling back some ten or twenty yards. Moments later, Murdo said, he 'heard a shot behind him and heard [his uncle] several times repeat those words, "Oh, I am dead!"'.[36]

Wheeling round, Mungo rode back to the factor and found him slumped over his horse's neck. 'He's going to shoot you,' the wounded man managed somehow to say to his nephew. 'Take care of yourself!'[37]

But for all his horror at what had happened, Murdo was in no mood to exercise caution. Pushing through the scrub above the road in the hope of seeing who had fired on his uncle, the young man, as he wrote a week or so later, 'saw the villain with a firelock in his hand'. Subsequently, Murdo was to add that the gunman, who was running uphill, had been wearing 'a short, dark-coloured coat'. He was also, it seems, extremely fit; despite being burdened with a heavy musket and despite the terrain being very steep and broken, the man glimpsed by the lawyer was moving at great speed, and had soon taken advantage of the lie of the land to put a piece of rising ground between himself and the watching Mungo – who, though he might have given chase, understandably returned to the aid of his wounded uncle.[38]

Lifting Colin from his horse, Mungo stretched him out on the gravelly surface of the track where John MacKenzie, coming up at this point, found his master 'lying on his back . . . with blood upon his clothes and [more blood] gushing out from his belly'. The factor, MacKenzie added, 'was groaning'. That is scarcely surprising, for the sniper, as a Barcaldine surgeon was to confirm the next day, had left his victim with stomach wounds of a type which, as well as being fatal, were agonisingly painful. 'He found that [Campbell of Glenure] had been shot by two bullets entering at his back,' the Barcaldine medical man reported, 'one on each side of the backbone; one [bullet] had come out about half-an-inch below the navel and the other about two inches from it, towards the right side.'[39]

Turning to John MacKenzie, Murdo ordered him 'to mount [their] best horse' – probably the dying factor's – and to go in search of John Campbell of Baleveolan, whom Colin and his party had been due to meet at Kentallen Inn that evening. Reaching the inn and discovering that Campbell was not there, MacKenzie pressed on for Glen Duror – which, at this point, had been in the Baleveolan laird's occupancy for about twelve months. Encountering some people in their fields at Achindarroch and asking them for word of John Campbell's whereabouts, John MacKenzie, as he put it, 'was told by one of the tenants of Achindarroch that probably James Stewart in Acharn would tell him whether [Campbell of] Baleveolan was come to Glen Duror or not'. Spurring his horse across the Water of Duror, MacKenzie accordingly made haste for James' Acharn home.[40]

With James at Acharn this Thursday evening, according to a Duror tradition that would persist into the twentieth century, was Robert Stewart, one of mid-eighteenth-century Duror's several millers. '*A Rob*,' James supposedly remarked to his companion on catching sight of the approaching MacKenzie, '*cò sam bith am marcaiche, cha leis fhèin an t-each*': 'Rob, whoever that rider may be, the horse is not his own.' And on hearing John MacKenzie's dramatic news, or so the story goes, Seumas a' Ghlinne, turning again to Robert Stewart, made a further comment so prescient that it might serve as his epitaph: '*A Rob, cò sam bith an ciontach, 's mise an crionlach.*' In other words: 'Whoever is the culprit, I shall be the victim.'[41]

Contemporary accounts of what took place at Acharn that night confirm Robert Stewart's presence there. The accounts are at odds, however, as to how James Stewart reacted to what John MacKenzie – now self-confessedly weeping as the shock he had experienced took its toll – had to say. By his prosecutors at his Inverary trial, James was said to have 'appeared noways surprised or concerned at the news of the murder'. By his defence counsel, in contrast, he was stated to have shown 'that surprise, that deep concern, which every innocent man must feel at so unexpected and so melancholy an accident'.[42]

What is clear, however, is that neither James nor his sons, Alan and Charles, went to the Wood of Lettermore on the evening of Thursday, 14 May, to see what, if anything, they might do to help Mungo Campbell. This – being contrary to Highland custom which demanded that neighbours should immediately rally round the bereaved at times of sudden death – was thought, even by relatively neutral observers, to point to James having had a hand in the crime. James himself was well aware of this. That is why he was at such pains to explain why he remained at home. On the evening of the day of Colin Campbell's murder, James said, 'several of the tenants in the neighbourhood, particularly the tenants of Achindarroch, and Duncan Stewart [from] Inshaig, and Robert Stewart, the miller, came to [him] to know what they should do'. He advised all those people to go at once to Lettermore, James went on, 'but . . . neither he nor his son, Alan, went there because he understood [as a result of what he had heard from John MacKenzie] that [Campbell of] Baleveolan and his sons were to be there, and . . . there was some chagrin betwixt him [James] and them, they having taken . . . the year before . . . Glen Duror'. When questioned separately about his own failure to offer assistance to Mungo Campbell, Alan Stewart took much the same line as his father. His mother, Alan added, 'also hindered his going [to the murder scene] and assigned for a reason that, if the friends of the deceased were there, and had arms, they might, in their passion, do hurt to him [Alan] and his father'.[43]

In the Wood of Lettermore, meanwhile, Mungo Campbell had been seized by fears that were the mirror image of Margaret Stewart's. Within minutes of John MacKenzie's departure, the mortally wounded Cailean Ruadh had died. Darkness was approaching. And with the surrounding countryside populated very largely by people whose evictions Mungo had come north to supervise, there was every reason – from Mungo's perspective – to be apprehensive as to what the night might bring. 'Judge my situation,' Mungo was afterwards to write to a friend, 'in the middle of Appin, surrounded by my enemies and the doleful spectacle of my dead uncle before me, expecting every moment to be attacked and entirely defenceless.'[44]

At about seven o'clock, the lawyer prevailed on his one remaining companion, Donald Kennedy, to retrace his steps towards Ballachulish in the hope that – with there still being no sign of John MacKenzie or John Campbell of Baleveolan – help might be found in that direction. Kennedy, who seems to have been even more terror-struck than Mungo, went off reluctantly. Within half-an-hour, however, he was back with Alexander Stewart and some of Alexander's Ballachulish tenants, these being joined shortly by the returning MacKenzie, Campbell of Baleveolan and the Duror men James Stewart had sent to the murder scene.

To the folk who now flocked about him, Mungo Campbell responded with understandable caution. None of those people, he felt, would have been anything other than 'pleased . . . had [he] shared [his] uncle's fate'. But the gathering crowd – despite, or maybe because of, its members' lack of any obvious sympathy for the dead factor or his nephew – proved willing enough to provide the manpower needed to carry Colin Campbell's corpse down the hill to the shore of Loch Linnhe. There a boat and oarsmen had been organised. The body was lifted aboard; Mungo followed, and soon the boat was heading, in gathering darkness, for Kentallen Bay. There Colin Campbell's remains were conveyed to the inn which had been his destination that day and where a shaken and grief-stricken Mungo was to sit up all night with, as he later recalled, 'not a mortal to consult or advise with but poor old [Campbell of] Baleveolan'. No record survives of what was said by the two men in the small hours of the day that should have seen them assisting the assassinated factor to install his, and their, relatives as the Ardshiel estate's principal tenants. But it would hardly be suprising, in the circumstances, if Mungo and John Campbell should have wondered whether Duror was worth so much trauma.[45]

Near nightfall on the evening of Thursday, 14 May, Donald Stewart, a nephew of Alexander Stewart of Ballachulish, a member of the Ballachulish laird's household and one of the men who in his own words had 'assisted in carrying the corpse of [Campbell of] Glenure to the boat', was approached, in Ballachulish House, by a woman, Catherine MacInnes, whose home was nearby and who told Donald 'that [some]one without wanted to speak with him'. 'When he went out,' Donald Stewart said, 'Catherine MacInnes informed him that it was Alan Breck that wanted him and that he [Ailean] was a little above the house in the brae.'[46]

This was the first definite glimpse anyone had had of Ailean Breac since Archibald MacInnes, the Ballachulish ferryman had watched him set off several hours before along the road that was shortly afterwards to be taken by Colin Campbell. Unsurprisingly then, Donald Stewart, on going 'up the brae' and meeting Ailean, immediately raised the matter of Cailean Ruadh's killing and, by his own account, 'said it could not be but that he, Alan Breck, was about it'. 'To which,' Donald went on, 'Alan Breck answered that he heard of the murder, but had no hand in it.'[47]

Although this would be Ailean Breac's consistent line thereafter, it is by no means certain that Donald Stewart – for all that his version of events was given under oath – was wholly forthcoming as to his own part in the proceedings of 14 May. Donald, an Appin Regiment veteran who had been wounded at Culloden, was close to Ailean Breac; he was believed by Duror tradition-bearers of a slighly later era to have been one of the leading participants in the Lochan Blar nan Lochan shooting match; and, in addition to his being Stewart of Ballachulish's nephew, he was the son-in-law of David Stewart of Annat, one of the several Jacobite lairds on whom James Stewart had called when bound for Edinburgh in April. While it is impossible now to prove that Donald Stewart was party to any plotting that may have preceded the shooting of Colin Campbell, it is wholly implausible – a point underlined by Ailean Breac having sought him out at this critical juncture – that his role in the affair was entirely that of an innocent bystander. By his own admission, after all, in the period immediately following Cailean Ruadh's death Donald was to do exactly as he was told by the man, Ailean Breac, whom Donald suspected, or so he said, of being Cailean Ruadh's murderer.

Ailean Breac, Donald Stewart insisted under later questioning, 'said he [Ailean] believed he would be suspected of the murder and, upon that account and as he was a deserter formerly from the army, it was necessary for him to leave the kingdom'. Ailean then told him, Donald informed his interrogators, that he was 'very scarce of money'. That was why, Donald explained, Ailean Breac asked him to go on his behalf to Acharn. There Donald was to tell James Stewart of his foster-son's plight and ask James to send such cash as he could spare to Ailean, who, for the next day or two, would be hiding out in the vicinity of Caolasnacoan, an isolated farmstead on the southern shore of Loch Leven.[48]

According to Isabel MacDonald, at about four o'clock on the morning following Ailean Breac's meeting with Donald Stewart, Ailean came to Isabel's home at Carnoch – some two or three miles short of Caolasnacoan – and 'knocked at the window'. As Isabel opened her door, she reported afterwards, she asked Ailean: 'What news up the country?' 'To which [Ailean] answered,' Isabel went on, 'a good deal of news; that [Campbell of] Glenure was killed the evening before in the Wood of Lettermore, that he [Ailean] was come to take farewell . . . [and] that he was to leave the country.'[49]

By dawn that morning, Friday, 15 May, Ailean Breac had installed himself in a wood on the hillside (the north-eastern flank of the Pap of Glencoe) above Caolasnacoan. Also by that time, Donald Stewart was on his way from Ballachulish House to Acharn with Ailean's message for James.

The previous evening had been a busy one at Acharn. Suspecting – correctly – that, in the aftermath of Colin Campbell's murder, his home would be among the first to be raided by the troops he knew would to be sent from Fort William to help with the search for the factor's killer, James had spent some time organising the concealment of such weapons as were held – illegally, of course – by his household. Those included four broadswords and two muskets – one of the latter, according to Iain Mòr MacColl, being a gun which 'he himself [had] received in Edinburgh at the time of the rebellion and [which he had] used . . . when in England [with the Jacobite army]'. By Iain Beag MacColl (the man who had spent much of Thursday travelling to and from Maryburgh) and by Dugald MacColl, both of them acting on James' orders, the weapons were hastily buried in a peat bog on rising ground a little to the south-east of Acharn's several buildings.[50]

This, for a time at least, removed the threat posed to James by his possession of illicit weaponry. But no sooner had James disposed of that difficulty than he was confronted by another – much larger – danger in the shape of Ailean Breac's request for the funds needed to finance his return to France. This request reached James, courtesy of Donald Stewart, early on Friday, 15 May. Although the risk inherent in complying with it would have been glaringly obvious to him, James at once took steps to do so. 'I do declare,' James said in explanation of this decision, 'that it was not from any conviction of his being guilty of [Colin Campbell's murder] I sent him money to carry him off the country, but out of [the] charity and friendship I had for him, not only as a relation, but likewise as a pupil left to my charge by his father, and as a person who kept close to my brother [Charles Stewart of Ardshiel] when lurking [in the hills] before he got off.'[51]

Although eager to get money to Caolasnacoan and the waiting Ailean, James had first to lay his hands on a sufficiently sizeable sum. This could only be done by calling in a debt of £4 owed him by his brother-in-law, a Fort William or Maryburgh merchant, William Stewart, on whose behalf James had recently bought some cattle. The task of making the necessary approach to William fell on Alexander Stewart, another Appin Regiment veteran who, during the months following Culloden, was resident at Achara and who, both then and in 1752, was described as a 'packman' or 'pedlar'. Alexander Stewart was well known to James, whose Acharn home Alexander visited often. But this was equally true of many other Duror folk, and what probably persuaded James to give Alexander Stewart the job of recovering the needed funds for Ailean Breac was the fact that the packman and Ailean, their fathers having been brothers, were cousins. Because of this relationship, James might well have reasoned, Alexander was more likely than anyone else available to be favourably disposed to the fugitive. James, Alexander subsequently recalled, asked the packman to make haste for Maryburgh where he was 'to tell . . . William Stewart that he must send . . . money, tho' he should borrow it from twenty purses'.[52]

By midday on Friday, 15 May, the packman was in Maryburgh. But William Stewart, it now transpired, was as short of ready cash as James. As a result, it was not until well into the next day, Saturday, 16 May, that Alexander – who had gone off on other business to Glen Nevis in the interim – was provided by the Maryburgh merchant with three guineas. This, being just over £3, fell short of the sum James had sent Alexander to Fort William to obtain. But judging that he would get no more the packman, taking the three gold coins offered to him, set off again for Duror, reaching Acharn that evening.

At Acharn, Alexander Stewart was met by James' wife, Margaret, and by the news that both James and his eldest son, Alan, had minutes before been arrested by the military at Taigh na h-Insaig, where the packman and Margaret now hurried. There, said Alexander, 'they found [James] a prisoner'. But fortunately for James and still more fortunately for Ailean Breac, the troops who had taken the two Acharn men into custody were commanded by an officer who was not averse to the prisoner having a few moments, in private, with his wife and with his wife's companion. Huddling together with Margaret and the packman – and speaking, of course, in Gaelic which the waiting soldiers, being English, would not have understood – James asked Alexander 'what money he brought from Fort William'. 'On [his] telling [James] that he brought three guineas,' Alexander Stewart stated, '[James] pulled a green purse out of his pocket, out of which he took two guineas.' These were handed to the packman, who now had five guineas, in total, in his possession. This sum, James told Alexander, he was to take personally 'to . . . Alan Breck to see if he could make his escape'.[53]

While her husband and son were led off by their captors to Fort William, where both James and Alan were to be imprisoned the following morning, Margaret Stewart returned to Acharn with Alexander Stewart. There the latter, as he recalled, 'got his supper' prior to being handed, by Margaret, Ailean

Breac's French clothes, consisting of 'a blue side coat, red waistcoat, black breeches, a hat and some shirts'. These, the packman was told, he was to take immediately to Caolasnacoan, along with the three guineas he had obtained from William Stewart and the further two guineas he had been given by James. At Caolasnacoan, Margaret further instructed the packman, he was to hand over clothes and money, if not to Ailean Breac personally, then to the Caolasnacoan farmstead's occupant, John MacColl.

Caolasnacoan at this time was in the possession of the Appin chief, Dougal Stewart, who had installed John MacColl in the place as his *bouman*. Boumen, in the terminology of the eighteenth-century Highlands, were people who managed landholdings on behalf of those holdings' owners and who received, instead of a wage, a stipulated proportion of such output as resulted from their efforts. To be a bouman, then, was to be a sharecropper. It was also to be in an extremely vulnerable position tenurially. This may have made John MacColl more than usually susceptible to pressure from the men who were soon to be inquiring into Colin Campbell's murder. And since several of those men were Colin's close relatives, they would also have had something of a hold over Caolasnacoan's owner, Dougal Stewart, because of their ability to foreclose on the debts he had owed the dead factor. It is probably no coincidence, then, that the Caolasnacoan bouman was eventually to be a key prosecution witness at James Stewart's trial – where he testified to Ailean Breac having told him all manner of things pointing to James Stewart's complicity in the Wood of Lettermore shooting.

On Sunday, 17 May, however, those matters lay in the future. When the Duror packman, Alexander Stewart, who had walked north overnight from Acharn, reached Caolasnacoan that morning, he was received hospitably enough by John MacColl, with whom Ailean Breac had already been in contact more than once. Depositing Ailean's clothes 'at the root of a fir tree'[54] near the Caolasnacoan homestead, the packman asked MacColl to direct him to Ailean's hiding place. 'MacColl', Alexander said later, 'told . . . him to go to a hill above the house and whistle, [adding that] Alan Breck would [then] come to him.' But the packman – who had gone without sleep for more than 24 hours and who had tramped from Acharn to Fort William, from Fort William to Acharn and from Acharn to Caolasnacoan – clearly felt, as he put it, that 'he had gone far enough after . . . Alan Breck already'. Entrusting Ailean's five guineas to John MacColl, the packman 'slept for some time and thereafter dined' prior to begin setting off on his return trek to Duror.[55] 'He . . . came back to Acharn upon the evening of Sunday, the 17th day of May,' Alexander Stewart was afterwards to state. There Margaret Stewart 'asked him if he had seen Alan Breck and, upon his answering he had not [but] telling that Alan Breck was in

Caolasnacoan . . . and that he [Alexander] had given the clothes and the money to John [MacColl], she appeared satisfied'.[56]

At Caolasnacoan the same evening, Ailean Breac received, from John MacColl, the five guineas which had been got to him at such risk and with so much trouble. Characteristically, Ailean complained that his foster-father – whom he knew, by this point, to have been imprisoned – had sent him 'but little money'. With somewhat better grace, Ailean next accepted the Caolasnacoan bouman's offer of 'a noggin [of] milk and water' before once again striking up the hillside. There he retrieved his French clothes and put them on in place of the 'short black coat [and] trowsers' which he had borrowed from his foster-father and which John MacColl found outside his house next morning. Of Ailean, the bouman declared subsequently, there was by then no sign.[57]

That was because Ailean, in another demonstration of his ability to move across wild country at remarkable speed, managed during Monday, 18 May, to get himself from Caolasnacoan to Rannoch, where he put in an appearance before nightfall at the Ardlarach home of his uncle, Alan Cameron.

'Cuime 'm biomaid gun eudail,' runs a Rannoch song of that time, 'Agus sprèidh aig na Gallaibh': 'Why should we lack booty as long as Lowlanders have livestock?' Much the same note is struck by the words of a government official who knew mid-eighteenth-century Rannoch very well: 'Rannoch lay in the centre of the Highlands, with wide, extended hills [all around], and [there was] scarce a . . . man in [the district] but either stole or connived at theft. It was the common rendezvous for thieves and stolen cattle.' There could have been no better place, it is clear, for Ailean Breac to find sanctuary than this Highland equivalent of the criminal settlements – populated mainly by rustlers, smugglers and other undesirables – which were to develop in the nineteenth-century American West. In Rannoch, a man on the run was most unlikely to encounter, in any shape or form, the forces of law and order. And if such a man was in search of a gun, Rannoch was the sort of place where – the British government's Disarming Act notwithstanding – guns were always to be readily had.[58]

During the couple of days he spent at Ardlarach, situated on the north shore of Loch Rannoch and a mile or two from the loch's western end, Ailean Breac, it seems, spent some of James Stewart's five guineas on a firearm – for, when he turned up 'about twilight' on what was probably Wednesday, 20 May, at a dramshop in Innerhadden, the dramshop's owner, James Mann, 'saw a holster under [Ailean's] left arm'. 'Alan Breck', Mann said, 'declined to come in, being in a hurry [and intending] to go further down the country that night.' Mann accordingly brought out some bread and cheese which Ailean ate before striding off into the gathering darkness.[59]

Innerhadden is located a mile or so to the east of Kinlochrannoch, itself about ten miles east of Ardlarach. Beyond this point, an eastward-bound traveller would have had in the eighteenth century (as such a traveller still has today) the choice of several routes to Pitlochry, Dunkeld and, ultimately, to Scotland's North Sea ports. Which of those routes Ailean Breac took will forever remain a mystery. All that is certain is that, after he left Innerhadden, Ailean was never again sighted in Scotland by anyone prepared to admit to having seen him.

On Tuesday, 26 May, Colin Campbell was interred at Ardchattan Priory on the north shore of Loch Etive, the burial ground of his Campbell of Barcaldine forebears since the fifteenth century. The funeral, which had been delayed for several days with a view to enabling mourners from a wide area to gather at Glenure House and at other Campbell residences in the vicinity, was a large one. Among the numerous accounts which rolled into Glenure in the burial's aftermath was one for twelve dozen bottles of 'old claret', six dozen bottles of 'white port' and three dozen bottles of sherry. Given those quantities, it is hardly suprising that Colin's widow felt it prudent to lay in six corkscrews as well as, among other comestibles, 'two loaves of sugar weighing eleven pounds fifteen ounces', tea, coffee, 'one pound of aniseed', 'flour of mustard', 'twelve bricks [of] bread', 53 dozen eggs and 93 newly slaughtered hens. Cailean Ruadh's Campbell kin, to be sure, were not without real regret for a man whose 'wisdom and vision', as a sympathetic poet put it at the time, had failed to safeguard the factor from 'spiteful men of violence'. But Campbell grief, it is evident from the bill of fare laid on at Glenure House on 26 May, was not allowed to get in the way of some serious eating and drinking.[60]

However, the dish that Colin Campbell's mourners wished to taste above all others was vengeance. Three men were central to the huge effort that went into making this wish a reality. The three were John Campbell of Barcaldine, Cailean Ruadh's elder half-brother, known locally as *Iain Dubh* (Black John) because his hair was as dark as his dead half-brother's had been red; Duncan Campbell, Colin's younger brother and Perthshire's sheriff-substitute, who was to inherit the Glenure estate together with Cailean Ruadh's interests in Glen Duror and Lagnaha; and Alexander Campbell, one of Colin's several nephews, Duncan Campbell's son and the man whom Cailean Ruadh had been intending to install in Duror on 15 May as tenant of Ardshiel.

Iain Dubh and Alexander, soon to be known to others of this Barcaldine–Glenure grouping as Sandy Ardshiel, were already in North Argyll when the Wood of Lettermore killing occurred. To Sandy there fell the task of summoning his father Duncan, then resident in Killin, to join them. Writing to Duncan on the morning of 15 May, Sandy urged: 'Immediately on receipt of this, make the best of your way hither. Lose no time, I beg of you. What need

I keep you in suspense? Poor Glenure was shot by some damned villains out of a bush yesterday at four o' clock in Duror. Haste to us with all the expedition you can.'[61]

This letter, handed by Sandy to a mounted letter-carrier, reached Killin the day it was written. Responding the same day, Duncan pledged: 'I'm resolved to be revenged or perish in the attempt.' This, understandably, was the universal Campbell sentiment. For much of the summer of 1752, John Campbell noted on 15 August, he, Duncan and Sandy were 'constantly employed' in 'endeavouring to discover' the 'bloody authors' of his half-brother's 'barbarous assassination' – spending in the process, as John afterwards calculated with typical exactitude, the then enormous total of £1,334 9s 2½d.[62]

From a modern perspective it seems odd that Colin Campbell's relatives were permitted to assume key roles in the hunt for his killer, or killers. The Scotland of the 1750s, however, did not make twenty-first-century distinctions between public and private interests in matters of this kind. Besides, even if the authorities of that time had wanted to attempt such a thing, which they did not, it would have been impossible – given Clan Campbell's overwhelmingly dominant position in the administration of eighteenth-century Argyll – to keep men with the name of Campbell out of the business of trying to discover who had been behind what had occurred, on the afternoon of 14 May, in the Wood of Lettermore.

To underline this point, it is necessary only to mention that the machinery of justice in Argyll in 1752 was the responsibility of the county's sheriff, Archibald Campbell of Stonefield, a man whose background, attitudes and conduct serve perfectly to illustrate a further, and absolutely vital, truth about the processes which were to culminate in James Stewart's execution. Those processes were, at every stage, intensely and inescapably political – the politics in question being inextricably enmeshed in Hanoverian–Jacobite enmities of the type which had also underlain the events of 1745–46. For the duration of that earlier crisis, it must be stressed in this connection, Archibald Campbell of Stonefield had worked ceaselessly to bring about Charles Edward Stuart's defeat and Jacobitism's destruction. At bottom, no doubt, the sheriff's anti-Jacobite stance – a stance every bit as pronounced in 1752 as it had been six or seven years earlier – was rooted in his own ideological convictions. But those convictions owed some of their intensity to the closeness of Archibald Campbell's links with the most prominent of all Scotland's pro-Hanoverian politicians – this being that other Archibald Campbell, who was both the Duke of Argyll and the chief of the Argyll sheriff's clan.

Campbell of Stonefield and Duke Archibald knew each other intimately, the sheriff having been employed as chamberlain, or manager, of the duke's extensive estates. That is why, on his being called to London following Charles Edward Stuart's landing in the summer of 1746, it was to Campbell of Stonefield that Duke Archibald assigned the duty of ensuring the safety of Clan Campbell's Argyll heartlands. This trust, as Duke Archibald had known would be the case, was discharged punctiliously. Having first helped to raise the Argyll Militia, the sheriff had collaborated closely with General John Campbell both in supplying the Duke of Cumberland with those militia detachments which served at Culloden and in deploying the further militia units which, in Culloden's aftermath, had been given the job of reimposing Hanoverian authority on pro-Jacobite localities like Duror. When dealing with post-Culloden Duror, where he helped supervise the disarming of the district's population, Archibald Campbell of Stonefield had behaved less like a legal functionary, more like the emissary of a conquering power. On returning there in 17 May 1752, Argyll's sheriff clearly continued to think of himself as operating very much in enemy territory. In a manner that would not have been tolerated in most other parts of the mid-eighteenth-century United Kingdom, he made extensive use of troops to conduct searches, effect arrests and intimidate potential witnesses. And far from discouraging those other Campbells, notably John of Barcaldine and John's close kin, who had their own, highly personal, reasons for offering him assistance, Sheriff Archibald at once integrated them into his team. This team's eventual success, a representative of the Barcaldine laird maintained gleefully, was thereby assured: 'The appearance of [Campbell] gentlemen joined with the . . . military . . . struck a terror into the people of the country and made them, even against their inclinations, tell so much of the truth as, by degrees, brought the whole to light.'[63]

By the Monday following the Thursday that Colin Campbell was shot, Archibald Campbell, sheriff of Argyll, had installed himself in Taigh na h-Insaig and had given instructions for a series of Duror people to be brought before him one by one: Solomon MacColl, merchant; Donald MacColl from Achindarroch; Duncan MacColl, servant to Mildret MacColl, also from Achindarroch; Dugald Carmichael; John MacColl, shoemaker; John MacColl and Mary MacColl, his wife; a further John MacColl with his wife; Catherine MacPhail, widow. And so it went on hour after hour, day after day, at Taigh na h-Insaig to begin with, then in lots of other locations. Question after question was asked; response after response was noted down; facts were checked, rechecked, checked again. At the close of each interview, a sworn statement – in the shape of one of the documents which, in Scots law, are called precognitions – was produced. Many of those statements, as copied by Archibald Campbell's clerks, run to several, tightly inscribed, pages. And it is a measure of the almost unprecedented scale of the investigation which he launched at Taigh na h-Insaig on 18 May that when, well into June, the sheriff finally got home from what he described as 'a long and fatiguing expedition to the country of Appin', he had something like 700 separate precognitions to collate, cross-index and consider.[64]

Not all those precognitions, of course, resulted from Archibald Campbell's unaided efforts. Other law-enforcement officers were involved. So, as already indicated, were John, Duncan and Sandy Campbell – the murdered factor's kinsmen having been given carte blanche by the sheriff of Argyll to seek out and interview potential witnesses, suggest lines of inquiry and generally shape, influence and direct the search for Colin Campbell's killer.

The Glenure laird's relatives were duly appreciative. They were appreciative, too, of the backing they got from Colonel John Crawford of Pulteney's Regiment, the man in charge, by 1752, of the Fort William garrison. On 17 May, three days after the Wood of Lettermore shooting, Sandy Campbell, describing Crawford as 'a warm, interested friend', observed of Fort William's commander: 'Colonel Crawford sent a party [of troops] yesterday to Duror and desired that some of us should go to meet [their] officer.' The troops in question, Sandy Campbell's words make clear, reached Duror on Saturday, 16 May. And it is reasonable to suppose, given the tenor of Sandy's comments, that when, within hours of their arrival in Duror, those same troops took James Stewart and his son into custody at Taigh na h-Insaig, this was in part at the instigation of men – not least Sandy Campbell and his associates – whose Duror 'landgrabs' James had been trying to forestall. Neither the soldiers nor the junior officer responsible for the Taigh na h-Insaig arrests could have been expected – the troops in question merely obeying the orders they had been given in Fort William – to ask whether they were enforcing British justice, which was legitimate, or furthering a Campbell vendetta, which was not. But their superiors, both civilian and military, might have done well, on occasion, to pose precisely this question. Argyll's sheriff, or so the surviving evidence suggests, only once came close to doing so. 'There was a general jealousy entertained by [Campbell of] Glenure's relations against James Stewart and his family,' Archibald Campbell wrote when perusing his hundreds of precognitions in the seclusion of his study, 'as ... James ... was the chief person that managed the plea for the [Ardshiel estate] tenants, in order to support them in their possessions, by offering [the Court of Session] a bill of suspension.'[65]

While at the Duror front line, however, Sheriff Archibald seems to have engaged in no wider reflection of this kind – reflection which might have persuaded him to rely a little less on men who had their own reasons for wanting James Stewart taken out of their way. As it was, the sheriff, far from reining in his Campbell allies, seems mostly to have given them their head. On one occasion, Mungo Campbell, the dead Colin's lawyer nephew, was permitted to send 'a sergeant and a party of soldiers' to James Stewart's Acharn home 'with orders to search, and particularly to search for writings'. On a second occasion, Patrick Campbell, another of Colin's nephews and Sandy Campbell's brother, was given the use of a further military detachment, this one headed by Captain David Chapeau of Pulteney's, in order to ransack Acharn and its environs for weapons. Mungo's raid turned up papers which were to be produced at James' trial. (These are preserved today among the records of Scotland's High Court and have been quoted on preceding pages.) Patrick's Acharn foray uncovered the broadswords and firearms James Stewart had ordered hidden on the evening of Cailean Ruadh's killing – Captain Chapeau noting that one of the guns his men found showed signs of having been fired prior to its being buried. But for all that James' correspondence helped illuminate the nature of the campaign he had waged against Colin Campbell's projected evictions, and for all that the discovery of concealed weaponry at Acharn constituted evidence of law-breaking in its own right, none of this Campbell activity – much as it may have gratified Mungo and Patrick – took Sheriff Archibald, as he was well aware, much closer to the man who had actually carried out the Wood of Lettermore murder. That man, as everyone accepted, could not have been James Stewart, who was known to have been at home when the fatal shot was fired. Hence the importance attached by Archibald Campbell, almost from the moment of his arrival at Taigh na h-Insaig, to finding the person in whose direction accusing fingers had been pointed within hours of Colin Campbell dying. This person, of course, was James' foster-son, Ailean Breac.[66]

While Ailean Breac – unbeknown to his pursuers – was still at Caolasnacoan, Sandy Campbell was attempting to block Ailean's getaway routes to the east. From Sunday, 17 May, if not before, Sandy was getting reports from people 'searching the Braes of Glencoe and watching the passes there', from a second party scouring 'the forests of Glen Etive', and from a contingent busily criss-crossing 'the moor betwixt Glencoe and Rannoch'. None of Sandy Campbell's searchers, needless to say, as much as caught a glimpse of Ailean Breac. And though news was eventually to filter through of Ailean's having been in the Rannoch area, his trail, long before it could be followed to Ardlarach and Innerhadden, had grown hopelessly cold. By the Barcaldine Campbells and their allies, a number of individuals – some of them, it was noted, concealing their identities 'under the character of chapmen'[67] – were next employed to look for traces of Ailean in Atholl and in the Angus glens. But this quest, too, proved fruitless. While Ailean Breac may have been briefly in the localities in question, one Campbell agent wrote on 17 July, it was 'certain that he is not now skulking in those parts'. 'The success of endeavours', this man added philosophically, 'does not depend upon us but upon the Great Governor of the world.'[68]

The 'Great Governor's' apparent disinterestedness notwithstanding, port officials all along Scotland's east coast were told to do everything possible to prevent Ailean Breac getting abroad. 'There being reason to apprehend that the murderer may attempt to escape by sea out of the kingdom,' Dunbar's customs officer was informed on 19 May, 'we order you . . . to examine very strictly every person offering to take passage on board any ship going out of this kingdom, and to stop any person who cannot give a good account of himself.' Distributed with dispatches of this sort, and inserted in newspapers the length and breadth of Scotland, were detailed descriptions of the wanted man. 'The person suspected of [Colin Campbell's] murder,' runs one of these, 'is . . . Alan Breck Stewart, a French cadet [meaning junior officer], who was in Appin at the time. He is about five feet, ten inches high; his face much marked with the smallpox, black bushy hair put up in a bag, a little in-knee'd, round shouldered, has full black eyes and is about 30 years of age. He is . . . shabby with an inclination to be genteel.'[69]

This last, if he saw it, would have infuriated Ailean. But it did nothing to facilitate his capture. In early June, a man was 'taken out of a ship in Leith' and committed to Edinburgh Castle on a charge of 'being concerned in the murder of [Campbell of] Glenure'. This unfortunate, however, turned out to be John MacGregor, 'a Perthshire man, and lately a gentleman's servant' – just as a further dubious character, seized in Annan in July and conveyed to prison in Carlisle on suspicion of being Ailean Breac, proved, when inquiry was made, to be George Blair, 'a sergeant in the Dutch service'.[70]

Sheriff Archibald, by this stage, was aware of rumours – which may well have been true – to the effect that Ailean Breac 'had [already] left the kingdom from the coast of Fife'. Also by this stage, the sheriff had begun to ask himself if, in devoting so much effort and resource to a ceaseless quest for the elusive Ailean, both he and his Campbell collaborators might be doing exactly as the Appin Stewarts wanted. Among the latter, as is obvious from Sheriff Archibald's precognitions, there had certainly been no lack of enthusiasm for the notion that the hunt for Colin Campbell's killer should begin and end with the pursuit of Ailean Breac. 'He suspects Alan Breck . . . for the murder,' the sheriff had jotted down when questioning Alexander Stewart of Invernahyle. 'Nor does he suspect anybody . . . but Alan Breck,' Sheriff Archibald had noted when interviewing Alexander Stewart of Ballachulish. 'When he first heard [of] it [the murder],' ran the sheriff's notes of his encounter with the

Ballachulish laird's elder son, 'he . . . suspected that Alan Breck Stewart had done it.' 'When [he] heard of [Campbell of] Glenure's murder,' Sheriff Archibald recorded at the close of an hour or so spent with John Stewart of Fasnacloich, 'he suspected . . . Alan Breck Stewart to have been guilty of it.' This unanimity of view was superficially impressive. The sheriff, however, was by no means convinced. Indeed, the more he and his fellow investigators thought about what they had been told by the leading men of the Appin Stewarts, the less plausible they found it.[71]

What appeared especially unbelievable to the men in charge of the Lettermore murder inquiry was the idea that Ailean Breac had planned and carried out the 14 May shooting entirely by himself. Mungo Campbell, within a week of his having witnessed his uncle's death, had come to the conclusion that the crime, far from being the work of a single individual, was the end product of 'a horrid chain of roguery' involving several of the leading men among the Appin Stewarts. 'The odium seems to be put on Alan Breck Stewart,' Mungo commented caustically, 'but numbers were his associates.' Colonel John Crawford, Fort William's commander, agreed. 'Above twenty people must have known of the murder,' he observed. And the colonel was at one with Mungo Campbell in thinking that the 'Appin potentates', as Mungo called men like the Stewarts of Ballachulish and Fasnacloich, were party to a well-organised conspiracy of which Ailean Breac's flight from Duror and from Scotland was an integral component. 'This', Crawford wrote of Ailean's disappearance, 'seems to me calculated to divert our attentions from objects [meaning the Stewart gentry] more in our power; and the way his [Ailean's] name has been mentioned . . . by the Stewarts fully convinces me that his . . . absconding was intended as a peace-offering by the rest of his friends.'[72]

Crawford's opinion, interestingly enough, has the endorsement of Duror tradition. 'He received a reward for fleeing and [for] allowing the killing of Colin of Glenure to be imputed to himself,' it was said of Ailean Breac in nineteenth-century Duror. While the belief that Ailean received a cash payment for his services as scapegoat can be dismissed as a distorted folk memory of the complex transactions surrounding the five guineas which eventually reached Ailean at Caolasnacoan on 17 May 1752, much in this verdict rings true. By Duror tradition-bearers, of course, Ailean's conduct in the aftermath of Colin Campbell's murder was seen as having followed on from his participation in the Lochan Blar nan Lochan shooting match. That shadowy episode, tradition-bearers insisted, had involved a number of Clan Stewart's 'principal men'. It had culminated, they further insisted, in one of those 'principal men' being selected as Colin Campbell's assassin; this assassin was not Ailean Breac, but he had agreed or been persuaded to make a very public getaway, 'for the purposes of lessening inquiries concerning the rest of the [Stewart] gentlemen by directing suspicion to himself'.[73]

This thesis has the merit of explaining much that is otherwise inexplicable about Ailean Breac's behaviour during the weeks, days and hours preceding the Wood of Lettermore shooting. A man aiming simply to kill Colin Campbell would surely not, as Ailean did, have boasted in a dozen Duror and Appin drinking establishments of his intention to do Colin harm. But a man who positively wanted to make himself suspect might well do that very thing – just as such a man might, for the same reason, hang around Ballachulish ferry on the day of Cailean Ruadh's murder, asking needless questions about the factor's movements.

Nor is it hard to see why, if some Stewart combine wished to have matters muddied in this way, Ailean Breac was the obvious man to do the necessary muddying. As both Ailean and his foster-father stressed at the time, whether or not Ailean Breac had a hand in what happened in the Wood of Lettermore, he would have had no alternative, the moment Cailean Ruadh was shot, but to get out of North Argyll as fast as possible. With some 200 of Colonel John Crawford's soldiers stationed in its immediate vicinity and with Sheriff Archibald Campbell and his colleagues taking dozens of its inhabitants in for questioning, Duror, towards the end of May 1752, was no place for a known deserter from the British army – a deserter who, if apprehended, would hang irrespective of any connection he may or may not have had with Colin Campbell's killing. By singling out Ailean Breac as their number one suspect, then, the various Stewarts who cast Ailean in this role were not forcing him into absconding. He would have absconded anyway. And their knowledge of Ailean's ability to look after himself would have mitigated any unease his Stewart accusers may have experienced when selling out Ailean. This was a man who had hidden in the hills for many months in 1746; a man who'd managed, during 1747, to escape to France; a man who had been in and out of Scotland illegally more than once since then. If there was one person in Duror who could be relied on to get safely abroad even if he had half of Scotland in pursuit of him, it is easy to imagine someone saying as the Lochan Blar nan Lochan shooting match drew to a close, then that man was Ailean Breac.

For what it is worth, this interpretation of the events of 1752 accords with Ailean's last recorded comment on the subject – a comment made, half a lifetime after the Wood of Lettermore murder, to Alexander Campbell, a son of one of Colin Campbell of Glenure's many nephews. In 1787, when spending some time in Paris, Alexander was visited in his lodgings, as he informed his father, by 'a tall, thin, ugly man' who introduced himself as Ailean Breac and who at once raised the topic of Cailean Ruadh's killing. 'He denied the murder,'

Alexander Campbell reported of what the self-declared Ailean (who would then have been in his sixties) had to say of the events of 35 years previously, 'and swore by all that was sacred that it was not him, [saying] that he knew who it was, [but that he] was bound by oath to conceal it.'[74]

One obvious difficulty remains, however. If Ailean Breac's precipitate departure for the continent – where he rejoined the French army with which he was to serve for another twenty-five years – had indeed been factored into a wider conspiracy well in advance of this conspiracy coming to fruition on 14 May, why was Ailean so short of cash on the day in question as to oblige him to waste valuable time waiting for his foster-father, James Stewart, to scrape together the five guineas which the Duror packman, Alexander Stewart, finally delivered to Caolasnacoan on Sunday, 17 May?

However one marshals the known facts, then, unresolved issues continue to emerge. They always will. And yet the surviving evidence suggests every bit as strongly in the twenty-first century as it did in the eighteenth that the shooting of Cailean Ruadh is unlikely to have been a solitary act on the part of an unaided gunman. Absolutely critical in this context is the wider background to that shooting – for it is here, as already indicated, that there are to be discovered the origins of the powerful emotions engendered in senior members of Clan Stewart by the actions Colin Campbell took in the period preceding his assassination.

Colin, to recapitulate, belonged to the Barcaldine Campbells, a family with whom the Appin Stewarts had been at loggerheads since they had usurped, as the Stewarts saw it, the Lordship of Lorn. Underpinning this 300-year-old feud, on the Stewart side, were fears that the Campbells of Barcaldine nurtured designs on what, subsequent to the loss of Lorn, had become Clan Stewart's heartland – the territory lying between Loch Creran and Loch Leven. By the Appin Stewarts, in times past, battles had been fought to prevent Campbell encroachments on this heartland. Now, without a blow being struck, Colin Campbell of Glenure, whose half-brother was Campbell of Barcaldine himself, looked to be masterminding just such an encroachment. In not much more than twelve months, Colin had both acquired ownership of Lagnaha and obtained a stake in the tenancy of Glen Duror; he was on the verge of placing the majority of what remained of the Ardshiel estate in the tenancy of men such as his half-brother's son, Sandy, and had also put himself in a position – by virtue of the loans he had made to Clan Stewart's semi-bankrupt chief, Dougal – to add substantially to these gains at a moment of his choosing. Colin Campbell, in other words, was on the verge of accomplishing something that had eluded his forebears for three centuries – he was on the verge of incorporating a large slice of Appin into the Campbell of Barcaldine empire.

And such a development, it's clear from everything that is known about the mind-set and attitudes of the leading Stewarts of that time, is one that many Stewarts would have been willing to take huge risks to stop. This, at bottom, is why there is nothing inconceivable about the concept of Colin Campbell's murder having been the outcome of Clan Stewart plotting, and why Colin's kinsmen, who knew better than anyone the extent of the ill-feeling they had stirred up by moving into Duror, were not surprised that such plotting should have occurred.

Thus Sandy Ardshiel, both a Barcaldine Campbell and a major beneficiary of Colin's plans for Duror, was convinced, almost from the moment of the Wood of Lettermore slaying, that his uncle had fallen victim to a conspiracy. In his more embittered moments, Sandy blamed 'the whole damned race' of Stewarts for what had happened. But two men seemed to him to be especially implicated. They were John and James Stewart, heirs to Alexander Stewart of Ballachulish and John Stewart of Fasnacloich.[75]

Like Sandy, the Fasnacloich and Ballachulish heirs were in their twenties; like Sandy, John and James had seen active service in the course of Prince Charles Edward's rebellion. The pro-Jacobite Stewarts, however, were Appin Regiment veterans, while the staunchly Hanoverian Sandy, like many other Campbells, had joined, in 1745, the Argyll Militia. In assuming control of Ardshiel township and what little Captain Caroline Scott had left standing of Ardshiel House, therefore, Sandy, from a Stewart perspective, was not only a Barcaldine Campbell occupying Clan Stewart land; he was also a pro-government man who had had the temerity to take charge of what had been the home of the Appin Regiment's former colonel, Charles Stewart. Hence the array of animosities on display when, during the winter preceding Cailean Ruadh's murder, James Stewart, the Fasnacloich heir, happened to encounter one of Sandy Ardshiel's close associates, John Campbell, whom Cailean Ruadh had very recently named as tenant of a part of Lettermore.

'The conversation,' John Campbell said of his chance meeting with James of Fasnacloich, 'turned upon him [John] and his friends coming to possess some of the estate of Ardshiel.' 'You are greedy people,' James allegedly told John, 'and will not be contented with your own land but will remove other poor people from their possessions.' To which John Campbell, by his own account, replied: 'We will be in the middle of Appin in spite of you.' 'If he was a son or near relation of [Stewart of] Ardshiel,' James Stewart retorted in his turn, 'he would be the death of them [the Campbells] before they would get settlement there.'[76]

Comments of this sort – and there were probably a lot of them – would have come to Sandy Campbell's attention before the events of 14 May 1752. After those events, however, such comments took on a new significance in Sandy's mind, as did various other bits of information, such as the fact that the laird of Fasnacloich's elder son (the source of the barely veiled threat made to Sandy's colleague, John Campbell) was a good friend of Ailean Breac; that Ailean and James had been in each other's company at Fasnacloich the weekend prior to Cailean Ruadh's killing; and that, following the Wood of Lettermore episode, James had been keeping what was – from a Hanoverian or Campbell standpoint – some very dubious company. 'He has not been at home since [the] melancholy accident [of 14 May],' Sandy Campbell noted of the Fasnacloich laird's heir on 25 May. James, he added, was in the south, where, Sandy believed, he was in discussion with the self-same Jacobite families his namesake, Seumas a' Ghlinne, had visited in April. It was 'highly probable,' Sandy concluded, that James of Fasnacloich 'knew every step intended' by Colin's murderers.[77]

Sandy believed that John Stewart of Ballachulish and his father, Alexander, were equally in the know. 'Both Ballachulishes are extremely busy,' Sandy wrote in July. 'The young man has frequent expresses [letters] from the south, and the old is closeted twice or thrice with the ladies Glencoe and Callart.' The women referred to were Isabel MacDonald and Helen Cameron, the sisters of Charles Stewart of Ardshiel with whom Ailean Breac had spent time – just as he had spent time with Alexander Stewart of Ballachulish – before Cailean Ruadh's killing. To Sandy, increasingly frustrated by his inability to discover what exactly was being said at the Stewart gatherings going on all around him, the very fact that so many known Jacobites – Alexander and John Stewart of Ballachulish, James Stewart of Fasnacloich, Isabel MacDonald and Helen Cameron – were regularly in conclave was justification enough for stern measures. 'I really think,' he commented of the Ballachulish laird and his son, 'they ought . . . both to be laid fast.'[78]

The Fasnacloich heir, it was felt by the Barcaldine contingent, should be arrested also. And on this – as on much else – they were at one with Fort William's commanding officer. 'I have been talking to Colonel Crawford about apprehending [James of] Fasnacloich,' Mungo Campbell reported, 'and he thinks it very proper to commit him.'[79]

But on what grounds exactly? John Crawford and his Campbell allies may have been persuaded that several of the Appin Stewarts had conspired to kill Cailean Ruadh. They were aware of ceaseless to-ings and fro-ings between Jacobite households in Appin, Glencoe, Callart and Stirlingshire. They had even heard mention of the Lochan Blar nan Lochan shooting match. But none of this – certainly not what had gone on at Lochan Blar nan Lochan – could be properly pinned down. For all that plenty of people in Duror and Appin –

the district's Stewart gentry included – were willing enough to pin the Wood of Lettermore murder on the missing Ailean Breac and to talk at length about Ailean's alleged boasts and threats, nobody was prepared to say a word about what might have occurred at Lochan Blar nan Lochan or at any other of the locations where leading men of Clan Stewart were known to have got together during the opening months of 1752. Unsurprisingly, therefore, Colonel John Crawford, for one, thought it legitimate – in the face of so much calculated defiance – to abandon legal niceties. 'In the short experience I have had of this part of the country,' Fort William's commander observed, 'I have found that in order to come at the bottom of any villainy many methods are necessary to be put into practice to give the law an opportunity of exerting its force; for we find very few who act merely from the love of justice.'[80]

With those sentiments, Sandy Campbell and his kin agreed wholeheartedly. And in their desperation to uncover some at least of what they knew was being concealed from them, they even contemplated trying to win over the one man in a position to explain all. If Ailean Breac – in return for his promising to reveal the exact nature of his dealings with his Stewart relatives – were to be offered a pardon in respect of his desertion from King George's forces at Prestonpans, it was suggested to the authorities in Edinburgh by John Campbell of Barcaldine, then the extent of Clan Stewart's involvement in Cailean Ruadh's death might finally be laid bare. John's contacts among Scotland's political and legal establishment were not unsympathetic. As lawyers and politicians always do, however, they feared setting a precedent. 'The only thing I can think of', observed one very senior official, 'would be to let [Alan] Breck's avowed friends understand that, if he did deliver himself up . . . and would tell the truth, he would find true intercessions for him.'[81]

Since it was never made, there is no knowing whether Ailean would have responded positively to such an offer, though the chances must be that he would have ignored it. As it was, having abandoned all hope of adding substantially to their haul of suspects, the Barcaldine Campbells, Argyll's sheriff and the sheriff's political superiors began, during June and July 1752, to frame the strongest possible case against the single Stewart of consequence already in their power. This, of course, was Seamus a' Ghlinne, whom Mungo Campbell – mindful of his family's need to see someone hang for Colin's murder – now declared to be 'the chief contriver of the whole scene of villainy'.[82]

'Oh!' says I, willing to give him a little lesson, 'I have no fear of the justice of my
country.' 'Man, I whiles wonders at ye,' said Alan. 'This is a Campbell that's been
killed. Well, it'll be tried in Inverara, the Campbells' head place; with fifteen Campbells
in the jury-box and the biggest Campbell of all (and that's the Duke) sitting cocking
on the bench.'

Robert Louis Stevenson, *Kidnapped*

When first imprisoned in Fort William, James Stewart had high
hopes of an early release. In a letter of 19 May to John
MacFarlane, the Edinburgh lawyer who had acted for him in
connection with his previous month's case in the Court of Session, James
expressed some expectation of being bailed – remarking that Donald Campbell
of Airds, among others, would bail him 'in any sum whatever' and urging
MacFarlane to 'spare no pains' in contacting both the Airds laird and other
prospective sources of cash. 'What makes my confinement very uneasy to me',
James added, 'is that this is the time of the year that my business would require
my presence most; having bought cattle (wherein I yearly deal) in different
countries, and taking grazings [in the] south for the cattle which I must pay
[for] if I should never send a beast upon [them].' Soon, however, James
Stewart's worries as to the fate of his cattle-trading operations were to give way
to much more pressing concerns. Far from planning to set him free, it soon
became clear to James, his captors were calculating how they might most
effectively set about depriving him of life as well as liberty.[1]

James Stewart's position would have been precarious enough had his
Campbell enemies been acting in isolation. Making his plight still more
serious, however, was the fact that they enjoyed political backing at the highest
level. 'It is with great satisfaction,' the barons of exchequer were informed by
the United Kingdom's prime minister, Henry Pelham, 'I have heard that the

relatives of Mr Campbell of Glenure are using their utmost endeavours to bring his murderers to justice.' And Pelham's satisfaction on this point, it appears, was shared by no less a personage than King George II himself, the monarch's 'gracious approbation' being given to 'the steps . . . taken in order to discover and to bring to justice the barbarous murderers of Mr Colin Campbell of Glenure'.[2]

Had the Wood of Lettermore killing been seen in London as an incident likely to produce merely local consequences, it would scarcely have registered in the nation's capital, murders being fairly routine occurrences in eighteenth-century Britain. What concerned the most senior of the country's politicians, however, was the possibility, as they saw it, that the shooting of Colin Campbell – a government servant administering an estate seized by the government from a prominent Jacobite – might become the signal for a resurgence of Jacobite activity right across the Scottish Highlands. Over and over again, this apprehension surfaces in the correspondence of cabinet ministers of the time. 'There never was a more daring attempt against a government,' commented Robert d'Arcy, Earl of Holdernesse and one of Pelham's close colleagues. To Philip Yorke, Earl of Hardwicke and England's Lord Chancellor, the killing of Colin Campbell seemed 'an audacious and outrageous insult upon the government'. The Wood of Lettermore shooting, the prime minister acknowledged, 'undoubtedly' deserved 'serious and vigorous attention'.[3]

One immediate outcome was an insistence on all sides that someone had to pay a high price for Colin Campbell's murder. Holdernesse declared himself 'fully sensible of the dangerous consequences of suffering such a notorious attack upon government to remain unpunished', while Pelham considered it 'ruin to think of quieting the Highlands' if those responsible for Colin's death were not 'severely punished'. Before the end of May 1752, therefore, the authorities in Edinburgh were ordered to 'bring to condign punishment the actors and accomplishers in this insidious and cruel action'. If the 'spirit of revenge and disaffection' underlying Colin Campbell's murder were to receive the 'encouragement' which would result from the murderer going unpunished, administrators and officials in Scotland's capital were warned by their London superiors, the 'most pernicious consequences' might all too readily manifest themselves.[4]

Adding hugely to the pressures on the men responsible for the governance of Scotland was their awareness of the extent to which their own loyalties were being called into question by none other than Culloden's victor, the Duke of Cumberland. What had provoked the duke were government proposals to take over, or annexe, in perpetuity forfeited estates of the Ardshiel type – with a view to utilising the resulting 'rents and profits . . . for the better civilising and improving [of] the Highlands'. Their so-called Annexing Bill, ministers insisted, would have the effect of 'promoting amongst [Highlanders] the protestant religion, good government, industry and manufactures, and principles of duty and loyalty to his majesty [King George], his heirs and successors'. To the Duke of Cumberland, however, the measure smacked of mollycoddling rebels. And it infuriated the duke – who thought himself something of a Highland expert – that Henry Pelham should have embarked on such a course without prior discussion with him. Cumberland's consequent disenchantment with Pelham's Highland policy was summarised thus by one of his close collaborators, Horace Walpole: 'The duke, who had conquered the Scotch like an able general, who had punished them like an offended prince, and whose resentments were not softened by the implacability of their hatred to him, was not a little disgusted at seeing measures of favour to them adopted, and himself totally unconsulted upon these measures.' When the Annexing Bill came before the House of Lords in March 1752, therefore, the Duke of Cumberland made it his business to engineer a great deal of opposition to it.[5]

Much of this opposition took the form of suggestions to the effect that all sorts of government posts in Scotland were occupied by Jacobite sympathisers. 'Nobody who has spent their life here [in London], and has not been in that country and seen their practices, can have any notion of them,' Cumberland commented darkly of what he had seen of society to the north of the Anglo-Scottish border. And though the duke refrained from intervening personally in March's House of Lords debates, his several political allies among the nation's peers gave his prejudices a thorough airing. 'Some pretty strong reflections upon the government were thrown out,' the Earl of Holdernesse reported, 'and some instances were given of supposed neglect in the king's servants as to the administration of affairs in Scotland.' 'It [was] in general objected', Holdernesse went on, 'that non-jurors [meaning Episcopalians] and other disaffected persons meet with countenance and support, and even preferment.' It was also alleged, the earl added, 'that universally the sheriffs, or their deputies, are very negligent of their duty in omitting to secure [meaning imprison] persons wearing the Highland dress or carrying arms'.[6]

Among the Scottish office-holders whom the Duke of Cumberland believed to be less than sound, ironically enough, were John Campbell of Barcaldine and his half-brother, Colin Campbell of Glenure. 'He [the duke] owned his suspicions of them,' the Earl of Hardwicke noted of the Campbell brothers following his having met with Cumberland in the early part of 1752. Hence the bitter note struck by one of the Glenure laird's Campbell relatives on the day news came of Colin's murder: 'This is the man who was represented to . . . ministers as a Jacobite. He has given a fatal proof to the contrary.'[7]

But if his death had the effect of posthumously exculpating Colin Campbell from the charge of harbouring pro-Jacobite sentiments, it rendered other prominent Scots more vulnerable to the same accusation. Had those Scots been doing their jobs properly, after all, it would have been impossible, or so the Duke of Cumberland and those who thought like him could readily argue, for a government official to be gunned down in one of the very localities which since 1746 had supposedly been disarmed, pacified and generally restored to order. And if, or so the Cumberland clique could equally readily maintain, nobody was brought to justice in connection with Colin Campbell's killing, this would constitute proof positive that, as the Duke of Cumberland and his friends had been insinuating, Scotland's administrative machine was indeed in the hands of men who could not be trusted to keep the Hanoverian dynasty's opponents under control. During the summer of 1752, it followed, practically nobody in authority in Scotland was inclined to deal open-mindedly and disinterestedly with James Stewart. On all sides, carefully nurtured careers and reputations depended on finding someone to hang in connection with the Wood of Lettermore murder. And since James, in the absence of Ailean Breac, seemed the obvious candidate for execution, he was, as one of his defence lawyers remarked in the Inveraray church where James was tried, under a crippling disadvantage from the outset. 'What I mean', this lawyer elaborated, 'is an impression . . . has been industriously raised and artfully propagated as if it were somehow necessary that [James Stewart] should be found guilty, and as if his being acquitted might bring a reflection on this part of the kingdom.'[8]

Among the individuals with an interest in creating exactly this impression were two of the men James Stewart faced across Inveraray's church-cum-courtroom in September 1752. One of these was Archibald Campbell, Duke of Argyll, who – as mentioned earlier – had opted, in his capacity as Scotland's Lord Justice General, to preside at James' trial. The other was William Grant of Prestongrange, Scotland's lord advocate or leading law officer, who had chosen to head the team conducting James' prosecution. It had 'not been frequently practised by [his] predecessors in office' to attend 'in person' at a trial such as James Stewart's, the lord advocate acknowledged. Nor had it been any more usual, William Grant might have added, for Lords Justice General to sit in judgement on men such as James. As a result of what had been said in London by the Duke of Cumberland, however, both Grant and Duke Archibald were highly conscious of a pressing need to demonstrate their unswerving loyalty to Britain's Hanoverian regime. The Duke of Argyll, by far the most important Scottish ally of Henry Pelham, the prime minister, was one of the Scots whom Cumberland considered to have shown 'favour to Jacobites'.

And the lord advocate was ultimately responsible for numerous appointments – of sheriffs and the like – which the Duke of Cumberland and his fanatically anti-Jacobite friends thought extremely questionable.[9]

As it happened, neither William Grant nor Duke Archibald – as would have been instantly evident to anyone more in tune with Scottish realities than King George II's younger son – were tainted in the least by Jacobite feeling. But both were of the opinion, as members of a Scottish aristocracy which had been deeply permeated by Jacobitism for several generations, that it would ultimately be helpful to the king and his family – the Duke of Cumberland included – to have some at least of the Hanoverian dynasty's Scottish enemies won over to its side. That is why, when exercising their considerable powers of patronage, both the Duke of Argyll and Grant of Prestongrange had given jobs to men who, if Cumberland's opinions had prevailed, would forever have remained beyond the political pale.

Their policies having been attacked and their loyalties questioned in London, both William Grant and Duke Archibald thought it prudent to ensure that James Stewart was hanged. In the highly charged circumstances of 1752, after all, the last thing the Duke of Argyll or the lord advocate needed were whispers and rumours to the effect that they had dealt less than ruthlessly with this known Jacobite, who had also been alleged to have had a hand in Colin Campbell's murder. Hence the unctuously pro-Hanoverian speech – featuring the Duke of Cumberland in the guise of a renowned soldier and 'great prince' – with which Duke Archibald sent James to the gallows. Hence, too, the professions of profound devotion to king and country with which William Grant of Prestongrange prefaced his remarks to the Inveraray trial jury. 'Upon my first hearing of the murder . . . of . . . the king's factor upon certain of the forfeited estates,' Grant declared, 'I was greatly shocked and considered the murderers, whoever they were, as having been guilty not only of a horrid crime against the laws of God and humanity, but, together with this, of a most audacious insult against . . . the king's government . . . Under this impression, I then resolved, whenever a discovery should be made of any persons concerned in this wickedness, to attend at the trial, wherever it should be, and to do all that in me lay, consistently with law and justice, to convince the disaffected part of the Highlands of Scotland that they must submit to this government which they have several times in vain endeavoured to subvert.'[10]

On 17 August 1752, the case against James Stewart was summed up thus by one of James' principal antagonists, John Campbell of Barcaldine: ' The proof points chiefly at Alan Breck Stewart . . . as the assassin who committed the murder and against James Stewart . . . as the person who contrived and assisted the barbarous design.' This represented something of a withdrawal from the earlier Campbell contention that a much larger group of Stewarts had helped plan Cailean Ruadh's murder. But for all that they continued to cling to the notion of wider involvement in the Wood of Lettermore killing, it was now apparent, to the Barcaldine Campbells as well as to the various politicians with whom they were in close touch, that it might make sense to proceed with a trial of the one Clan Stewart member whose hostility to the dead factor could easily be demonstrated. 'He was moved by revenge against [Campbell of] Glenure,' John of Barcaldine observed of James Stewart, 'first, for having accepted the [Ardshiel estate] factory at all and, second, for [the factor's] having turned out the said James Stewart and some of his favourites who were in possession of parts of the estate of Ardshiel.'[11]

To show that James harboured a grudge against Colin Campbell, however, was not to prove that he had been implicated in Colin's death. During August, therefore, a great deal of work went on behind the scenes in an attempt to provide William Grant of Prestongrange and his fellow prosecutors with a narrative containing – or so it was hoped – reasons why it might plausibly be concluded by a jury that James' dislike of Cailean Ruadh had reached such a pitch as to cause James to have the factor killed. By the month's end, this document – drawing extensively on Sheriff Archibald Campbell's several hundred precognitions – had been completed and was being circulated around the many influential individuals who had an interest in seeing James Stewart hang.

The resulting 'abstract of precognitions', as the August narrative was entitled, begins by asserting 'that the friends of Mr [Charles] Stewart of Ardshiel and the tenants upon his estate [James Stewart included] were very much discontented at [Campbell of] Glenure's being appointed [the estate's] factor'. But James, the abstract notes, nursed an additional grievance, 'James Stewart . . . and his family [being] extremely discontented with [Campbell of] Glenure for removing them from . . . Glen Duror'. Those tensions, the August abstract implies, wre heightened by the factor's decision – for good managerial reasons, it is stated – to eject 'some other tenants'. This caused discontent to spread across Duror, with the result that James, scenting an opportunity to get back at Colin, 'set himself to oppose these removings'.[12] As the eviction crisis developed, the abstract maintains, James' state of mind became increasingly dangerous, repeated mention being made of precognition evidence to the effect that 'James Stewart uttered strong threats against [Campbell of] Glenure's life'.[13]

Having thus set the scene, the abstract introduces its alleged murderer, Ailean Breac, stressing that he 'was in great intimacy and familiarity with James Stewart and his family and lived often at [James'] house'. Like James, the abstract continues, 'Alan Breck Stewart expressed strong resentment against [Campbell of] Glenure,' and encouraged by James, Ailean began to plan the detested factor's murder.[14]

'On the 8th of May,' the abstract observes, 'Alan Breck ... came to [Stewart of] Fasnacloich's house which lies opposite [Campbell of] Glenure's house ... After [Campbell of] Glenure left his own house to go to Fort William on Monday the 11th of May, Alan Breck went directly to James Stewart's house ... changed [out of] his own clothes and put on a black short coat, trousers and blue bonnet belonging to James Stewart.' There follows a detailed account of Ailean's subsequent movements, culminating in his arrival, on the evening of Wednesday, 13 May, at Stewart of Ballachulish's home.[15]

On the day of Colin Campbell's death, the abstract next points out, 'Alan Breck went to fish upon a burn that runs by [Stewart of] Ballachulish's house ... He fished the burn into a woody place where he was in cover but, as the ground rose, [it] gave him an opportunity of seeing [Ballachulish] ferry and all the road that [Campbell of] Glenure would take after he crossed the ferry until he entered the Wood of Lettermore where he was killed, and from the place Breck was he had a very short cut to that wood.'[16]

The abstract, of course, is unable definitively to place Ailean Breac at the murder scene. But the clothes which Ailean had borrowed from James on the Monday and which he was still wearing on the Thursday were akin in cut and colour, the document insists, to the clothes worn by the gunman whom Murdo Campbell glimpsed seconds after his uncle was shot.

Finally, the abstract takes up the issue of James' behaviour in the immediate aftermath of the killing. 'James Stewart', it remarks, 'soon after being acquainted of the murder showed no surprise or concern for it, neither did he or his son ... go to ... the corpse.' More damning still, the abstract comments, was James' willingness, at this critical juncture, to come to Ailean Breac's assistance. 'Immediately upon the murder's being known,' the abstract reminds its readers, 'it was the general belief in the country that Alan Breck Stewart had committed it.' But James, while knowing this, had sent Ailean both money and Ailean's own clothes – thus facilitating the escape, from his temporary hiding place at Caolasnacoan, of the man whom the abstract assumes to have been Colin Campbell's killer.[17]

There remained one or two further circumstances of which, or so it was hinted by the August abstract's compilers, the lord advocate and his colleagues might be able to make something – notably the discovery of guns, one of them showing signs of recent use, at James' Acharn home. Overall, however, William Grant and his assistant prosecutors must have read their copies of the 'abstract of precognitions' with a growing sense of despondency. The mass of information gathered so painstakingly by Sheriff Archibald Campbell and distilled with such care by the abstract's authors had, in the end, yielded very little that was incontrovertibly detrimental to James Stewart. While it was a fact that James possessed illegally held firearms, it could not be proved that the weapons in question had played any part in Colin Campbell's murder – there being all sorts of reasons, having to do with the commonplace shooting of game, why one of James' guns might have been discharged legitimately. And while it was also a fact that James had aided Ailean Breac's getaway, the defence team at his trial would doubtless advance the argument (as they did) that James, knowing Ailean was wanted as a deserter, had merely yielded to an understandable, if legally dubious, desire to help his foster-son keep out of the army's reach. As for the rest, what was not the most circumstantial of circumstantial evidence was hearsay, speculation, even gossip. And as if that were not bad enough, there remained the huge stumbling block of Ailean Breac's seemingly successful flight – a flight which put James Stewart's prosecutors in the extremely awkward position of having to charge James, in effect, with being an accessory to a murder whose supposed perpetrator had himself not been tried, let alone found guilty.

Irrespective of their lack of hard evidence that James Stewart had committed any capital crime, the authorities dealing with his case needed – for reasons already touched on – to have him executed. This being so, they set about depriving James of such meagre rights as eighteenth-century Scotland's justice system conferred on him. For much of June, July and August 1752, James Stewart was held in Fort William. For lengthy periods, he and the other Duror men who had been apprehended by the military – a group including James' sons, Alan and Charles, and his Acharn employees, Iain Mòr MacColl, Iain Beag MacColl and Dugald MacColl, together with Alexander Stewart, the packman James had sent to Caolasnacoan with cash for Ailean Breac – were kept, or so it was claimed by James' friends, 'in shackles or handcuffs'. No warrant for James' arrest was issued until 7 July – more than seven weeks after his seizure at Taigh na h-Insaig. Before and after that date, moreover, James was generally refused visitors. For example, not until he had been in custody for more than a month was his wife, Margaret, permitted to see him. And even this privilege, if privilege it was, was withdrawn in early July when Fort William's governor, as James himself put it, 'turned my wife twice from the fort'. Nor was James allowed so much as a word with his sons – for all that they were imprisoned within yards of him. 'I use all possible precautions to keep the prisoners from having any sort of intercourse with one another,' John Campbell of Barcaldine was informed by Fort William's senior military man, Colonel John Crawford.[18]

By keeping James Stewart in close confinement, the authorities were not seeking simply to impose gratuitous hardship on their prisoner. They were endeavouring, James suspected correctly, to make it as difficult as possible for him to prepare for his trial. 'Any who could be supposed to be of any service to me in making my defences', James said, 'were not permitted access to me.' Initially, James' backers hoped that the Maryburgh lawyer or public notary, Charles Stewart, with whom James had been in regular contact when trying to forestall Colin Campbell's evictions, might be prepared to make representations on his behalf. 'But the timid notary', it was reported of this lawyer (who had already let James down at least once), 'declined the employment and left the place.' The task of doing what could be done to mitigate James' plight appears as a result to have been taken up by John Stewart, son of the Ballachulish laird, Alexander Stewart, and a man whom – as noted previously – the Barcaldine Campbells suspected of knowing far more about Cailean Ruadh's murder than he had admitted publicly.[19]

First, John Stewart sought out John Campbell of Barcaldine in an attempt to ascertain the precise grounds on which James Stewart was being held. This, the Barcaldine laird told John, was none of his business. 'If he [John Stewart] acted any further in this matter,' John Campbell was said to have added, 'he himself should be taken up and imprisoned.'[20] Next, John tried to get an interview with James in Fort William. To this end, the Ballachulish heir wrote to Colonel John Crawford 'earnestly begging to be allowed to converse with the prisoner'. 'You are represented to [the colonel],' John Stewart was informed by one of Crawford's aides, 'as a person entirely in the confidence and secrets of Alan Breck Stewart.' For that reason, the aide went on, there was no question of John being granted a meeting with James.[21]

The young man persisted, however. Refused access to Fort William, he travelled south to find lawyers who – unlike Maryburgh's Charles Stewart – would be prepared to act on James' behalf. This took time. But by August, John had obtained the services of Alexander Stewart of Edinglassie, a man who had close connections with the Jacobite families James himself had visited in Stirlingshire in the spring. Having agreed to act as James Stewart's agent, Alexander Stewart immediately applied to the authorities for the details of the charges which John Stewart had earlier requested in vain – and which, despite his having now been imprisoned for three months, had been kept from James also. At the root of those prevarications, Alexander Stewart of Edinglassie believed, was a successful attempt by the men then administering Scotland – the Duke of Argyll and William Grant, the lord advocate, among them – to lengthen the already substantial odds against James Stewart getting a fair trial. Alexander pointed out that on James being formally charged, the law, as it then stood, insisted on him being brought before a court within 60 days. If this 60-day period were to have elapsed before the High Court was next due (in mid-September) to visit Argyll, James would have had to be tried in Edinburgh – and an Edinburgh jury, as Alexander Stewart observed and as the Scottish authorities of the time were well aware, might not have been out of sympathy with him. Hence the point-blank refusal to charge James until all possibility of an Edinburgh trial had passed.[22]

By way of substantiating Alexander Stewart's suspicions on this point, it is necessary only to have recourse to the correspondence of the Barcaldine Campbells and their backers. 'I hear there is a subscription made at Edinburgh to support the [Fort William] prisoners,' one Campbell ally wrote on 16 June. 'It is amazing that anybody can be so imprudent (not to give it a much worse name) and when such things are heard in London is it to be wondered at that the English call Scotland a Jacobite country?' For this reason, if no other, James Stewart's Campbell enemies were right to feel, as their letters show they did, that it might be prudent from their perspective to keep James out of Edinburgh – the more so since, if James were brought before the High Court in Argyll, he had be tried in the court's regular Argyll stopping-place, which, as luck would have it, was the Clan Campbell capital of Inveraray.[23]

But not even an Inveraray trial of James Stewart, it was feared by the Barcaldine Campbells and by their political supporters, could be guaranteed to produce the desired outcome – especially as Alexander Stewart of Edinglassie, at John Stewart's instigation, was clearly intent on providing James with a carefully crafted defence. Knowing this, Sandy Campbell, John of Barcaldine's nephew, canvassed the notion of arresting John Stewart on his way home to Ballachulish from Edinburgh – in the hope, as Sandy explained, of finding on him 'some papers that may throw light into what they [John and Stewart of Edinglassie] are about'. In the event, no such arrest was authorised. During the weeks immediately preceding James Stewart's appearance in court, however, all sorts of other obstacles were placed in his defence team's way.[24]

For example, when Alexander Stewart sought permission to meet his still-imprisoned client, the necessary sanction was refused repeatedly. And on its being finally -- though grudgingly – granted, steps were at once taken to have James removed from Fort William before his lawyer could get there. This particular piece of obstructionism failed, as it happened, solely because Alexander Stewart, on his way from Edinburgh to Fort William, happened to encounter the military party escorting James from the fort to his new quarters in Inveraray's jail. Had they chosen the most direct road, the soldiers taking James south from Fort William would have passed through Duror en route for the Shian and Bonawe ferries. But, doubtless thinking it best to avoid James' home territory at such a time, they conveyed the prisoner to Inveraray by way of Glencoe, Tyndrum and Dalmally. Thus it came about that – thanks to the generosity of the English officer in charge of James' escort – James was able, in the vicinity of Tyndrum, to snatch a few words with his northward-bound agent.

At this chance meeting James appears to have asked Alexander Stewart to press on to Acharn where he could expect to find a good deal of documentation relating to matters likely to loom large at James' now imminent trial. Stewart of Edinglassie duly rode on from Tyndrum to Duror. 'But what was his surprise', the lawyer[25] wrote later, 'when, arriving at Acharn, [James Stewart's] dwelling-house, he found that his [James'] repositories had been opened and examined, three different times, and without any warrant, by near relations of the prosecutors [meaning the Barcaldine Campbells] assisted by a military force.' Such papers as the raiders 'thought might suit their purpose', Alexander Stewart went on, had been 'carried away'. His detour having thus achieved little other than to demonstrate the strength of the forces James Stewart was up against, the weary lawyer – James' trial now just days away – had no choice but to remount his horse and turn the animal's head in the direction of Inveraray.[26]

Alexander Stewart's Tyndrum encounter with James Stewart had taken place on 2 September 1752. The next day, however, was 14 September. The British government had opted at this point to bring the United Kingdom's calendar into alignment with the differently calculated dating method used in most of continental Europe. This upheaval – which, incidentally, was so unpopular as to provoke riots in several parts of the country – had certainly not been initiated with a view to inconveniencing Alexander Stewart of Edinglassie. But it was yet another difficulty which James Stewart's legal agent could have done without – for the date-change meant that by the time Alexander got from Tyndrum to Duror and from Duror to Inveraray, it was the evening of Monday, 18 September. With the High Court due to convene in the town on the morning of Thursday, September 21, time was running out for James Stewart and his defenders.

Finding advocates prepared to represent James had taken a great deal of effort on Alexander Stewart's part. He had 'rode about . . . day and night' in search of individuals with the necessary skills, Alexander reported. 'Of the men of greatest note,' he continued, 'most were pre-engaged by the agents of the other side.' Of those who had not been hired by the Campbells, the majority advanced all manner of excuses as to why they could not possibly be in Inveraray on 21 September. 'Some were afraid of the rainy weather and the length of the journey,' Alexander Stewart commented caustically, 'others of resentment from a certain quarter; and many refused altogether.' The 'certain quarter' Alexander referred to, of course, was Scotland's ruling establishment in the form of Duke Archibald and his associates. And it says a good deal either for Stewart of Edinglassie's persuasive powers or their own independence of mind that four men eventually agreed to risk some setback to their careers by appearing in opposition to Lord Advocate Grant and his several colleagues in a case which, as the lord advocate appreciated all too well, he simply had to win.[27]

Of the four men in question, one, Walter Stewart of Stewarthall, was part of the Stirlingshire-centred Jacobite nexus to which Stewart of Edinglassie himself belonged. The other three – Thomas Miller, George Brown and Robert MacIntosh – appear to have had no particular political axe to grind. They could have been under few illusions, however, as to the potentially explosive nature of the High Court trial in which they were shortly to be embroiled. And if Miller, Brown or MacIntosh harboured any doubts on that point, those were removed on their arrival at Inveraray. 'When his counsel came to this [James'] place and wanted to see him,' Walter Stewart commented bitterly of the initial attempts made by himself and his colleagues to gain access to James Stewart's Inveraray prison cell, 'we were told that none were to be admitted without a warrant from the Duke of Argyll.'[28]

That was on Monday, 18 September, the day Alexander Stewart of Edinglassie also reached town. And it was well into Tuesday before the bar on meetings with James was removed. When his agent and his four advocates were finally allowed to talk with the man they aimed to save from the gallows, therefore, James' legal representatives had only one-and-a-half days available to concert their response to a prosecution case on which their state-backed opponents had been working for the best part of four months.

In 1752, Inveraray as it is today did not exist. At that time the rebuilding programme which was to result in the emergence of the modern town had just commenced, at the instigation of the locality's leading resident, Duke Archibald. Supplying that programme's initial impetus was the duke's determination to provide himself and his successors with a stately home, as opposed to the medieval fortification which his Campbell predecessors had occupied over the centuries since they had made Inveraray their principal Highland base. Work on this home, the present-day Inveraray Castle, was underway in 1752. But nothing had yet been done to give effect to the duke's still more ambitious plans for the settlement which had grown up in the vicinity of his ancestral seat. This settlement, the medieval burgh of Inveraray, lay between the site of the duke's new castle and Loch Fyne. Because the town – as long as it remained there – blocked the wide and open vistas its architect thought essential to the new castle, Duke Archibald had decreed that the ancient burgh should be demolished. In its place, there was to be laid out, a little to the west, the carefully planned village which became the basis of twenty-first-century Inveraray. It is impossible, therefore, to form any first-hand impression nowadays of the town where James Stewart's trial occurred.

The bulk of this town consisted, as one of its eighteenth-century visitors observed, 'of the most wretched hovels that can be imagined'. But the original Inveraray also contained the jail where James was held, the church where he was tried and the inns or lodging houses where the numerous personnel without whom no High Court sitting could be held were accommodated. Since the Duke of Argyll invariably travelled 'with a great retinue', and since his two fellow judges – to say nothing of the lord advocate and all the other senior lawyers present in Inveraray by 20 September 1752 – would have had their own set of clerks and servants on hand, the old town, for the duration of James' trial, must have been seriously overcrowded. It would have been all the more overcrowded as a result of the High Court sitting having coincided with the late-summer herring fishery on Loch Fyne. This involved, as was noted at the time, 'hundreds of boats' and thousands of people. It seems likely, therefore, that when the High Court assembled in Inveraray's church on the morning of Thursday, 21 September, there would have been no lack of bystanders to observe the consequent stir and bustle.[29]

First to appear in front of the court's three judges (the Duke of Argyll, Patrick Grant of Elchies and Sir James Fergusson of Kilkerran) that day was Mary McCombie, a young, unmarried woman who came from Muckairn, to the south of Loch Etive, and who was alleged to have committed 'the crime of child-murder'. Consideration of her case, it was announced, would be delayed until the court had dealt with matters arising from the killing of Colin Campbell. Accused of complicity in this killing, it was further announced, were 'James Stewart in Acharn in Duror of Appin . . . and Alan Stewart commonly called Alan Breck'. Ailean having failed – unsurprisingly – to come forward on his name being shouted repeatedly from 'the outer door of the court-house', was formally declared 'an outlaw and fugitive'. James, for his part, was brought before the court where the charges against him were read out. At the end of this proceeding Duke Archibald asked James to respond to the charges. 'My Lords,' James Stewart told his judges, 'I am not guilty of the crime of which I am accused, and I refer to my lawyers to make my defence.'[30]

Commencing this defence, the lawyers argued, as expected, that it was not permissible in law for the High Court, in effect, to try James Stewart on a charge of having incited Ailean Breac to carry out a crime which Ailean, being unavailable for trial, had not been shown to have committed. Argument on this point raged for much of Thursday. But it raged to no great purpose from James' perspective. The Duke of Argyll and his colleagues eventually ruled, first, that it was perfectly legitimate for James to stand trial on the charges which had been stated and, second, that his trial proper should commence at five o'clock the following morning.

When they met again before dawn on Friday, 22 September, Duke Archibald, Lord Elchies and Lord Kilkerran began by selecting a fifteen-strong jury from among the thirty-four prospective jurors ordered to attend the High Court by Argyll's sheriff, Archibald Campbell. The sheriff, as anxious as everyone else in authority in Scotland to have James Stewart found guilty, had done his best to provide the court with a jury that could be guaranteed to reach the desired verdict – going so far as to take advice on this jury's potential membership from John Campbell of Barcaldine, Colin Campbell's half-brother and the sheriff's close collaborator during the summer-long inquiry into Colin's murder. In a letter which effectively invited John Campbell to nominate prospective jurors from his own locality of Lorn, Sheriff Archibald informed the Barcaldine laird: 'I shall be glad to know which of the people in that country you consider fittest.' This, even by eighteenth-century standards, was extraordinary. But it achieved the intended outcome, helping to deliver a jury which, on its finally taking shape in the early hours of 22 September, included eleven men by the name of Campbell.[31]

With the exception of James Campbell, a prominent resident of Inveraray itself, those men – Colin Campbell of Ederline, Neil Campbell of Dunstaffnage and Duncan Campbell of Southhall among others – were Argyll lairds whose background was virtually identical to that of the man whose death James Stewart was accused of plotting. They were men, in many instances, who had known Cailean Ruadh personally. They were men, without exception, who had shared his views, his attitudes, his overall outlook. They were men, for the most part, who had served in the Argyll Militia during 1745–46 and who, for this reason and for other reasons stemming from what had been done to their families and their properties in the course of earlier Jacobite rebellions, were implacably hostile both to the Appin Stewarts and to the political cause – that of restoring the Stuart monarchy – with which Clan Stewart had been so long associated. Last but not least, the jurors thus empanelled by the Duke of Argyll and his two flanking judges were men – and this applied to the four non-Campbells among them, as well as to the rest – who had been accustomed all their adult lives to taking a lead on issues of importance from Duke Archibald or his predecessors.

Something of the atmosphere of a show trial, then, hung about the Inveraray court hearing of September 1752. This was not entirely due to Sheriff Archibald Campbell's behind-the-scenes efforts to ensure the compliant character of Inveraray's High Court jury, however. Equally suggestive of bias and malpractice was the Duke of Argyll's tetchy response to a suggestion from one of James' advocates, Walter Stewart, that Donald Campbell of Airds, from whom James rented his Acharn and Keil landholdings, 'might be interrogated as to [James'] moral character in the country'. What the advocate wished to highlight, with the help of the one Campbell who seems to have felt some sympathy for James, was the extent to which James enjoyed (as a result of his having come to the aid of so many orphaned children, for example) a positive reputation among the generality of folk in North Argyll. This the duke was violently opposed to. 'Would you pretend, sir,' he is reported to have stormed at Walter Stewart, 'to prove the moral character of the [accused] after [his] being guilty of rebellion, a crime that comprehends almost all other crimes? Here you will find treasons, murders, rapines, oppressions, perjuries, etcetera!' At the close of this tirade, which occurred just an hour or two into the High Court's evidence-taking session, an understandably demoralised James Stewart apparently remarked to one of his legal team: 'It is all over now. My lawyers need give themselves no further trouble about me. My doom is as certain as if it were pronounced.' On this point, James was absolutely right. But for all that, reaching a verdict was to take a long, long time.[32]

Because eighteenth-century Scotland's criminal courts were obliged to hear evidence in single sittings, the High Court session which began in Inveraray at five on the morning of Friday, 22 September, was to last – without any formal break or interruption – until seven on the morning of Sunday, 24 September. During those fifty hours, the High Court heard from more than sixty witnesses, most of whom, because they spoke only Gaelic, had to be questioned through interpreters. But little said in the course of that weekend could have done much to detract from James Stewart's belief – as expressed at the outset of proceedings – that matters were moving inexorably towards a predestined conclusion. Nor could James' well-founded suspicion that his trial was no more than a painstakingly contrived charade have been in any way diminished by the trial's failure to grapple, in any meaningful sense, with what had been at stake in Duror during the months preceding Colin Campbell's murder. For instance, practically nothing was said in Inveraray, on 22, 23 or 24 September which acknowledged the far-reaching nature of Cailean Ruadh's plans for Duror.

This, to be fair, may have been because details of those plans had been deliberately kept from William Grant of Prestongrange, reckoned by his contemporaries to have been a fundamentally decent man as well as an effective lord advocate. Writing some weeks after his successful prosecution of James Stewart, William Grant commented of Colin Campbell: 'The whole salary of the poor gentleman ... for doing the duty whereof he was assassinated ... was no more than £10 10s 7d per annum. [This] made me wonder how he accepted [the job of factor], and [I] was told, for answer, that those forfeited lands [meaning the Ardshiel estate] lay in his neighbourhood and he did not love to be idle.' Grant mentions nothing in this letter of the mechanisms whereby Cailean Ruadh aimed to make Duror – and possibly much of the rest of Appin also – a Campbell preserve. Nor were those mechanisms explored at James Stewart's trial. Instead the impression was conveyed there – by the lord advocate pre-eminently – that Colin, far from administering the Ardshiel estate in ways calculated to advance his own and his family's interests, had been a well-meaning man whose only fault, if he possessed one, had lain in an over-developed sense of duty. 'It is not easy to conceive that there was any reason or just cause given by [the] conduct of [Campbell of] Glenure for resentment or hatred from [James Stewart],' William Grant told the Inveraray jury on the morning of Sunday, 24 September. In fact, especially if it is kept in mind that James and others of the Appin Stewarts thought themselves morally entitled to resist a Campbell seizure of their territories, there were obvious and adequate explanations for James' all-too-evident detestation of the Ardshiel estate's factor. But not knowing of these, or thinking it prudent to keep quiet about them, the lord advocate stuck firmly to a version of events so simplified as to verge on the fictional. In adherence to public policy as laid down by the exchequer barons in Edinburgh, the lord advocate maintained, Campbell of Glenure had ejected James Stewart from Glen Duror prior to organising the removal – and here Grant was so vague as to be positively misleading – of another 'four or five' tenants from their Duror landholdings. Because he blamed Colin Campbell for the loss both of his Glen Duror tenancy and of the managerial role he had earlier exercised in relation to the Ardshiel estate, the lord advocate continued, James – conscious that Colin had made it impossible for him to keep supplying his exiled half-brother with subventions from Ardshiel's tenantry – had become selfishly obsessed with avenging himself on the factor. Ailean Breac, Grant said, was duly fashioned into the willing instrument of James' vengeance. And Colin Campbell, the lord advocated concluded, died as a result.[33]

Unfortunately for James Stewart, countering this farrago with the truth was not an option. Had James' lawyers outlined the means by which Colin Campbell sought to obtain control of Duror, Colin would have been shown as rather less reputable than William Grant of Prestongrange portrayed him. But at the same time a whole set of issues which it was in James' best interests to keep firmly under wraps would have been opened up. Had the Inveraray trial focused on the animosities engendered both in Duror and in Appin at large by Colin Campbell's conduct during the winter of 1751–52, it might have become all too apparent why, from a Clan Stewart perspective, Cailean Ruadh posed so major a threat. This would not have helped James Stewart; instead of being accused of wanting to do away with Colin Campbell for personal reasons, he could have been accused of wanting Colin killed in order to safeguard what remained of his clan's territories. If James were to have pointed out that, while certainly seeking to protect Clan Stewart's position, he had operated always within the law, he would immediately have been confronted with the question of who among the Appin Stewarts might not have felt themselves so constrained; Ailean Breac, perhaps, or the other men who had accompanied Ailean to the rumoured Lochan Blar nan Lochan shooting match. These were topics, it can safely be assumed, that James Stewart had no desire to see explored, not least because their exploration might simply result in other Stewarts hanging alongside him. Even if they had been his most distant relatives, James – for such were the duties and obligations of clanship – would have hesitated to embroil those other potential Stewart candidates for execution in his troubles. As it was, additional Stewart victims, had the wider background to the Lettermore killing been exposed more fully to the light of day, could well have included James Stewart's own son, Alan. He had long been close to Ailean Breac, had probably participated in the Lochan Blar nan Lochan gathering, and was already under arrest – Alan having been held, since May, in Fort William, where, it is relevant to note, the fort's commander had commented in July that there were good grounds for thinking Alan Stewart 'would be hanged as well as his father'.[34]

James Stewart, therefore, permitted the Inveraray trial to go exactly as the authorities wanted. He listened quietly while witness after witness described how Colin Campbell was shot. He said nothing when other witnesses repeated his own, often intemperate, remarks about Colin. He made no challenge to suggestions that he and Ailean Breac had jointly planned both the factor's murder and Ailean's subsequent escape. 'My silence at the bar', James afterwards acknowledged of his behaviour in the Inveraray courtroom, 'was said to have proceeded from conviction of guilt.' This he denied, going on to emphasise that much of the testimony heard by the High Court had consisted, in his opinion, of 'untruths'. He did not blame his Duror and Appin neighbours for saying what they did in Inveraray, James went on. 'There were plenty of bribes and rewards offered to several,' he commented. Besides, James added, 'all the poor people were put in such a terror by a military force . . . that they – I mean the poor country people – would say whatever they thought pleased my prosecutors best'.[35]

For all that they were made just prior to James Stewart's execution, those remarks were a renewed evasion of the issue James had been avoiding from the moment of his arrest. If James was convinced that the High Court had not heard the full truth about Colin Campbell's killing, it followed that he possessed information which he chose not to reveal – either at his trial or, as far as is known, on any subsequent occasion. Having accepted that irrespective of what he did he was bound to die anyway, James Stewart seems to have made it his mission to ensure that no one else joined him on the gallows.

When, in the early hours of the morning of Sunday, 24 September, one of James Stewart's lawyers, George Brown, was making his closing speech in Inveraray's church-cum-courtroom, he was noisily interrupted by a juror, Duncan Campbell of Southhall. 'Pray, sir, cut it short,' this Cowal laird is said to have urged. 'We have [had] enough . . . and are quite tired, the trial having lasted long.' Although Campbell of Southhall was right about the duration of James' trial, which the lord advocate described as Scotland's lengthiest in a hundred years, the peremptory manner of his intervention, or so Alexander Stewart of Edinglassie reported, disconcerted Brown and shocked those of Duncan Campbell's hearers naïve enough to have expected jurors – even in a case as politicised as this one – to affect unmade-up minds. But James Stewart, whose gloomy forebodings as to his eventual fate had already been communicated to Stewart of Edinglassie, could not have been greatly taken aback by Campbell of Southhall's outburst. Nor would James have been surprised when, having deliberated from seven to twelve that same Sunday morning and having returned to the reconvened High Court, as instructed, at 11 a.m. on Monday, 25 September, Duncan Campbell and his colleagues formally pronounced him guilty as charged. 'On which verdict,' an Edinburgh periodical of the time reported, 'the court sentenced [James Stewart] to be hanged on Wednesday, the 8th of November, New Style,[36] on a conspicuous eminence, near to the place where the murder was committed, and adjoining to the ferry of Ballachulish, being the most frequented passage between the countries of Appin and Lochaber; and ordained his body to be hung in chains at the place of execution.'[37]

At last, James Stewart spoke. 'My lords,' he said to his judges, 'I tamely submit to my hard sentence. I forgive the jury and the witnesses who have sworn things falsely against me, and I declare before the great God and this auditory that I had no previous knowledge of the murder of Colin Campbell of Glenure, and am as innocent of it as a child unborn. I am not afraid to die, but what grieves me is my character, that after ages should think me capable of such a horrid and barbarous murder.'[38]

Clearly aggravated by James' protestations of his innocence, and especially by his claim that the High Court had been subjected to a good deal of suspect evidence, the Duke of Argyll, as Alexander Stewart of Edinglassie observed in a letter penned that same day, 'turned [at this point] to Lord Elchies and expressed great surprise at the [prisoner's] behaviour'. Hence, perhaps, the strength of feeling evident in what the duke called his 'exhortation' to James – this exhortation taking the form of the already quoted speech in which Duke Archibald reflected so wrathfully on the Jacobite antecedents both of James and of his clan. But for all his confidence – voiced privately as well as in public – that, by presiding over James' trial, he had helped send a Jacobite rebel to a well-merited death, the Duke of Argyll was by no means convinced, interestingly enough, that all the circumstances surrounding the Wood of Lettermore killing had been made known to the High Court. This much is clear from comments made by the duke in the course of a dispatch he sent to London within twenty-four hours of James' trial ending. 'We are all of the opinion,' Duke Archibald wrote, 'that many of his clan were privy to this murder.'[39]

This was, and would remain, the common view among Scotland's political establishment. But given the impossibility of finding evidence strong enough to justify the execution of more Appin Stewarts, James' accusers were more than happy to celebrate the now certain hanging of the one Appin Stewart, Seumas a' Ghlinne, against whom they had been able to construct a case. Their celebrations were delayed slightly as a result of the High Court being obliged to return to the adjourned case of the alleged child-murderer, Mary MacCombie. She, however, was rapidly found guilty, the court agreeing to 'banish [her] to one or other of His Majesty's plantations in America, never to return'. This left James Stewart's prosecutors free, as Alexander Stewart of Edinglassie noted disgustedly, to spend Monday evening 'in great jollity and mirth'.[40]

That night, and the following ten nights, James remained (as did Mary MacCombie for whom no immediate transatlantic passage was available) in jail at Inveraray. From his cell, on Wednesday, 5 October, James – 'tied on a horse and guarded by 80 soldiers' – began his return journey, made in accordance with the terms of his sentence, to Fort William. There, if the wishes of England's Lord Chancellor, the Earl of Hardwicke, held any sway in Scotland, James Stewart was subjected to a singularly harsh regime. 'I hope', Hardwicke remarked on getting news of the Inveraray verdict, 'that [Fort William's] officers will take care that the prisoner be kept by himself, free from any resort of company and with low diet, which may perhaps at last induce him to confess his guilt and [help us] to discover his accomplices.'[41]

When, some years after those events, Robert Forbes, the episcopalian clergyman whose accounts of post-Culloden repression in the Highlands were cited earlier, visited the home of Alexander Stewart of Ballachulish, the talk turned, naturally enough, to the fate of the man who had been hanged just a few hundred yards from the Ballachulish laird's front door. 'We were told,' Forbes recorded of this conversation, 'that a gentleman of the name of Cameron charitably visited James Stewart when a prisoner in Fort William, after sentence of death had been pronounced, and generously offered to rescue him, with fifty men only, from the command [the military escort] that might be appointed to guard him to the place of execution, which proposal . . . James as generously refused, alleging that such an attempt would, no doubt, be attended with more hurt to his country than his life was worth; and, therefore, expressly desired such a thing might never be mentioned again. The spot where the attempt was to have been made was pointed out to me, and, from its situation, I am fully persuaded that it would have succeeded, especially as the day proved most tempestuous and rainy, and poisoned [meaning soaked] the muskets of the [escorting] party – two companies – so that they could not have been discharged.'[42]

Although this story may have grown somewhat in the telling before it reached Robert Forbes' ears, it is by no means implausible. The Lochaber Camerons – whose lands James Stewart's escorts unavoidably traversed when taking James from Fort William to Ballachulish ferry's northern terminus – were no better disposed either to Britain's Hanoverian government or to its Campbell backers than were the Appin Stewarts. And there were, of course, particularly close connections between Clan Cameron and Seumas a' Ghlinne – whose half-sister, Helen, was the widow, as already mentioned, of the prominent Culloden veteran, Alan Cameron of Callart. Might Helen Cameron – whose confiscated estates straddled the Fort William–Ballachulish road – have sent a gentleman of her clan to ask for her imprisoned half-brother's collaboration in a daring rescue attempt? Quite possibly. And might James have refused to sanction such an attempt? Again, quite possibly – the more so as, with every day that passed, James appears to have become increasingly reconciled to his execution.

Preparations for that execution, meanwhile, were proceeding apace. In charge of them, as October 1752 drew to a close, was Argyll's sheriff, the tireless Archibald Campbell of Stonefield, whose meticulous accounts show that he expended on the arrangements for James Stewart's hanging the then substantial sum of £108 17s 10d.

Erecting a gibbet on Cnap a' Chaolais, the 'conspicuous eminence' mentioned in the High Court judgement of 25 September, was no easy task. The knoll, a little overshadowed nowadays as a result of its proximity to the modern Ballachulish Bridge, is, as the sheriff commented in 1752, 'a steep rock' where construction work of any kind was inherently difficult. As a result, the job the sheriff had on hand – a job undertaken by a number of his own officers and a party of the military – was demanding in the extreme. It required the building of a gibbet, reckoned by Sheriff Archibald to be 'about thirty feet high', on the summit of a hillock where space was at a premium. Nor could there be any skimping on the quality of the materials involved. Since James Stewart's corpse, on the High Court's orders, was to be sheathed in iron chains – made for Archibald Campbell by an Inveraray blacksmith at a cost of £8 – and left to dangle indefinitely above the place of his execution, the Cnap a' Chaolais gibbet had to be capable both of bearing a heavy weight and withstanding the repeated gales to which it would be subjected.[43]

He 'was himself obliged to go to Fort William to buy timber [to] form the gibbet and to employ tradesmen for the making thereof', Sheriff Archibald reported. Although the necessary timber was readily obtained, joiners and carpenters were to be got only by paying premium wages – in consequence, the sheriff noted wearily, of 'the backwardness of tradesmen to be employed in a work of this nature'. Adding to Archibald Campbell's troubles was the weather, 'which happened to be very boisterous and wet', and growing worries as to how the Cnap a' Chaolais gibbet, following James Stewart's hanging, was to be protected from James' many sympathisers. 'As it was apprehended that the gibbet might be cut down,' it is noted alongside one more of the items of expenditure incurred by Sheriff Archibald in Ballachulish, 'he was advised . . . that it should be plated with iron.' The sum of £13 19s 10d was accordingly laid out on the Fort William blacksmith who was brought to Cnap a' Chaolais 'to put on the plates'.[44]

There was, it seemed, no end to the anxieties plaguing Archibald Campbell that October and November. No sooner was his ironclad gibbet firmly in place above Ballachulish ferry than he began to be uncomfortably aware of all the many things that might go wrong with the mechanics of a hanging which – given the political sensitivities surrounding it – had to be absolutely flawless. 'Lest the execution of the sentence should fail by bad weather or any other accidents,' Sheriff Archibald wrote, 'it was judged advisable to have two executioners to attend, one from Glasgow and another from Inverness, there being no executioner at the time in Argyllshire.'[45]

A set of accounts dealing with military expenditure at Fort William during 1752 includes this item: 'To expense [of] fixing up iron bars in a barrack[room] window [and to the provision of] irons and bolts for the safekeeping [of] James Stewart, confined [while awaiting] execution, £1 16s 6d.' The only other surviving information concerning James' final period of imprisonment is a statement to the effect that on Tuesday, 7 November, he was taken from Fort William and, surrounded by a hundred heavily armed infantrymen, conveyed along the road leading, by way of Onich, to North Ballachulish. It had been intended that James and his escorts, commanded by a Captain Welch, would cross Ballachulish ferry that afternoon. 'But it blew so hard,' it was reported, that this plan had to be abandoned. Where exactly James Stewart spent his last night alive is not recorded. It is clear, however, that the weather, by the morning of Wednesday, 8 November, had abated sufficiently to make it possible for James and the redcoated troops accompanying him to be brought across Loch Leven. 'A little after twelve,' it was observed by one of the many people waiting at Cnap a' Chaolais for the arrival of the military and their prisoner, 'they got to the place of execution.'[46]

James Stewart, the same eyewitness commented, was attended by 'a few of his friends' and by two clergymen, 'Mr Malcolm MacAskill, minister of Kilmallie, and Mr John Couper, minister of Maryburgh'. On the summit of Cnap a' Chaolais, crowned now by the darkly looming shape of Sheriff Archibald's gibbet, there had been put up a small tent – made from a boat's sail – which the two ministers and the prisoner promptly entered. There, concealed briefly from the 'great number of . . . country people' who had gathered to witness his hanging, James Stewart doubtless received such spiritual consolation as Presbyterian clerics were able to administer to a man who was, as he had always been, a devout Episcopalian.[47]

On re-emerging into the open air, James Stewart must surely have looked south, towards Ballachulish House and Beinn a' Bheithir. Had the day been clear, James would easily have been able to pick out the most westerly of the Beinn a' Bheithir horseshoe's three peaks, the summit called Sgorr Dhonuill. Below this summit, though on its far side and thus hidden from James' view, lay the two or three homes at the centre of the landholding which had loomed so large in his life – this holding that had given him the name of Seumas a' Ghlinne, by which he was known to everyone in the crowd that day at Cnap a' Chaolais.

Although there is no contemporary evidence on which to base such a supposition, it is appropriate to imagine James pausing, for just a second or so, as he walked towards the gibbet on which he was to hang – pausing and looking out across Ballachulish's fields to Sgorr Dhonuill's lower slopes. In that direction lay Glen Duror. And in that direction James Stewart must have gazed for one last time.

Although James was familiar enough with Cnap a' Chaolais' surroundings to have known exactly where Sgorr Dhonuill's summit was located, he is unlikely to have actually glimpsed it during the minutes preceding his death. Tuesday's gale may have eased slightly that Wednesday morning, but as the hour of James' execution approached the storm returned with such ferocity that the tent in which James had taken refuge with the two ministers was ripped apart. At the time of James Stewart's hanging, then, Cnap a' Chaolais must have been scoured and buffeted repeatedly by savage gusts of wind. And since storms of this sort are invariably accompanied in the West Highlands by lowering cloud and driving rain, Beinn a' Bheithir's higher reaches, for much of James Stewart's final afternoon, were probably invisible.

Days later, in faraway Edinburgh, there was published a letter – dated Thursday, 9 November 1752 – which had been rushed south from Ballachulish. 'I was present yesterday', this letter's writer informed Scotland's capital, 'at James Stewart's execution, who behaved with great decency and resolution. He read a paper, which he afterwards signed and delivered to the sheriff, containing a long narration of facts, and denying . . . in the most solemn manner . . . his accession to, or knowledge of, Mr Campbell of Glenure's murder.'[48]

'I die an unworthy member of the Episcopal Church of Scotland,' James Stewart said towards the close of his speech from the Cnap a' Chaolais scaffold, 'in full charity with all mortals, sincerely praying God may bless all my friends and relations, benefactors and well-wishers, particularly my poor wife and children who, in a special manner, I recommend to His divine care and protection; and may the same God pardon and forgive all that ever did or wished me evil, as I do from my heart forgive them. I die in full hopes of mercy, not through any merit in myself, as I freely own I merit no good at the hands of my offended God; but my hope is through the blood, merits and mediation of the ever-blessed Jesus, my redeemer and glorious advocate, to whom I recommend my spirit. Come, Lord Jesus, come quickly.'[49]

Then James Stewart climbed the ladder leading to the noose which, on its being slipped over his head and on all support being knocked away, would – if the attendant hangmen had done their work well – instantly break his neck. As he mounted the Cnap a' Chaolais gibbet's steps, or so it was insisted afterwards in Duror, James recited verses from Psalm 35 – a psalm which, for as long as Duror folk spoke Gaelic, was known to them as *Salm Sheumais a' Ghlinne*. 'False witnesses did rise up,' Psalm 35 proclaims. 'They laid to my charge things that I knew not. They rewarded me evil for good . . . Lord, how long wilt thou look on? Rescue my soul from their destructions.'

CHAPTER EIGHT

'Well,' says he, 'ye ken very well that I am an Appin Stewart, and the Campbells
have long harried and wasted those of my name; ay, and got lands off us by
treachery — but never with the sword,' he cried loudly, and with the word brought
down his fist upon the table.

Robert Louis Stevenson, *Kidnapped*

From the British government's standpoint, the hanging of James Stewart
had less to do with retribution than with intimidation. Everything
about the Cnap a' Chaolais execution, from the sheer scale of Sheriff
Archibald Campbell's carefully constructed gibbet to the High Court's decision
to have the hanged man's body suspended indefinitely in public view, was
intended — just as the British army's post-Culloden terror tactics had been
intended — to drive home the message that Highland dissent would forever be
met with the harshest and most brutal of responses. That is why it was so
important to the Hanoverian authorities to ensure that nothing was done to
interfere with the Cnap a' Chaolais gibbet after James' execution. The many
people who passed Cnap a' Chaolais each day were meant to be exposed to the
gruesome spectacle of James Stewart's chained-up and slowly rotting corpse,
and were meant, as a result, to be left in absolutely no doubt as to the futility of
challenging Hanoverian rule. But the repressive effect thus produced by the
Cnap a' Chaolais gibbet and its grisly burden would have been instantly
negated had James Stewart's clansmen managed, as they may have planned, to
remove James' body or, failing that, to hack down the timbers on which the
body hung.

Hence the requirement to have Cnap a' Chaolais watched night and day by
a military detachment consisting, as army order books reveal, of 'an officer with
one sergeant, one corporal and sixteen men'. Those soldiers' existence, it
appears, was miserable in the extreme. Sheriff Archibald, according to army

dispatches of the time, had ordered 'the country people' living around Ballachulish to provide Cnap a' Chaolais with 'a hut' in which the gibbet's sentries could be accommodated. But the Ballachulish residents in question, or so it was reported to army headquarters in Edinburgh, had 'staved off the performance with fair promises'. 'The motive for so gross a neglect in them', it was suspected of the Ballachulish folk by the military, 'must be . . . their hoping . . . that the troops would be withdrawn.' This, needless to say, did not happen. Cnap a' Chaolais' little garrison remained firmly in place – as, incidentally, did the corporal and four men who had been stationed in Duror to minimise the risk of any further trouble from the Ardshiel estate's tenantry.[1]

Months passed, then years. Cnap a' Chaolais' guards were withdrawn during 1754. And eventually, in January 1755, some 50 months after his death, what was left of James Stewart's body – reduced by this time to a skeleton – fell from the gibbet. In Edinburgh it was immediately suspected that, by one means or another, this 'insult upon the law' had been engineered by dissident Highlanders who had somehow managed both to scramble up the gibbet and to cut through the corpse's securing chains. The long-suffering Archibald Campbell of Stonefield consequently found himself under orders to head, once again, for Ballachulish, where he was to find out the names of 'any person or persons' who might have conspired to bring about the body's fall – and where the sheriff was also to see to it that James' remains were 'properly hung up again'.[2]

James Stewart's corpse, Sheriff Archibald quickly concluded, had in fact been blown down by a winter gale. But restoring it to its previous position, he reported, had been no simple matter. He had had to have a long ladder brought specially from Fort William, 'there being no other way of getting up the gibbet'. And he had also had to instruct the fort's commander to supply him with a platoon of soldiers, 'as none of the country people could be got to touch the body'. Not that the military proved much more co-operative, Archibald Campbell complained. 'As neither [Fort William's] governor or commanding officer would give directions to the [Cnap a' Chaolais] party to put up the body [on the gibbet],' the sheriff observed angrily, he had been obliged to spend twenty shillings on alcohol in order to induce the members of his borrowed platoon 'to undertake putting up the body cheerfully'.[3]

Further years passed. Gradually, a bone at a time, James Stewart's skeleton fell once more to earth. Unobstrusively, each fragment was gathered up by John Stewart, Culloden veteran, heir to the Ballachulish estate and the man who had put so much effort into ensuring that James, when he stood trial, at least had lawyers on hand to defend him. By persevering determinedly with this last endeavour on James' behalf, John Stewart was able gradually to assemble at his home, Ballachulish House, the bulk of James' mortal remains. At one point John's then ten-year-old daughter, or so Robert Forbes was told when he visited Ballachulish House in the summer of 1770, washed 'the skull with her own hands'. And eventually, John Stewart was in a position to make arrangements for James Stewart's burial. This, appropriately enough, took place in Duror. There James' bones were placed inside the crumbling walls of Duror's ancient church at Keil – alongside those of his widow, Margaret, who had died at some point prior to John Stewart's recovery of her husband's corpse.[4]

The Duror to which James Stewart thus returned was one where his Campbell enemies appeared to have achieved the dominance Colin Campbell of Glenure had sought for them. Within weeks of Colin's murder, his nephew, Mungo Campbell, had been appointed Ardshiel factor in Colin's place. Mungo, understandably enough in the circumstances, promptly set about reinforcing the pro-Campbell, pro-Hanoverian thrust of his predecessor's Ardshiel policies. That most anti-Jacobite of Church of Scotland clerics, John MacAulay, was confirmed in 1752 as tenant of one-half of Achindarroch and, a little later, was also installed as tenant of Achara. Colin's younger brother and Mungo's uncle, Duncan Campbell, who had succeeded Cailean Ruadh as laird of Glenure, followed Colin both as proprietor of Lagnaha and as part-tenant of Glen Duror, which Duncan, like Colin, occupied jointly with John Campbell of Baleveolan.

As for the former home of James Stewart's still exiled half-brother, Charles, the Ardshiel estate's original proprietor and the Appin Regiment's ex-colonel, it remained firmly in the occupancy of Sandy Campbell, Duncan of Glenure's son and the Campbell who had been more prominent than any other in the hunt for Cailean Ruadh's killers during 1752. 'During his possession', it was reported in 1765 of Sandy's tenancy of Ardshiel, '[he] has improved his farm to better advantage than any of his neighbours, and made several fences of stone, and proper ditches, and built [a] farm[house] and [other buildings], the best in that country.' But for all that Sandy Campbell was clearly intent on making his family a permanent feature of the Duror scene, and for all that he appeared to have succeeded in this ambition when his own tenancy of Ardshiel was transferred in 1767 to his younger brother, Patrick, there was, in the end, to be no permanent Campbell annexation of Duror – still less of the rest of Appin.[5]

When the semi-bankrupt chief of the Appin Stewarts, Dougal Stewart, died in 1765, Dougal's creditors – who had once included Colin Campbell of Glenure – sold his estate to Hugh Seton of Touch, one of the Stirlingshire Jacobite lairds to whom James Stewart had turned for support and advice in 1752. Seton – a colourful character who had made his money in the French wine trade, and who was to end his days wandering through India 'in the dress of a Mahometan' – apparently purchased Dougal Stewart's lands, in part at least, with the intention of expelling Colin Campbell's heirs and successors from Duror. During the late 1760s or early 1770s, by one means or another, Hugh Seton bought out the Campbell interest in Lagnaha. During this same period, Seton – in addition to investing heavily in the development of his own possessions – did a great deal to promote and facilitate the sequence of events which culminated in much of Duror being returned first to Stewart occupancy, then to Stewart ownership.[6]

It was of considerable help to Hugh Seton and his Stewart associates that in 1765, John MacAulay, by this point part-tenant of Achindarroch and sole tenant of Achara, was invited by the Duke of Argyll to become minister of Inveraray. MacAulay's successor as Church of Scotland representative in the Appin area, Donald MacNicol, a prominent Gaelic scholar and a nephew of Alexander Stewart of Invernahyle, was interested neither in accumulating Duror tenancies nor in assisting Duror's Campbell settlers to tighten their grip on the locality. Equally disinclined to make Campbell causes his own was the man appointed manager of the Ardshiel estate in succession to Mungo Campbell when, in 1758, Mungo relinquished his Ardshiel factorship and took a commission in the army. This man was Henry Butter who became, in effect, the means by which Campbell expansionism of the Cailean Ruadh type was put into reverse. Originally from Pitlochry and having – in consequence – no personal stake in the ultimate outcome of the feuding in which he found himself embroiled in Duror, Butter was no Stewart stooge. But unlike Mungo and Colin Campbell, to whom the Ardshiel factorship was of value principally because it enabled them to advance their family's territorial ambitions, Henry Butter was a professional land manager. His key aim – one assisted by properties of the Ardshiel sort having been taken out of the hands of the exchequer barons and placed under the jurisdiction of a new, and more developmentally minded, Commission for the Forfeited Estates – was to maximise rental income while, at the same time, modernising agricultural structures he thought hopelessly outmoded. And if his approach resulted – as it did – in Duror's Campbell tenants being ejected from holdings they had hoped would be theirs in perpetuity, then that, to Henry Butter, seems to have been neither here nor there.

When, in 1765, John MacAulay left for Inveraray, his vacated Duror tenancies were let by the Ardshiel estate's factor to two younger brothers of the Prestonpans and Culloden veteran, Alexander Stewart of Invernahyle. One brother, James Stewart, took over MacAulay's part of Achindarroch; the other, Alan Stewart, received a lease of Achara. But if this – from a Campbell perspective – was bad enough, it was as nothing to what occurred in 1771 when, to the evident fury of Colin Campbell's surviving relatives, Henry Butter agreed to lease Glen Duror to none other than Isabel Stewart, whose connection with the Ardshiel estate, it was generally assumed up to this point, had been severed for all time by her decision in 1748 to join her exiled husband, Charles, in France.

Isabel, whose spirit had not broken even when Captain Caroline Scott was expelling her from her half-demolished home, was not the sort of woman to give up on a cause – however hopeless that cause might seem to others. Although there must have been occasions when – as a result of the execution of her husband's half-brother and as a result, too, of so much of the Ardshiel estate passing into Campbell hands – Isabel came close to abandoning hope of ever reinstating her family on their ancestral lands, she never quite relinquished that ambition. Hence the protracted correspondence which Isabel, and the various allies she enlisted, conducted with Henry Butter's superiors in the Edinburgh offices of the Forfeited Estates Commission.

This correspondence started within months of Charles Stewart's death at Sens in 1757. To begin with, Isabel's letters mostly concerned the annual payment (of £27 15s 6½d) which Isabel claimed had been settled on her by her husband at the time of their wedding. Since this payment, in terms of the marriage contract between Isabel and Charles Stewart, was a fixed charge on the Ardshiel estate rental, then the Forfeited Estates Commission, or so Isabel maintained, had no legal alternative but to remit it regularly to her. With Charles' death, she assured the Forfeited Estates Commission, she had been left in a 'destitute condition' and the commission, in consequence, represented her only chance of providing 'for the subsistence of herself and eight helpless children'. This, to put it mildly, was not quite the case, Isabel having been granted a Jacobite widow's pension of 1,500 livres annually by the French monarchy. But the pleas of Lady Ardshiel, as Isabel continued to be styled by her sympathisers, were rewarded nonetheless. Some modest funds began to flow in her direction from the Forfeited Estates Commission. And when, in 1771, the commission was asked by Hugh Seton, acting on Isabel's behalf, to award her the tenancy of Glen Duror, this concession, too, was eventually sanctioned.[7]

In 1771, Glen Duror was effectively tenanted by Patrick Campbell, who had taken over from his father, Duncan, the stake in the glen which Duncan, back in 1752, had inherited from his murdered brother, Cailean Ruadh. And since Red Colin had been instrumental in turning James Stewart out of Glen Duror in 1751, Isabel, by having herself made Glen Duror's tenant, had succeeded – twenty years on – in doing to Patrick what Patrick's uncle, Colin, had once done to Seumas a' Ghlinne.

Although Patrick Campbell remained in occupation of Ardshiel, where he had succeeded Sandy, his brother, as tenant some years before, he was outraged by his loss of Glen Duror. Taking issue with Hugh Seton's contention that Isabel, together with her sons and daughters, had struggled with 'many difficulties . . . in the course of many years', Patrick, in a 'memorial' he sent in protest to the Forfeited Estates Commission, insisted that 'one and all of that family are in the most affluent circumstances'. With his brother Sandy, Patrick went on, he had come to Duror at their late uncle's invitation at a time when, as loyal supporters of the British government, they had run the risk of being done to death by Duror's Jacobites. Now an agency of this same government was ejecting him from Glen Duror to make way for a woman whose Stewart husband and Stewart in-laws had repeatedly engaged in the 'most violent opposition' to Britain's legally constituted authorities. This was, from Patrick Campbell's perspective, a perfectly reasonable argument to advance. But it availed him nothing. From the Forfeited Estates Commission, in respect of Glen Duror, Patrick received no further communication beyond successive notices to quit.[8]

Isabel Stewart, it should be made clear, did not actually take up residence in Glen Duror either in 1771 or subsequently. Although she had left Sens shortly after her husband's death, Isabel continued to live in France – residing, for the most part, in either Boulogne or Dunkirk. From France, however, she made arrangements to have Glen Duror managed on her behalf – and, from 1771 until her death in 1779, doubtless derived a reasonable income from sales of the glen's livestock.

Nor was Isabel Stewart content with this triumph. In 1775, the Forfeited Estates Commission agreed to a further manoeuvre whereby James and Alan Stewart of the Invernahyle family transferred their tenancies of Achindarroch and Achara to one of Isabel's younger sons, John. Between them, in consequence, Isabel and John were in occupation, by the mid-1770s, of more than half the estate which Charles Stewart, Isabel's husband and John's father, had been obliged to relinquish nearly thirty years before. Isabel, to be sure, had not quite won a total victory over her Campbell antagonists, but she had made some remarkable gains.

Had the members of Clan Stewart who re-established the clan's hold on Duror during the 1760s and 1770s been regarded by British governments of the period as constituting a threat of the sort Clan Stewart had posed to those governments' predecessors, this reassertion of Stewart influence would not have been permitted. But the Stewarts who moved back into Duror were Stewarts whose outlook and attitudes had altered enormously in the course of the twenty or so years following the Battle of Culloden.

This is most obvious in the case of Alan Stewart, who obtained the tenancy of Achara in 1765 and who, in 1775, transferred that tenancy to John Stewart, Isabel's son. Like his elder brother, Alexander Stewart of Invernahyle, Alan had been one of the Appin Regiment's officers. He had fought for Charles Edward Stuart at Prestonpans, Falkirk and Culloden. And in Culloden's aftermath, Alan – along with his namesake, Ailean Breac – had joined Charles Stewart of Ardshiel in France. The Alan Stewart of the 1740s, then, was at war with Britain's political establishment. The Alan Stewart of the 1760s, however, was a part of that establishment himself. He came to Achara in 1765 as an officer lately retired on half-pay from the British army following his participation in a highly successful campaign which had culminated in the ejection from North America of those same French forces he had regarded as his allies, backers and protectors not so many years previously. As was true of lots of other former Jacobites, Alan Stewart owed his rehabilitation, ironically enough, to a man who had played a key role, as a prosecutor, in the Inveraray trial of James Stewart.

This man was Simon Fraser. In 1746, at the age of nineteen, he had commanded the several hundred men committed to Charles Edward Stuart's army by his father, Lord Lovat, chief of Clan Fraser. At Culloden, those men had occupied positions immediately to the left of the Appin Regiment in the Jacobite front line. They had consequently fought alongside James Stewart, who, Simon told the High Court in September 1752, deserved 'the most severe and exemplary punishment' for his part in an 'assassination' which had 'offered . . . the most daring and barefaced insult' to King George II and his government.

Whether or not Simon Fraser was personally present at Culloden is unclear. What is certain is that he surrendered to the British military at Fort Augustus in August 1746, that he was then imprisoned in Edinburgh Castle, and that, while in custody, he was told of the beheading, on treason charges, of his elderly father. But far from plotting vengeance on the Hanoverian politicians responsible both for his own imprisonment and for his father's execution, Simon – a coldly calculating invidual who saw much more clearly than James Stewart where the future of the Highlands now lay politically – set out to curry favour with them. While still a prisoner in Edinburgh, Simon deployed his considerable influence with his Fraser clansmen in such a way as to ensure that franchise-holders among those clansmen used their votes in an Inverness-shire parliamentary election in such a manner as to secure the return of the candidate favoured by ministers in London. His pro-Hanoverian credentials having been thus established, Simon Fraser gained release from custody, took a law degree at Glasgow University and, on graduating, tried to find ways of further enhancing his reputation as a Highlander on whom the Hanoverian authorities could rely. Hence his willingness to join the lord advocate's prosecution team at Inveraray, and his decision, when a new war broke out between France and Britain in 1756, to raise a Highland regiment for service in the British army.

This regiment was to have a major role in the campaign which led to Britain taking Quebec and the rest of Canada from the French. Its soldiers, known as Fraser's Highlanders, duly found themselves fêted, on their return to the United Kingdom, as men who had contributed hugely to the expansion of the British empire. Among those homecoming heroes was Alan Stewart who had held the rank of lieutenant in Fraser's Highlanders and who, at the war's close, became tenant of Achara. His was a career path which was to be taken by many of his Appin Stewart kin, and by many more Highlanders, in the decades that lay ahead. In consequence, the figure of the kilted clansman, once seen in the south as synonymous with rebelliousness and barbarity, became identified increasingly with courage, military prowess and all the other virtues which the British Empire sought to nurture. As this happened, Clan Stewart's upper echelons – in other words, the Stewarts of Ballachulish, Achnacone, Invernahyle, Fasnacloich and Ardshiel – gradually became more and more integrated into the fabric of the Hanoverian state which, in 1745 and on a number of previous occasions, Clan Stewart had tried so hard to subvert and destroy.

Something of the ensuing transformation is evident in a Victorian clan history which, having rehearsed Stewart involvement in all the many Highland rebellions and uprisings of the seventeenth and eighteenth centuries, lists the more recent achievements both of male members of the clan and of the husbands chosen by female Stewarts. Imperial soldier after imperial soldier is mentioned proudly. So are: a 'chaplain to the British embassy at Vienna'; a 'barrister of Lincoln's Inn'; a 'chairman of quarter sessions for Huntingdonshire and Cambridgeshire'; a 'merchant in London'; a 'vicar of St James, Manchester'. In the course of the hundred or so years following Culloden, then, the leading Stewart families – all of them formerly involved in repeated attempts to overthrow successive British governments – had merged into the United Kingdom's ruling order. By so doing, the more senior representatives of the Appin Stewarts had accomplished what their Campbell counterparts had managed to achieve rather earlier. They had got themselves on to history's winning side. Ceasing to be Jacobite rebels, they had become, instead, respectable – adopting, in the process, the attitudes, the politics, even the language, accents and dress code, of exactly the sort of people their ancestors, in 1745 and 1746, had battled against.[10]

This, inevitably, had the effect of rendering obsolete much of what had seemed hugely important to men like Seumas a' Ghlinne. While the Stewarts of Victorian times and later would continue to commemorate – though with less and less fervour as time went on – the victories their forebears had won in the course of their age-old quarrel with the Barcaldine Campbells, that quarrel's underlying causes had ceased to matter very much within a decade or two of James Stewart's death. As clanship of the old variety crumbled and as Stewarts and Campbells began to fight regularly alongside one another on the British Empire's ever-expanding frontiers, conflict between clans was replaced in the Scottish Highlands by conflict between classes. On one side of this new battleground were lairds and commercially minded farmers – folk to whom land was simply an asset to be exploited economically. Opposing this capitalist-inclined grouping were those Highlanders – mostly descended from the older society's lower ranks – who continued to cling to the strictly non-capitalist notion that simply to occupy territory was to have rights in it. The latter group, needless to say, were ultimately to lose out to the former – with consequences made brutally plain in the shape of the mass evictions known as the Highland Clearances. And among the numerous casualties of this process were the ties which had once bound chief and clansfolk, gentry and commons. The respect, even the affection, which the generality of clanspeople felt for men like Charles Stewart of Ardshiel and his many Highland counterparts was steadily withdrawn from those men's sons and grandsons – individuals who, all too often, were casually to dispossess and expropriate community after community to make way for sheep. All this was famously foreseen by Samuel Johnson when, some twenty years after James Stewart's execution, he came north to find that the tribal society he had hoped to see at first hand in the Highlands was already in an advanced stage of dissolution. 'Their chiefs', Johnson wrote by way of lamenting the passing of clans which had endured for centuries, 'have already lost much of their influence; and as they gradually degenerate from patriarchal rulers to rapacious landlords, they will divest themselves of the little that remains.' And so it turned out, with social tensions of the kind Johnson predicted beginning to be apparent in Duror as early as the 1760s.[11]

These tensions resulted in the hostility expressed by a group of folk in Achindarroch to James Stewart, the laird of Invernahyle's younger brother, when he took over the lease of a large part of this Duror township in 1765. The folk in question were subtenants – people to whom Achindarroch's principal tenants, whether Seumas a' Ghlinne in the 1740s or John MacAulay in the 1750s, had customarily rented out portions of their holdings. James Stewart, Achindarroch's subtenants complained to the Commission for the Forfeited Estates, was determined 'to turn them, their wives and children out of their possessions'. This was despite their being 'punctual in the payment of their rents'; it was also despite Achindarroch's subtenant families – who included MacColls, Carmichaels and MacCombies – having lived there for several generations. 'It is a very hard case', the Achindarroch people commented in the course of their submission to the Forfeited Estates Commission, 'to bring such numbers of honest, industrious, poor people to misery and distress in order to accommodate or gratify one man.'[12]

Although it indubitably signalled a reassertion of Stewart influence, then, the reappearance fourteen years after Seumas a' Ghlinne's removal from the place of a James Stewart in Achindarroch did not imply a return to what had gone before. On the contrary, the gradual recovery of Duror by Clan Stewart was to be accompanied, during the 1760s, 1770s and 1780s, by many more upheavals of the kind Achindarroch's subtenants found so hard to accept.

The leasing of Achindarroch and Achara to James and Alan Stewart was followed, as already noted, by the leasing of Glen Duror to Isabel, Lady Ardshiel. It was followed, too, by Alexander Stewart of Invernahyle becoming the proprietor of Acharn, Keil, Bealach, Achabhlar and those other Duror lands which Donald Campbell of Airds, just before the rebellion of 1745, had bought from the Appin chief, Dougal Stewart. Why exactly Stewart of Invernahyle made this move is uncertain. But in 1778 he negotiated with John Campbell of Airds, the late Donald's heir, an arrangement whereby John acquired Alexander Stewart's original possessions, including Invernahyle itself, in exchange for John Campbell's Duror landholdings – of which Alexander now became laird. Eventually, if somewhat confusingly, a new Invernahyle House[13] was constructed in Duror on a site not far from Seumas a' Ghlinne's former home at Acharn. And by 1778, Duror – with Isabel Stewart and one of her sons tenanting much of the Ardshiel estate, and with another Stewart owning those parts of the district which had previously belonged to the Campbells of Airds – was well on its way to becoming again the Stewart preserve it had been prior to the 1740s.

This recovery of the Stewart position was completed in 1784, when, in celebration of its own success in neutralising and absorbing the formerly Jacobite clans, the British state returned to the heirs of their previous owners the Highland properties declared forfeit in the wake of Culloden. This gesture resulted in the Ardshiel estate being acquired by Duncan Stewart, the eldest surviving son of the man who had been both the Appin Regiment's colonel and the long-dead Seumas a' Ghlinne's half-brother. Ardshiel's new laird, appropriately enough, was the very model of those Highlanders MPs had in mind when, in a preamble to the British parliament's Disannexing Act of 1784, they made mention of the 'signal services' performed by the 'loyal' and 'dutiful' younger generation of Highland families once notorious for their Jacobitism.

Having emigrated to Britain's North American colonies as a young man, Duncan had become collector of customs in New London, Connecticut, and, when the American Revolutionary War broke out in 1775, had unhesitatingly taken the side of the same Hanoverian monarchy his father had spent so many years attempting to remove from the United Kingdom's throne. Unsurprisingly, then, there was to be no Jacobite sword school of the old kind re-established at Ardshiel by Duncan Stewart, who had returned to Britain when Americans obtained their independence and whose only significant gesture in the direction of earlier Clan Stewart causes was his decision to build a new Ardshiel House[14] and to buy out the leases of the one or two remaining Campbell tenants he had inherited from the Forfeited Estates Commission.[15]

Exactly forty years after he had left the place in his mother's company, Duncan Stewart once again took up residence in Duror. It was now 1788, and his home locality, since Duncan's last sight of it, had altered enormously – even in appearance. The Water of Duror, long subject to very frequent floods, had been directed into a new channel excavated by one of the firms responsible for the construction of the Forth and Clyde Canal and funded jointly by Hugh Seton and the Forfeited Estates Commission. The retaining walls and embankments with which Duror's river was thus provided, at a total cost of around £150, were so robustly engineered that they were to remain unbreached until badly damaged by a freak flood in 1953. Surviving even this deluge unscathed was the arched and stone-built bridge – another improvement financed both by the Forfeited Estates Commission and by Hugh Seton – which, during the 1770s, was put in place across the Water of Duror about a quarter of a mile downstream from Inshaig. This bridge, unused since 1959 but still standing, helped make possible, or so it was reported at the time, 'an excellent line of road . . . from Shian Ferry [to] . . . Glencoe'. Along this road, traffic was moving by the 1780s at a previously undreamed-of speed, with a letter, as one local clergyman noted in amazement, taking just three days or even two-and-a-half days to get from Edinburgh to Duror. Nor were such letters necessarily destined solely for the high-ranking individuals who had earlier tended – whether in Duror or elsewhere in the Highlands – to have a monopoly of literacy. Since the 1760s, Duror had possessed a school where 29 'scholars' from a wide range of backgrounds were declared, in 1777, to have reached a satisfactory standard in 'reading of English and writing'.[16]

But if the Duror in which Duncan Stewart set up home in 1788 had acquired a bridge, river embankments, a new road, enhanced postal services and a school, it had also lost farming townships of the sort that had been standard during Duncan's childhood – townships of the sort that had been standard, in fact, for several centuries. This was the inevitable consequence of developments such as those instigated by James Stewart when he became tenant of Achindarroch in 1765. His eviction of Achindarroch's subtenants had rendered their closely clustered homes and outbuildings redundant. Those homes and outbuildings were consequently swept away. In their place there was constructed a substantial farmhouse – 'stone and lime, two storeys high and slated,' it was observed in 1774. This Achindarroch farmhouse, still standing and still occupied, was first inhabited by Alan Stewart himself. Soon it was to have counterparts all over Duror – at Keil, Acharn, Inshaig and elsewhere – as township after township went the same way as Achindarroch and as farms of the sort that have survived into the present began to be created.[17]

At first, Duror's new-style farms were mostly given over, like their predecessors, to cropping and cattle. During the 1770s, however, Duror's cattle herds – among them herds which Seumas a' Ghlinne had once managed – began to be displaced by sheep. Some of the resulting sheep farms, it was commented, were 'very extensive'. Prominent among those was the substantial unit created, around 1780, when Achindarroch was amalgamated with the formerly independent holding of Glen Duror. 'The farm of Achindarroch is partly corn land and partly grass,' it was reported in 1784, 'and the farm of Glen Duror is wholly a grazing [with] no tillage.' Having first been 'conjoined in one possession', the two farms had then been 'converted into a sheep walk'. Much the same was to happen to Acharn, Achara, Cuil, Keil, Bealach, Achabhlar and Ardshiel itself. And as always occurred in the Highlands when sheep replaced cattle, family after family were deprived of land, homes and livelihoods in consequence. Hence the loss of population which Duror began to experience in the course of the 1770s.[18]

Some of the families who left Duror at this time probably moved no further than Laroch – the modern Ballachulish – where, by the 1790s, a lot of men were employed in that community's rapidly developing slate quarries. Others, however, went further afield, people from Duror and the rest of Appin constituting the bulk of the 200 or so folk who embarked, in 1775, on the *Jupiter*, a ship which sailed that spring from the West Highlands to Wilmington, North Carolina.

Those emigrants were 'unanimously to declare that they never would have thought of leaving their native land could they have supported their families in it'. Many of them, however, had been 'obliged to quit their lands', or so they told the colonial authorities in Wilmington, as a result of the lands in question having been put under sheep. 'Those in particular from Appin', a Wilmington official noted of the *Jupiter* party, 'say that, out of about one hundred merkland that formerly was occupied by tenants who made their rents by rearing cattle and raising grain, thirty-three merkland of it is now turned into sheep walks, and they seem to think [that], in a few years more, two-thirds of that country at least will be in the same state, so, of course, the greatest part of the inhabitants will be obliged to leave it.'[19]

The sources of such statements probably included some of Achindarroch's former subtenants. The surviving evidence, to be sure, is insufficiently detailed to show the exact place of origin, within the wider parish of Appin, of particular emigrant families. But Duror folk definitely sailed for America aboard the *Jupiter*. And when one strolls today – as this book's author did on a hot and humid August afternoon in 1996 – through Stewartville Cemetery, Scotland County, North Carolina, looking at names on tombstones, it is impossible to be other than convinced that among the Scotland County settlers buried below this cemetery's sheltering trees are folk who knew James Stewart. Those settlers – Carmichaels, MacLarens, Colquhouns and, of course, MacColls – were eventually to be joined, in their new homeland, by many more emigrants from the Appin area. Inevitably, descendants of the pioneer families in question have since spread across the United States. But such onward migration notwithstanding, communities like Scotland County's Laurinburg, or nearby Marlboro County's McColl, still contain, as their telephone directories confirm, plenty of the surnames which have featured in this book.

This, ironically, is more than can be said about modern Duror, which, in the course of the last 200 years, has continued to evolve in directions which have made it more and more unlike the Duror of Seumas a' Ghlinne's lifetime. That locality's comparative isolation, first breached by new roads of the late-eighteenth-century type, was reduced further by the steamers which began plying Loch Linnhe during the nineteenth century and by the railway which reached Duror just after 1900. Those developments brought many incomers to the district. So did the afforestation of Glen Duror – acquired, from the last of its sheep-farmer occupants, by the then newly established Forestry Commission in 1919.[20] Loch Linnhe's steamer services, to be sure, were withdrawn a long time ago; Duror's railway closed in 1966; and forestry – for all that much of Acharn, Achara, Keil, Achabhlar and Bealach have followed Glen Duror into Forestry Commission ownership – no longer employs the numbers it once did. However, with Loch Etive, Loch Creran and Loch Leven all bridged and with roads to Fort William and Oban becoming faster with each year that passes, Duror continues to attract new residents. Today more people live there than at any point in recent times. That's good. But so complete has been the exodus of the folk who inhabited the place in the past that there is in twenty-first-century Duror just a single family – the family of Innes and Agnes MacColl – whose members can trace their ancestry to men and women who were acquainted with Seumas a' Ghlinne. Such have been the long-term consequences of the population movements set in train by what occurred in Duror during the three or four decades following the Cnap a' Chaolais execution of November 1752.

Had Seumas a' Ghlinne lived, it is possible that he would have embraced late-eighteenth-century Duror's new order with enthusiasm. As his cattle-trading activities demonstrate, James Stewart was nothing if not commercially minded. And his tenancy of Acharn – which, during the week that ended with his arrest, he was in the process of combining with a part-tenancy of Keil – had given him the means, even after his expulsion from Glen Duror, of producing livestock on a substantial scale. It isn't difficult, then, to imagine James – had the events of May 1752 not occurred – becoming one of those entrepreneurs and innovators who, in the course of the eighteenth century's closing decades, propelled localities like Duror down the road that led inexorably to many of their inhabitants being obliged to take themselves off to North America. Had he lived, one can readily hypothesise, James Stewart would have made a good match for his daughter, Elizabeth, and would have encouraged his sons, Alan and Charles, to follow their fellow clansmen into Fraser's Highlanders. James, one can further postulate, would have urged those sons – assuming they had survived the Quebec campaign – to embrace the possibilities opened up, during the 1770s, by the beginnings of sheep farming.

But these are might-have-beens. As it was, James Stewart's family were to suffer greatly as a result of his prosecution and death. When, in 1753, Alexander Stewart of Edinglassie published an account of the Inveraray trial of the year before, that account carried an announcement to the effect that it had been 'printed for the benefit of a poor widow and her five children'. The widow and children in question, it can be assumed, were Margaret Stewart, her sons Alan and Charles, her daughter, Elizabeth, and two further, presumably younger, children whose names are unknown. Margaret, as noted previously, died while James' corpse still hung above Cnap a' Chaolais. Alan and Charles, who had been arrested along with their father in 17 May 1752, were released from Fort William prior to that year's end – Charles to become, in time, a shoemaker in Edinburgh, Alan to disappear from the historical record. A daughter of James and Margaret Stewart – perhaps Elizabeth, but not necessarily so – is known to have been a milliner, or hatmaker, in Fort William in 1770. What happened to the two nameless children mentioned by Stewart of Edinglassie is, of course, a mystery – though it is conceivable that one at least of them lies today beneath the longleaf pines in Stewartville Cemetery, Scotland County.[21]

What exactly, his children may have wondered, caused James Stewart to undertake the actions which led directly to his death? While no categorical answer can be given to that question, their father, in doing what he did in 1751 and 1752, was motivated principally, or so this book has argued, by his belief in the importance of maintaining the longstanding connection between Duror and Clan Stewart. This connection, in the event, was terminated. And when Stewarts eventually resumed control of the greater part of Duror, as happened in the 1760s and subsequently, they had themselves broken so sharply with the past that they set about disposing of folk like Achindarroch's subtenants with a ruthlessness which Colin Campbell, at his most aggressive, never matched. Had he not been executed, James Stewart, as immediately preceding paragraphs have suggested, may one day have conducted himself in much the same self-interested fashion. But James, for better or worse, never had that opportunity, having been hanged in advance of the land-management revolution which, within thirty years of his death, both changed Duror irrevocably and rendered James' ideals hopelessly out of date. Even in 1752, admittedly, those ideals were starting to look decidedly old-fashioned in that they derived from an era whose end had been signalled by the Battle of Culloden and what followed from it. But in choosing to act as he felt the loyalties integral to clanship obliged him to, James Stewart, while arguably embracing an outmoded cause, was by no means behaving ignobly. Clanship of the sort which had prevailed in Duror for so long was certainly not without its downside. However, it made for a degree of security which the post-Culloden Highlands – so profoundly and so universally disrupted by evictions, clearances and enforced emigration – were to lack entirely. And if security is a virtue, as James Stewart thought and as the Highlanders scattered across the world during the period following his death would have agreed, then James, in trying to keep things as they had previously been, was acting in his neighbourhood's best interest.

After Seumas a' Ghlinne's execution, nobody – certainly nobody of James' class and background – would defend Highland clanship with quite the same determination, quite the same commitment, ever again. Hence this book's contention – made explicit in its title – that, when they hanged James Stewart on the afternoon of Wednesday, 8 November 1752, the Hanoverian authorities also hanged the last clansman.

ACKNOWLEDGEMENTS

Many people helped with my researches. They included: my Duror friends Innes and Agnes MacColl; Mairi Smith, Ronnie Laing, Sylvia Laing and their colleagues in the Appin Historical Society; John Todd of Duror Community Council; Hugh Dan MacLennan of the Gaelic Society of Inverness; Alastair Campbell of Airds; Muriel Walker of the Stewart Society; Fiona Marwick of the West Highland Museum, Fort William.

My interest in Duror – to which this book is dedicated with the greatest possible affection – derives from my having been born and brought up there. I first heard of James Stewart, Colin Campbell and related matters from my late parents and from other Duror residents – especially Angus MacColl, our Duror neighbour and Innes MacColl's late father. My earliest copy of *Kidnapped*, which I read repeatedly, came from Duror schoolhouse where my aunt and primary school teacher, Mary McLachlan, then lived. That copy of Robert Louis Stevenson's great novel was carried home by way of Insaig which I passed every day on my way to school and where – though I didn't know this at the time – James Stewart was taken into army custody on the evening of Saturday, 16 May 1752.

I first visited James Stewart's one-time home in Glen Duror in the company of my father, Donald Hunter, who, like his own father and my grandfather, James Hunter, was Forestry Commission trapper or ranger in the glen. Acharn, where James lived latterly, was the home in the early 1950s of Alastair Ferguson, who, when we were both five or six, was my closest friend. At Acharn, Alastair and I played in the ruins of the house where James Stewart lived in the period immediately prior to his arrest and execution. Keil, Achara, Cuil, Achindarroch and Lagnaha – all of them familiar to James Stewart – were places I knew well. It has been good to revisit those places when working on this book – and to do so, on occasion, in the company of my wife, Evelyn, who has tempered her support for this project with an insistence that there's got to be more to life than Highland history. I agree – but not, I'm afraid, with much conviction.

Notes

CHAPTER ONE

1. This office was abolished in the nineteenth century.
2. Meaning the hillock by the strait or narrows.
3. D.N. MacKay (ed), *Trial of James Stewart*, Edinburgh, 1931, 289.
4. MacKay, *Trial*, 289.
5. Murray of Polmaise Papers: Letter from Stewart of Edinglassie [undated but from the context written on 25 September 1752].
6. Murray of Polmaise Papers: Letter from Stewart of Edinglassie; *A Supplement to the trial of James Stewart by a Bystander*, London, 1753, 68.
7. MacKay, *Trial*, 290.
8. MacKay, *Trial*, 290.
9. MacKay, *Trial*, 290.
10. MacKay, *Trial*, 290.
11. MacKay, *Trial*, 290–91.
12. MacKay, *Trial*, 291.
13. MacKay, *Trial*, 291.

CHAPTER TWO

1. E. Burt, *Letters from a Gentleman in the North of Scotland*, Edinburgh, 1998, 169–70.
2. Burt, *Letters*, 171–73.
3. D. MacNicol, 'United Parishes of Lismore and Appin', in D.J. Witherspoon and I.R. Grant (eds), *The Statistical Account of Scotland*, 20 vols, Wakefield, 1983, XX, 361.
4. A. Grant, *Letters from the Mountains*, 2 vols, London, 1845, I, 45–46; D. Wordsworth, *Recollections of a Tour made in Scotland in 1803*, London, 1997, 145.
5. J. Mackechnie (ed), *The Dewar Manuscripts*, Glasgow, 1964, 256.
6. Mackechnie, *Dewar Manuscripts*, 231.
7. J.H.J. Stewart and D. Stewart, *The Stewarts of Appin*, Edinburgh, 1880, 97–8,

107–08; J. Munro and R.W. Munro (eds), *Acts of the Lords of the Isles*, Edinburgh, 1986, 208, 214.

8. Stewart and Stewart, *Stewarts of Appin*, 76.

9. Burt, *Letters*, 115; W.B. Blaikie (ed), *Origins of the Forty-Five*, Edinburgh, 1975, 126; A. Lang (ed), *The Highlands of Scotland in 1750*, Edinburgh, 1898, 71.

10. Burt, *Letters*, 282–3.

11. The dating of these events is complicated by the fact that the French calendar postdated the British by eleven days during this period. The discrepancy was not eliminated until 1752 when Britain (Eurosceptic even then) was persuaded to adopt the continental system. The 1752 reform brought British (Old Style) dates into line with French (New Style) dates. In this book, for simplicity, British dating is used.

12. D. Nicholas (ed), *An Account of the Proceedings from Prince Charles' Landing to Prestonpans*, Edinburgh, 1958, 206; H.R. Duff (ed), *Culloden Papers*, London, 1815, 204.

13. Duff, *Culloden Papers*, 204; J. Home, *The History of the Rebellion in Scotland*, Edinburgh, 1822, 32.

14. In the nineteenth century, pro-Stewart historians commonly claimed that Dougal was a minor in 1745 and 1746. This story had the advantage of getting such historians round the (to them) awkward circumstance of the Appin chief's non-appearance at Culloden. The story's disadvantage lay in the fact that it was untrue.

15. Mackechnie, *Dewar Manuscripts*, 166.

16. Mackechnie, *Dewar Manuscripts*, 224; A. Stewart, 'The Last Chief: Dougal Stewart of Appin', SHR, LXXXVI, 1997, 289, 218–19.

17. Stewart, 'Last Chief', 209.

18. Some authorities, including Walter Scott, attribute this duel to another of the Appin Stewarts, Alexander Stewart of Invernahyle. However, an early nineteenth-century Stewart document explicitly corrects Scott on this point. *See*: 'Invernahyle Papers: Particulars Regarding the family of Invernahyle.'

19. A.M. Annand, 'Stewart of Appin's Regiment', *The Stewarts*, XI, 1961, 108–09; D.M. Rose (ed), *Prince Charlie's Friends: Jacobite Indictments*, Aberdeen, 1896, 26.

20. Blaikie, *Origins*, 54.

21. L. Scott-Moncrieff (ed), *The '45: To Gather an Image Whole*, Edinburgh, 1988, xii.

22. Mackechnie, *Dewar Manuscripts*, 167.

23. Wordsworth, *Recollections of a Tour*, 145–6

24. The precise extent of the Invernahyle Estate, as calculated by a government surveyor in Culloden's aftermath, was 4,006 acres. This measure, like those which follow, is converted here into the English or imperial acres which later became standard.

25. GD/87/1/42: Lord Glenorchy, Memorial for Barcaldine and Glenure, n.d.; RHP 3484: Plan of the Estate of Ardshiel, 1773; A.H. Millar (ed), *Forfeited Estates Papers*, Edinburgh, 1909, 271.

26. E737/1/5: Rental of Estate of Ardshiel, 1755; A.G. MacPherson, 'The Annexed Estate of Ardshiel', *The Stewarts*, X, 1956, 100.

27. Burt, *Letters*, 204.

28. S. Johnson, *A Journey to the Western Isles of Scotland*, London, 1984, 54–5.

29. T. Pennant, *A Tour in Scotland and a Voyage to the Hebrides in 1752*, Edinburgh, 1998, 217.

30. E. Cregeen, 'The Tacksmen and their Successors: A Study of Tenurial Reorganisation in Mull, Morvern and Tiree', *Scottish Studies*, 13, 1969, 125.

31. A. Lang (ed), *The Highlands of Scotland in 1750*, Edinburgh, 1898, 77.

32. These names are drawn from the invaluable researches of Angus and Flora Stewart as listed in this book's bibliography and published in *The Stewarts*, the magazine of the Clan Stewart society.

33. J. Allardyce (ed), *Historical Papers Relating to the Jacobite Period*, 2 vols, Aberdeen, 1995, I, 132; B.G. Seton and J.G. Arnot (eds), *The Prisoners of the '45*, 3 vols, Edinburgh, 1928, I, 271.

34. Lang, *Highlands of Scotland*, 77.

35. Stewart, 'Last Chief', 207.

36. Stewart and Stewart, *Stewarts of Appin*, 159.

37. W. MacLeod (ed), *A List of Persons Concerned in the Rebellion, Edinburgh, 1890*; MacKay, *Trial*, 41.

38. MacKay, *Trial*, 295.

39. MacKay, *Trial*, 86.

40. In *Kidnapped*, Robert Louis Stevenson translated Seumas a'Ghlinne as 'James of the Glens' – plural. Stevenson was in error.

41. Mackechnie, *Dewar Manuscripts*, 162.

42. MacKechnie, *Dewar Manuscripts*, 168.

43. A. Aufrere (ed), *The Lockhart Papers*, 2 vols, London, 1817, II, 441; Nicholas, *Account of Proceedings*, 209; R.F. Bell (ed), *Memorials of Murray of Broughton*, Edinburgh, 1898, 171.

44. GD87/1/42: Memorial for Barcaldine and Glenure, n.d.

45. GD87/1/42: Memorial for Barcaldine and Glenure, n.d.

46. W.A. Speck, *The Butcher: The Duke of Cumberland and the Suppression of the Forty-Five*, Caernarfon, 1995, 17.

47. Rose, *Prince Charlie's Friends*, 26.

48. Chevalier de Johnstone, *Memoirs of the Rebellion of 1745*, London, 1821, 26.

49. M. Hook and W. Ross, *The Forty-Five: The Last Jacobite Rebellion*, Edinburgh, 1995, 31; J. Home, *The History of the Rebellion in Scotland*, Edinburgh, 1822, 74.

50. Home, *History*, 78.

51. Bell, *Memorials*, 202.

52. Home, *History*, 87.

53. J.G. Lockhart, *The Life of Sir Walter Scott*, 10 vols, Edinburgh, 1903, I, 155; W. Scott, *Waverley*, London, 1972, 569.

54. Scott, *Waverley*, 567.

55. W.A.S. Hewins (ed), *The Whitefoord Papers*, Oxford, 1898, xviii, 50; R. Cadell, *Sir John Cope and the Rebellion of 1745*, Edinburgh, 1898, 231.

56. R. Chambers (ed), *Jacobite Memoirs of the Rising of 1745*, Edinburgh, 1834; Johnstone, *Memoirs*, 38.

57. R.L. Stevenson, *Kidnapped*, London, 1983, 54.

58. MacKay, *Trial*, 211.

59. MacKay, *Trial*, 211–12

60. MacKay, *Trial*, 41, 69, 295

61. MacKay, *Trial*, 69.

CHAPTER THREE

1. D. Warrand (ed), *More Culloden Papers*, 4 vols, Inverness, 1923, IV, 101.

2. Mackechnie, *Dewar Manuscripts*, 161.

3. J. Stuart, *March of the Highland Army*, Aberdeen, 1841, 291.

4. Adv 60.2.10: Order Book of the Appin Regiment, 13, 17, 35.

5, Adv 60.2.10: Order Book of the Appin Regiment, 1.

6. Adv 60.2.10: Order Book of the Appin Regiment, 14.

7. A.J. Youngson, *The Prince and the Pretender: Two Views of the '45*, Edinburgh, 1996, 11; Home, *History*, 75.

8. *Scots Magazine*, September 1745, 438; Adv 25.3.10: Precognitions Taken in the Murder of Colin Campbell, 22; J. Ferguson, *Argyll in the Forty-Five*, London, 1951, 56.

9. Speck, *The Butcher*, 53.

10. Speck, *The Butcher*, 54.

11. R. Clyde, *From Rebel to Hero: The Image of the Highlander, 1745–1830*, East Linton, 1995, 6; Speck, *The Butcher*, 95–97; W.B. Coley (ed), *Henry Fielding: The True Patriot and Related Writings*, Oxford, 1987, 146; E. Charteris, *William Augustus: Duke of Cumberland*, London, 1913, 227; W. Donaldson, *The Jacobite Song: Political Myth and National Identity*,

Aberdeen, 1988, 39.

12. Johnstone, *Memoirs*, 101.

13. Duff, *Culloden Papers*, 426.

14. Youngson, *Prince and Pretender*, 111.

15. A.W. Davison, *Derby: Its Rise and Progress*, London, 1906, 83–84.

16. F.J. McLynn, *The Jacobite Army in England*, Edinburgh, 1998, 119.

17. Speck, *The Butcher*, 88; McLynn, *Jacobite Army in England*, 137.

18. Home, *History*, 2.

19. Youngson, *Prince and Pretender*, 115.

20. McLynn, *Jacobite Army in England*, 193.

21. J. Black, *Culloden and the '45*, London, 1990, 146.

22. Blaikie, *Origins*, 149, 203.

23. Mackechnie, *Dewar Manuscripts*, 168.

24. A. Stewart and A.T.B. Stewart, 'The Appin Regiment', *The Stewarts*, XIX, 1993, 79.

25. The first Fort George occupied the town centre where Inverness Castle, a Victorian creation, now stands. The second, and surviving, Fort George, several miles to the east, was built in the years following Culloden.

26. W.B. Blaikie, *Itinerary of Prince Charles Edward Stuart*, Edinburgh, 1897, 120.

27. A. Maclean, 'Highlanders in the Forty-Five', TGSI, LIX, 1996, 331.

28. Chambers, *Jacobite Memoirs*, 106.

29. Most of what then remained of the original Fort William was destroyed, in the 1860s, by the builders of the West Highland Railway.

30. T. Pennant, *A Tour of Scotland in 1769*, Perth, 207; Grant, *Letters*, I, 58; B. Craven (ed), *Journals of the Episcopal Visitations of Robert Forbes*, London, 1923, 300.

31. J. Fergusson, *Argyll in the Forty-Five*, London, 1951, 112.

32. Fergusson, *Argyll*, 101, 142.

33. *Scots Magazine*, March 1746, 141; *Scots Magazine*, April 1746, 182; D.M. Rose (ed), *Captain Caroline Scott's Diary of the Siege of Fort William*, Edinburgh, 1900, 23.

34. Rose, *Scott's Diary*, 5.

35. J. Ray, *A Compleat History of the Rebellion*, Manchester, 1750, 354; Black, *Culloden*, 160.

36. Chambers, *Jacobite Memoirs*, 121.

37. M. Hughes, *A Plain Narrative or Journal of the Late Rebellion*, Londson, 1746, 33.

38. Chambers, *Jacobite Memoirs*, 130.

39. D. Stewart, *Sketches of the Character, Manners and Present State of the*

Highlanders of Scotland, 2 vols, Edinburgh, 1825, I, 244.

40. MacKay, *Trial*, 295; Home, *History*, 9.

41. J.L. Campbell (ed), *Highland Songs of the forty-Five*, Edinburgh, 1984, 178–79; J. Prebble, *Culloden*, London, 1967, 13, 26; E. Charteris (ed), *A Short Account of the Affairs of Scotland by Lord Elcho*, Edinburgh, 1973, 430.

42. *Scots Magazine*, May 1746, 248; Blaikie, *Origins*, 414.

43. *Scots Magazine*, May 1746, 218.

44. *Scots Magazine*, April 1746, 193.

45. Chambers, *Jacobite Memoirs*, 127.

46. *Scots Magazine*, May 1746, 247; A. Henderson, *The History of the Rebellion*, London, 1753, 327.

47. K. Tomasson and F. Buist, *Battles of the '45*, London, 1962, 177.

48. Black, *Culloden*, 170; Speck, *The Butcher*, 143.

49. Black, *Culloden*, 170.

50. Johnstone, *Memoirs*, 114.

51. Johnstone, *Memoirs*, 114.

52. *Scots Magazine*, April 1746, 193.

53. H. Tayler (ed), *The History of the Rebellion in the Years 1745 and 1746*, Oxford, 1944, 217–18.

54. *Scots Magazine*, Apirl 1746, 187; Tomasson and Buist, *Battles*, 178.

55. *Scots Magazine*, April 1746, 192.

56. Blacdk, *Culloden*, 166; *Speck, The Butcher*, 144.

57. MS 3735: D. Campbell to Stonefield, 22 April 1746.

58. MacKay, *Trial*, 303.

59. *Scots Magazine*, May 1746, 248; A. Campbell (ed), *Records of Argyll*, Edinburgh, 1885, 311.

60. Campbell, *Records of Argyll*, 311.

61. Blaikie, *Origins*, 215.

62. K. Tomasson, *The Jacobite General*, Edinburgh, 1958, 250–51; C. MacKenzie, *Prince Charlie*, London, 1934, 95.

63. Chambers, *Jacobite Memoirs*, 124; Tomasson, *Jacobite General*, 248; C. MacKenzie, *Prince Charlie*, London, 1934, 95.

64. MS 3735: Glenorchy to J. Campbell, 23 April 1746.

CHAPTER FOUR

1. Blaikie, *Origins*, 217; MacNicol, 'United Parishes', 347; Lang, *Highlands of Scotland*, 76.

2. O.D. Edwards, 'The Long Shadows: A View of Ireland and the '45', in Scott-Moncrieff, *The '45*, 77; R. Lodge (ed), *Private Correspondence of Chesterfield and Newcastle, 1744–46*, London, 1930, 130.

3. Black, *Culloden*, 146.

4. Speck, *The Butcher*, 112, 126–28, 168; G.B. Seton and J.G. Arnot (eds), *The Prisoners of the '45*, 3 vols, Edinburgh, 1928, I, 5; Blaikie, *Origins*, 161.

5. Fergusson, *Argyll*, 120.

6. Stewart and Stewart, *Stewarts of Appin*, 174–75.

7. Hughes, *Plain Narrative*, 56–57; *Scots Magazine*, June 1746, 287.

8. Speck, *Butcher*, 168.

9. P.C. Yorke (ed), *The Life and Correspondence of Philip Yorke, Earl of Hardwicke*, 3 vols, Cambridge, 1913, I, 542–43.

10. Speck, *Butcher*, 165.

11. R. Whitworth, *William Augustus, Duke of Cumberland*, London, 1992, 94.

12. MS 3735: J. Campbell to Cumberland, 3 May 1746.

13. MS 3735: E. Fawkener to J. Campbell, 13 May 1746.

14. Fergusson, *Argyll*, 194–95.

15. MS 3735: J. Campbell to E. Fawkener, 24 May 1746.

16. MacLeod, *List of Persons*, 385–86.

17. Prebble, *Culloden*, 184.

18. Bell, *Memorials*, 269; B.P. Lenman and J.S. Gibson (eds), *The Jacobite Threat: A Source Book*, Edinburgh, 1990, 226–27.

19. *Scots Magazine*, June 1746, 269.

20. Bell, *Memorials*, 290; MS 3736: J. Campbell to Cumberland, 15 May 1746; Stewart and Stewart, 'Appin Regiment', 76, 80; MacKay, *Trial*, 292.

21. C.S. Terry (ed), *The Albemarle Papers*, 3 vols, Edinburgh, 1893, I, 94.

22. *Scots Magazine*, June 1746, 285–86.

23. Terry, *Albemarle Papers*, I, 270.

24. Scott's father had been Britain's ambassador to the Hanoverian court in Germany just prior to Hanover's rulers becoming Britain's rulers also. Princess Caroline, wife of the future George II, was Scott's godmother and he was named after her. Hence, perhaps, his closeness to the Duke of Cumberland, who was Caroline Scott's godmother's son.

25. H. Paton (ed), *The Lyon in Mourning*, 3 vols, Edinburgh, 1893, I, 94.

26. Mackechnie, *Dewar Manuscripts*, 171, 196.

27. *Scots Magazine*, April 1746, 182; Terry, *Albemarle Papers*, I, 333; Mackechnie, *Dewar Manuscripts*, 172.

28. E737/10/1(2): Depositions of the Tenants of Achindarroch, 5 March 1750.

29. Terry, *Albemarle Papers*, I, 333.

30. Paton, *Lyon in Mourning*, I, 93–94.

31. E737/1/1: Rental of the Estate of Ardshiel, 12 September 1748.

32. E737/1/1: Rental of the Estate of Ardshiel, 12 September 1748.

33. MS3736: I. Stewart to J. Campbell, 25 August 1746.

34. Black, *Culloden*, 186.

35. Terry, *Albemarle Papers*, I, 25–26, 137, 309.

36. Stewart and Stewart, 'Appin Regiment', 78–79.

37. Terry, *Albemarle Papers*, I, 300, 333.

38. Terry, *Albemarle Papers*, 333; JC26/148/2768/5: Bill of Suspension presented to the Court of Session, 18 April 1752.

39. Stewart and Stewart, *Stewarts of Appin*, 139; Terry, *Albemarle Papers*, I, 332–33, 339; II, lxi.

40. Terry, *Albemarle Papers*, I, 297, 332.

CHAPTER FIVE

1. MS 3736: I. Stewart to J. Campbell, 25 August 1746.

2. MacKay, *Trial*, 91.

3. MacKay, *Trial*, 295

4. *Scots Magazine*, August 1746, 367; Speck, *Butcher*, 174; Stewart Papers: Notes on the Stewarts of Appin, n.d.

5. MacKay, *Trial*, 297.

6. Blaikie, *Origins*, 156; *Scots Magazine*, August 1746, 365.

7. E737/12/1: Petition of Isabel Haldane, 1758; E786/10: Memorial of C. Campbell, 6 May 1752; E737/4/3: C. Campbell to D. Moncrieff, 14 November 1748.

8. One pound Scots was equal to one-twelfth of that amount (1s 8d) in sterling.

9. E737/1/1: Rental of the Estate of Ardshiel, 12 September 1748.

10. E737/3/3: Valuation of the Estate of Ardshiel, 30 November 1761; RHP3484: Plan of the Estate of Ardshiel, 1773.

11 When tenant of Glen Duror, James Stewart occupied the most substantial of the glen's houses. Afterwards this house became a shepherd's cottage. Today it's a Forestry Commission bothy where walkers and backpackers can make overnight stays. This bothy is signposted as James of the Glen's birthplace. That's unlikely, but it was certainly his home for several years.

12. MacKay, *Trial*, 153; E737/10/1(2): Despositions of the Tenants of Achindarroch, 5 March 1750.

13. E737/1/1: Rental of the Estate of Ardshiel, 12 September 1748; MacKay, *Trial*, 219.

14. A.H. Millar (ed), *Forfeited Estates Papers*, Edinburgh, 1909, 281; E737/4/1: C. Campbell to W. Alison, 2 November 1749; E700/1: Minutes of Barons of Exchequer, 21 November 1749.

15. MacKay, *Trial*, 66.

16. MacKay, *Trial*, 213–14.

17. MacKay, *Trial*, 214.

18. MacKay, *Trial*, 153–55.

19. MacKay, *Trial*, 213.

20. E701/1: Book of Acts and Orders, 11 January 1750; E737/10/1(1): Petition of the Tenants of Achindarroch, 11 January 1750; E737/10/1(2): Depositions of the Tenants of Ardshiel, 5 March 1750.

21. E786/3/1: C. Campbell to D. Moncrieff, 28 March 1750.

22. E700/1: Minutes of Barons of Exchequer, 25 July 1751.

23. MacKay, *Trial*, 10; GD81/1/42: Memorial for Barcaldine and Glenure, n.d.

24. E701/1: Book of Acts and Orders, 25 July 1751; MacKay, *Trial*, 221.

25. Tayler, *History of the Rebellion*, 6; MacKay, *Trial*, 290; Lang, *Highlands of Scotland*, 93; D. Wimberley (ed), 'The Bighouse Papers', TGSI, XXI–XXIV, 1896–1900, XXIII, 36.

26. MacKay, *Trial*, 367; Mackechnie, *Dewar Manuscripts*, 195.

27. Fletcher, Lord Milton, was Scotland's Justice-Clerk.

28. E737/26/2: Memorial of Patrick Campbell, 1771.

29. E737/26/4(2): Case of Patrick Campbell, 16 December 1771.

30. It is one of the oddities of this story that it connects three of the nineteenth century's leading literary figures. Walter Scott visited Alexander Stewart of Invernahyle in Duror and made Stewart's recollections of the Jacobite rebellion the basis of Waverley. Robert Louis Stevenson visited Duror and put the killing of Colin Campbell at the centre of Kidnapped. Macaulay, though not touching explicitly on his grandfather's Duror links, wrote knowlegeably about the West Highlands in his multi-volume History of England.

31. I. Carmichael, *Lismore in Alba*, Perth, 1948, 143; E737/01/2: Petition of J. MacAulay, 3 March 1752.

32. Cregeen, 'Tacksmen and their Successors', 97–8; E737/26/2: Memorial of Patrick Campbell, 1771.

33. MacKay, *Trial*, 213.

34. The building in question, where this book's author played regularly when a small boy, was then mostly – and inexcusably – demolished.

35. MacKay, *Trial*, 155.

36. Adv 25.3.10: Precognitions in the murder of Colin Campbell, 28; MacKay, *Trial*, 208–09.

37. MacKay, *Trial*, 186.

38. Mackechnie, *Dewar Manuscripts*, 197.

39. MacKay, *Trial*, 163.

40. In printed versions of the documentation generated by James's trial, Acharn, not Achara, appears at this point. But it's obvious from the context that it was Achara that was meant.

41. MacKay, *Trial*, 162–64.

42. MacKay, *Trial*, 165.

43. MacKay, *Trial*, 190.

44. MacKay, *Trial*, 190.

45. MacKay, *Trial*, 165–66.

46. MacKay, *Trial*, 166.

47. E737/10/9: Petition of D. Colquhoun and others, 16 February 1764. A list of the people whom Colin Campbell planned to evict can be found in D.C. MacTavish (ed), *Inveraray Papers*, Oban, 1939, 61. Those names coincide with others to be found in documentation of the time.

48. S. Carney, *The Killing of the Red Fox: An Investigation into the Appin Murder*, Moffat, 1989, 24.

49. MacKay, *Trial*, 155.

50. MacKay, *Trial*, 69.

51. MacKay, *Trial*, 69.

52. MacKay, *Trial*, 70.

53. MacKay, *Trial*, 163.

54. MacKay, *Trial*, 140.

55. This comment is the basis of the notion, given currency by Robert Louis Stevenson in Kidnapped, that Colin Campbell was commonly called the Red Fox. He wasn't – being known simply, and universally, as Cailean Ruadh.

56. MacKay, *Trial*, 139; Adv 25.3.10: Precognitions in the Murder of Colin Campbell, 29–30.

57. Mackechnie, *Dewar Manuscripts*, 200.

58. Burt, *Letters*, 249.

CHAPTER SIX

1. Adv 25.3.10: Precognitions in the Murder of Colin Campbell, 8, 32, 58.

2. MacKay, *Trial*, 42, 196, 293.

3. MacKay, *Trial*, 159.

4. MacKay, *Trial*, 161–62

5. D. Defoe, *A Tour through the Whole Island of Great Britain*, 2 vols, London, 1962, II, 300; *Scots Magazine*, August 1752, 320; Pennant, *Tour in 1769*, 50.

6. MacKay, *Trial*, 202.

7. JC26/148/2768/12: Draft letter by J. Stewart, May 1752; MacKay, *Trial*, 262–63.

8. JC26/148/2768/5: Bill of Suspension, 18 April 1752.

9. JC26/148/2768/5: Bill of Suspension, 18 April 1752.

10. JC26/148/2768/5: Bill of Suspension, 18 April 1752.

11. J. Ramsay, *Scotland and Scotsmen in the Eighteenth Century*, 2 vols, Bristol, 1998, I, 85.

12. MacKay, *Trial*, 197.

13. MacKay, *Trial*, 155–56.

14. MacKay, *Trial*, 156.

15. JC26/148/2768/12: Instrument of Protest by Tenants of Ardshiel, 1 May 1752.

16. JC26/148/2768/12: Instrument of Protest by Tenants of Ardshiel, 1 May 1752.

17. MacKay, *Trial*, 104; JC26/148/2768/5: Answers to Bill of Suspension, 5 May 1752.

18. MacKay, *Trial*, 141–42.

19. MacKay, *Trial*, 155.

20. MacKay, *Trial*, 155.

21. MacKay, *Trial*, 142.

22. Adv 25.3.10: Precognitions in the Murder of Colin Campbell, 19.

23. MacKay, *Trial*, 195.

24. MacKay, *Trial*, 143.

25. MacKay, *Trial*, 219.

26. MacKay, *Trial*, 145, 156.

27. Adv 25.3.10: Precognitions in the Murder of Colin Campbell, 2; E737/16/1-3: Accounts of C. Campbell, 1752; MacKay, *Trial*, 135.

28. Mackechnie, *Dewar Manuscripts*, 203.

29. MacKay, *Trial*, 146.

30. MacKay, *Trial*, 146.

31. MacKay, *Trial*, 145.

32. MacKay, *Trial*, 44.

33. MacKay, *Trial*, 147.

34. RHP3484: Plan of the Estate of Ardshiel, 1752; MacKay, *Trial*, 153.

35. MacKay, *Trial*, 131.

36. MacKay, *Trial*, 131.

37. Adv 25.3.10: Precognitions in the Murder of Colin Campbell, 6.

38. J.R.N. MacPahil (ed), *Highland Papers*, 4 vols, Edinburgh, 1914–34, IV, 127; MacKay, *Trial*, 138.

39. Adv 25.3.10: Precognitions in the Murder of Colin Campbell, 2–3; MacKay, *Trial*, 138.

40. Adv 25.3.10: Precognitions in the Murder of Colin Campbell, 2, 6.

41. MacKay, *Trial*, 367.

42. Adv 25.3.10: Precognitions in the Murder of Colin Campbell, 2; MacKay, *Trial*, 45, 71.

43. MacKay, *Trial*, 195, 201.

44. MacPhail, *Highland Papers*, IV, 127.

45. MacPhail, *Highland Papers*, IV, 127.

46. MacKay, *Trial*, 147–8.

47. MacKay, *Trial*, 147.

48. MacKay, *Trial*, 148.

49. MacKay, *Trial*, 149–50.

50. Adv 25.3.10: Precognitions in the Murder of Coloin Campbell, 22; MacKay, *Trial*, 168.

51. MacKay, *Trial*, 292.

52. Stewart and Stewart, 'Appin Regiment', 79; MacKay, *Trial*, 179, 182.

53. MacKay, *Trial*, 180.

54. The term fir was applied in the eighteenth century to what would today be called a scots pine.

55. MacKay, *Trial*, 181.

56. MacKay, *Trial*, 182.

57. MacKay, *Trial*, 185.

58. R. Black, 'MacMhaighstir Alasdair in Rannoch: A Reconstruction', TGSI, LIX, 1996, 343; Adv 17.1.7: Factors' Reports on the Annexed Estates, 1755.

59. MacKay, *Trial*, 152.

60. GD170/3299/1: G. Douglas to A. Campbell, 16 May 1752; GD170/3275/1–8: Accounts for Glenure's Funeral, 1752; A. MacLeod (ed), *The Songs of Duncan Ban MacIntyre*, Edinburgh 1752, 68–69.

61. GD170/3298: A. Campbell to D. Campbell, 15 May 1752.

62. MS315: D. Campbell to J. Campbell, 15 May 1752; Adv 28.1.6: Memorial of J. Campbell, 71 August 1752; Adv 28.1.6: Account of Expenses Concerning Glenure's Murder, 1752.

63. MS315: Answers to the Objection made by Mr Moncrieff, n.d.

64. MS5077: A. Campbell to Lord Justice Clerk, 10 June 1752.

65. MS315: A. Campbell to J. Campbell, 17 May 1752; GD14/134: Memorial Relative to the Precognitions, n.d.

66. MacKay, *Trial*, 133.

67. Chapmen were itinerant sellers of pamphlets, religious tracts and the like.

68. GD170/3268: Account of disbursements by A. Campbell, 17 May 1752; GD170/3270: Account of D. Ferguson and A. MacCombie, 18 July 1752; GD170/3307: Unaddressed letter from A. Ferguson, n.d.

69. CE56/7/1: Orders to collector ad comptroller at Dunbar, 19 May 1752; MacKay, *Trial*, 308.

70. MacKay, *Trial*, 308, 310.

71. Adv 25.3.10: Precognitions in the Murder of Colin Campbell, 10, 12, 28, 32, 68.

72. MacPhail, *Highland Papers*, IV, 127–28; GD87/1/61: J. Crawford to J. Campbell, 20 May 1753; MS315: J. Crawford to J. Campbell, 22 May 1752.

73. Mackechnie, Dewar Manuscripts, 200, 207.

74. Carney, *Killing of the Red Fox*, 149.

75. GD87/1/44: A. Campbell to D. Campbell, 25 May 1752.

76. Adv 25.3.10: Precognitions in the Murder of Colin Campbell, 30.

77. GD87/1/44: A. Campbell to D. Campbell, 25 May 1752.

78. MS315: A. Campbell to J. Campbell, 28 July 1752.

79. MS315: M. Campbell to J. Campbell, 29 June 1752.

80. MS315: J. Crawford to J. Campbell, 22 June 1752.

81. MS315: C. Erskine to J. Campbell, 22 June 1752.

82. Adv 28.1.6(1): M. Campbell to D. Moncrieff, 10 June 1752.

CHAPTER SEVEN

1. MacKay, *Trial*, 212.

2. J.R.N. MacPhail, 'Further Notes on the Trial of James of the Glen', TGSI, XXIV, 1900, 143; MS5077: Hollernesse to Lord Justice Clerk, 30 June 1752.

3. J. Fergusson, 'The Appin Murder Case', *Scottish Historical Review*, XXXI, 1952, 125; MS5077: H. Pelham to Lord Justice Clerk, 28 May 1752.

4. MS5077: Holderness to Lord Justice Clerk, 26 May 1752; MS5077: Pelham to Lord Justice Clerk, 28 May 1752; Adv 28.1.6(1): N. Hardinge to Barons of Exchequer, 29 May 1752.

5. V. Wills (ed), *Reports on the Forfeited Estates*, Edinburgh, 1973, vi; MacKay, *Trial*, 216; H. Walpole, *Memoirs of King George II*, 3 vols, London, 1985, I, 178.

6. J. Fergusson, *The White Hind and Other Discoveries*, London, 1963, 160; MS5077: Holdernesse to Lord Justice Clerk, 30 June 1752.

7. Yorke, *Life and Correspondence of Philip Yorke*, I, 557; MS315: Breadalbane to J. Campbell, 16 May 1752.

8. MacKay, *Trial*, 259.

9. Walpole, *Memoirs*, I, 185; MacKay, *Trial*, 109.

10. MacKay, *Trial*, 109, 291.

11. Adv 28.1.6(1): Memorial of J. Campbell, 17 August 1752.

12. MS315: Abstract of the precognitions taken concerning Glenure's murder, n.d.

13. MS315: Abstract of the precognitions.

14. MS315: Abstract of the precognitions.

15. MS315: Abstract of the precognitions.

16. MS315: Abstract of the precognitions.

17. MS315: Abstract of the precognitions.

18. *Supplement to the Trial*, 14; MacKay, *Trial*, 294; MS315: J. Crawford to J. Campbell, 22 May 1752.

19. MacKay, *Trial*, 294; *Supplement to the Trial*, 9.

20. *Supplement to the Trial*, 9.

21. *Supplement to the Trial*, 10.

22. As can be deduced both from its contents and from the similarities it bears to a long letter he's known to have written from Inveraray at the close of James Stewart's trial, Alexander Stewart of Edinglassie, or so it's assumed here, was the author of A Supplement to the Trial of James Stewart by a Bystander. Published in London in 1753, this pamphlet was a powerful counterblast to The Trial of James Stewart which had been issued in Edinburgh some months before and which, being a Campbell-backed and semi-official account of the events preceding James's execution, was intended to show James in the worst possible light.

23. MacKay, *Trial*, 375.

24. MacKay, *Trial*, 18–19.

25. To disguise his identity, the author of the Supplement to the Trial refers to himself always in the third person.

26. *Supplement to the Trial*, 18.

27. *Supplement to the Trial*, 13.

28. MacKay, *Trial*, 65.

29. Pennant, *Tour in Scotland in 1769*, 218–19; I.G. Lindsay and M. Cosh, *Inveraray and the Dukes of Argyll*, Edinburgh, 1973, 67.

30. JC13/10: Justiciary Court, West Circuit Minute Book, 21 to 26 September 1752; MacKay, *Trial*, 62–63.

31. GD50/166: A. Campbell to J. Campbell, 25 July 1752.

32. *Supplement to the Trial*, 33–34.

33. Fergusson, *White Hind and Other Discoveries*, 139; MacKay, *Trial*, 221.

34. GD87/148: J. Crawford to J. Campbell, 12 July 1752.

35. MacKay, *Trial*, 292–94.

36. A reference to the then very recent change in Britain's dating system.

37. *Supplement to the Trial*, 64; *Scots Magazine*, September 1752, 460.

38. MacKay, *Trial*, 291.

39. Murray of Polmaise Papers: Letter from A. Stewart, n.d.; Fergusson, *White Hind and Other Discoveries*, 150.

40. JC13/10: Justiciary Court, West Circuit Minute Book, 21 to 26 September 1752; *Supplement to the Trial*, 67.

41. *Scots Magazine*, September 1752, 461; Yorke, *Life and Correspondence of Philip Yorke*, I, 558.

42. Craven, *Episcopal Visitations of Robert Forbes*, 306–06.

43. RH1/2/508: Account of expenses in putting up the body of James Stewart, February 1755; E737/11/1(1): Petition of A. Campbell, 1753.

44. E737/11/1(1): Petition of A. Campbell, 1753.

45. E737/11/1(1): Petition of A. Campbell, 1753.

46. West Highland Museum: Account of Sundry Disbursements by George Douglas, 1751 and 1752; *Scots Magazine*, November 1752, 555–56.

47. *Scots Magazine*, October 1752, 509; *Scots Magazine*, November 1752, 555–56.

48. *Scots Magazine*, October 1752, 509.

49. MacKay, *Trial*, 297.

CHAPTER EIGHT

1. MS309: Gen. Churchill's a.d.c. to Maj. Pym, 19 December 1752.

2. RH1/2/508: H. Erskine to A. Campbell, 4 February 1752.

3. RH1/2/509: Account of expenses in putting up the body of James Stewart, February 1755.

4. Craven, *Episcopal Visitations of Robert Forbes*, 305.

5. E737/10/11: Petition of A. Campbell, 1765.

6. B.G. Seton, *The House of Seton: A Study of Lost Causes*, 2 vols, Edinburgh, 1939, II, 481.

7. E737/12/1: Petition of I. Haldane, 1758.

8. E737/21/1: H. Seton to J. Hunter, 14 August 1771; E737/26/2: Memorial of P. Campbell, 1771.

9. MacKay, *Trial*, 90.

10. Stewart and Stewart, *Stewarts of Appin*, 144–50.

11. Johnson, *Journey to the Western Islands*, 97.

12. E737/10/9: Petition of D. Colquhoun and others, 16 February 1764.

13. Today the Stuart Hotel.

14. Nowadays the Ardsheal House Hotel.

15. B.P. Lenman, *The Jacobite Clans of the Great Glen*, London, 1884, 216.

16. E737/10/9: H. Butter to W. Barclay, 18 January 1773; MacNicol, 'United Parishes of Lismore and Appin', 360; Millar, *Forfeited Estates Papers*, 27.

17. E737/26/15(2): H. Butter to W. Barclay, 5 February 1774.

18. MacNicol, 'United Parishes of Lismore and Appin', 346; E737/19/4: Rental of the Estate of Ardshiel, 1784.

19. V. Cameron (ed), *Emigrants from Scotland to America, 1774–1776*, Baltimore, 1976, 91.

20. Among the folk who got jobs with the Forestry Commission in Glen Duror during the 1920s was the man taken on by the commission as Glen Duror's trapper or ranger. His name was James Hunter. He was the grandfather of this book's author.

21. *Supplement to the Trial*, title page.

BIBLIOGRAPHY

UNPUBLISHED SOURCES

In Scottish Record Office, Edinburgh:
Forfeited Estates Papers: (E 700–86)
Exchequer Documents: (E 405)
Plan of the Estate of Ardshiel: (RHP 3484)
Campbell of Stonefield Papers: (GD 14)
Campbell of Baleveolan Papers: (GD 13)
Campbell of Barcaldine Papers: (GD 170)
MacKay of Bighouse Papers: (GD 87)
John MacGregor Collection: (GD 50)
Minute Book of the Justiciary Court's West Circuit: (JC 13/10)
Justiciary Court: Papers relating to the trial of James Stewart: (JC 26/148/27/2768)
Account of disbursements for replacing the body of James Stewart: (RH 1/2/508)
Excise Board's orders to the board's collector at Dunbar: (CE 56/7/1)

In National Library of Scotland, Edinburgh:
Letter Books of Commanders-in-Chief Scotland: (Ms 304–09)
Original letters relating to the Appin Murder: (Ms 315)
Campbell of Mamore Papers: (Ms 3733–36)
Erskine Murray Papers: (Ms 5077)
Erskine Papers: (Ms 5127)
Factors' reports on the Annexed Estates: (Adv 17.1.6–7)
Copy of a letter concerning the murder at Appin: (Adv 22.2.23)
Precognitions taken in the murder of Colin Campbell: (Adv 25.3.10)
Correspondence of the commissioners for the forfeited estates: (Adv 28.1.66)
Order book of the Appin Regiment: (Adv 60.2.10)
Abstract of precognitions relative to the murder of Colin Campbell: (Ch 4452)

In Stirling Council Archives, Stirling:
Murray of Polmaise Papers

In Stewart Society headquarters, Edinburgh:
Ardshiel Papers
Invernahyle Papers
Notes on the Stewarts of Appin

In possession of Alastair Campbell of Airds:
Campbell of Airds Papers

In West Highland Museum, Fort William:
Account of sundry disbursements by George Douglas

PUBLISHED SOURCES

(Abbreviations: SHS, Scottish History Society; TGSI, Transactions of the Gaelic Society of Inverness.)

Allardyce, James (ed), *Historical Papers Relating to the Jacobite Period*, 2 vols, New Spalding Club, Aberdeen, 1895.

Arnot, Hugo, *A Collection and Abridgement of Celebrated Criminal Trials in Scotland*, Edinburgh, 1785.

Aufrere, Anthony (ed), *The Lockhart Papers*, London, 1817.

Bell, Robert F. (ed), *Memorials of John Murray of Broughton*, SHS, Edinburgh, 1898.

Blaikie, Walter B., *Itinerary of Prince Charles Edward Stuart*, SHS, Edinburgh, 1897.

Blaikie, Walter B. (ed), *Origins of the Forty-Five*, Edinburgh, 1975.

Boswell, James, *Journal of a Tour to the Hebrides*, London, 1984.

Burt, Edmund, *Letters from a Gentleman in the North of Scotland*, Edinburgh, 1998.

Burton, John H. (ed), *The Autobiography of Dr Alexander Carlyle*, Bristol, 1990.

Cameron, Viola C. (ed), *Emigrants from Scotland to America, 1774–1775*, Baltimore, 1976.

Campbell, Archibald (ed), *Records of Argyll*, Edinburgh, 1885.

Campbell, John L. (ed), *Highland Songs of the Forty-Five*, Edinburgh, 1984.

Chambers, Robert (ed), *Jacobite Memoirs of the Rising of 1745*, Edinburgh, 1834.

Chambers, Robert (ed), *History of the Rebellion of 1745–46*, Edinburgh, 1869.

Charles, George, *History of the Transactions in Scotland*, 2 vols, Leith, 1817.

Charteris, Evan (ed), *A Short Account of the Affairs of Scotland in 1744, 1745 and 1746 by Lord Elcho*, Edinburgh, 1973.

Cockburn, Henry, *Circuit Journeys*, Hawick, 1983.

Coley, W.B. (ed), *Henry Fielding: The True Patriot and Related Writings*, Oxford, 1987.

Craven, J.B. (ed), *Journals of the Episcopal Visitations of Robert Forbes*, London, 1923.

Defoe, Daniel, *A Tour through the Whole Island of Great Britain*, 2 vols, London, 1962.

Duff, Hugh R. (ed), *Culloden Papers*, London, 1815.

Grant, Anne, *Letters from the Mountains*, 2 vols, London, 1845.

Hamilton, Marion F. (ed), *The Loch Arkaig Treasure*, SHS, Edinburgh, 1941.

Henderson, Andrew, *The History of the Rebellion*, London, 1753.

Henderson, Andrew, *Memoirs of Dr Archibald Cameron*, London, 1753.

Henderson Andrew, *The Life of William Augustus, Duke of Cumberland*, London, 1766.

Hewins, W.A.S. (ed), *The Whitefoord Papers*, Oxford, 1898.

Home, John, *The History of the Rebellion in Scotland*, Edinburgh, 1822.

Howell, T.B. (ed), *A Complete Collection of the State Trials*, 21 vols, London, 1811–19.

Hughes, Michael, *A Plain Narrative or Journal of the Late Rebellion*, London, 1746.

Johnson, Samuel, *A Journey to the Western Islands of Scotland*, London, 1984.

Johnstone, Chevalier de, *Memoirs of the Rebellion of 1745*, London, 1821.

Lang, Andrew (ed), *The Highlands of Scotland in 1750*, Edinburgh, 1898.

Livingstone, Alistair and Aikman, Christian W.H. (eds), *Muster Roll of Prince Charles Edward Stuart's Army*, Aberdeen, 1984.

Lodge, Richard (ed), *Private Correspondence of Chesterfield and Newcastle, 1744–46*, Camden Society, London, 1930.

Macaulay, Thomas B., *The History of England*, 5 vols, Oxford, 1931.

MacGregor, Gregor, 'United Parish of Lismore and Appin', *New Statistical Account of Scotland*, Edinburgh, 1845.

MacKay, David N. (ed), *Trial of James Stewart*, Edinburgh, 1931.

MacKay, William (ed), 'Unpublished Correspondence between Lord Lovat, MacLeod of MacLeod, Lord Loudoun and Others', TGSI, XIV, 1887–88.

Mackechnie, John (ed), *The Dewar Manuscripts*, Glasgow, 1964.

Mackintosh, C. Fraser (ed), *Antiquarian Notes*, Inverness, 1865.

Mackintosh, C. Fraser (ed), *Antiquarian Notes: Second Series*, Inverness, 1887.

Mackintosh, C. Fraser (ed), *Letters of Two Centuries*, Inverness, 1890.

MacLeod, Angus (ed), *The Songs of Duncan Ban MacIntyre*, Edinburgh, 1952.

MacLeod, Walter (ed), *A List of Persons Concerned in the Rebellion*, SHS, Edinburgh, 1890.

MacNicol, Donald, 'United Parishes of Lismore and Appin', in, Withrington, Donald J. and Grant, Ian R. (eds), *The Statistical Account of Scotland*, 20 vols [XX], Wakefield, 1983.

MacPhail, J.R.N., 'An Interesting Copy of a Report of the Trial of James Stewart of Acharn', TGSI, XVI, 1890.

MacPhail, J.R.N. (ed), *Letters by Mrs Grant of Laggan Concerning Highland Affairs*, SHS, Edinburgh, 1896.

MacPahil, J.R.N., 'Further Notes on the Trial of James of the Glen', TGSI, XXIV, 1900.

MacPhail, J.R.N. (ed), *Papers from the Collection of Sir William Fraser*, SHS, Edinburgh, 1924.

MacPhail, J.R.N., *Highland Papers*, 4 vols, SHS, Edinburgh, 1914, 1916, 1920, 1934.

MacTavish, Duncan C. (ed), *Inveraray Papers*, Oban, 1939.

Marchant, John, *The History of the Present Rebellion*, London, 1746.

Matheson, Angus (ed), *A Traditional Account of the Appin Murder*, TGSI, XXXV, 1930.

Millar, A.H. (ed), *Forfeited Estates Papers*, SHS, Edinburgh, 1909.

Mitchell, Arthur (ed), *Macfarlane's Geographical Collections*, 3 vols, SHS, Edinburgh, 1907.

Munro, Jean and Munro, R.W. (ed), *Acts of the Lords of the Isles*, SHS, Edinburgh, 1986.

Nicholas, Donald (ed), *Intercepted Post: Letters Written in 1745*, London, 1956.

Nicholas, Donald (ed), *An Account of Proceedings from Prince Charles' Landing to Prestonpans*, SHS, Edinburgh, 1958.

Paton, Henry (ed), *Papers about the Rebellions of 1715 and 1745*, SHS, Edinburgh, 1893.

Paton, Henry (ed), *The Lyon in Mourning*, 3 vols, SHS, Edinburgh, 1896.

Pennant, Thomas, *A Tour of Scotland in 1769*, Perth, 1979.

Pennant, Thomas, *A Tour in Scotland and Voyage to the Hebrides in 1772*, Edinburgh, 1998.

Ramsay, John, *Scotland and Scotsmen in the Eighteenth Century*, 2 vols, Bristol, 1996.

Ray, James, *A Compleat History of the Rebellion*, Manchester, 1750.

Robson, James, *General View of Agriculture in the County of Argyll*, London, 1794.

Rose, D. Murray (ed), *Prince Charlie's Friends: Jacobite Indictments*, Aberdeen,

1896.

Rose, D.Murray (ed), *Captain Caroline Scott's Diary of the Siege of Fort William*, Edinburgh, 1900.

Scots Magazine, Edinburgh, 1745–1752.

Seton, Bruce G. (ed), *Commentary on the Expedition made to Scotland by Charles Edward Stewart*, SHS, Edinburgh, 1926.

Seton, Bruce G. and Arnot, Jean G. (eds), *The Prisoners of the '45*, 3 vols, SHS, Edinburgh, 1928.

Smith, Adam, *An Inquiry into the Nature and Causes of the Wealth of Nations*, 2 vols, Oxford, 1976.

Stewart, Angus and Stewart, A.T.B., 'The Appin Regiment', *The Stewarts*, XIX, 1993.

Stewart, David, *Sketches of the Character, Manners and Present State of the Highlanders of Scotland*, 2 vols, Edinburgh, 1825.

Stewart, Flora and Stewart, Angus, 'Appin's List', *The Stewarts*, XX, 1998.

Stuart, James, *March of the Highland Army*, Spalding Club, Aberdeen, 1841.

A Supplement to the Trial of James Stewart by a Bystander, London, 1753.

Tayler, Alistair and Tayler, Henrietta (eds), *Jacobite Letters to Lord Pitsligo*, Aberdeen, 1930.

Tayler, Alistair and Tayler, Henrietta (eds), *The Stuart Papers at Windsor*, London, 1939.

Tayler, Henrietta (ed), *Jacobite Epilogue*, London, 1941.

Tayler, Henrietta (ed), *Anonymous History of the Rebellion: Containing Elcho's Journal*, 1944.

Tayler, Henrietta (ed), *The History of the Rebellion in the Years 1745 and 1746*, Oxford, 1944.

Tayler, Henrietta (ed), *A Jacobite Miscellany*, Oxford, 1948.

Terry, Charles S. (ed), *The Albemarle Papers*, 2 vols, Spalding Club, Aberdeen, 1902.

The Trial of James Stewart in Aucharn in Duror of Appin, Edinburgh, 1753.

Walpole, Horace, *Memoirs of King George II*, 3 vols, London, 1985.

Warrand, Duncan (ed), *More Culloden Papers*, 4 vols, Inverness, 1923.

Wills, Virginia (ed), *Reports on the Forfeited Estates*, 1755–69, Edinburgh, 1973.

Willson, Beckles (ed), *The Life and Letters of James Wolfe*, London, 1909.

Wimberley, D. (ed), 'The Bighouse Papers', TGSI, XXI–XXIV, 1896–1900.

Wordsworth, Dorothy, *Recollections of a Tour Made in Scotland in 1803*, London, 1997.

Yorke, Philip C. (ed), *The Life and Correspondence of Philip Yorke, Earl of Hardwicke*, 3 vols, Cambridge, 1913.

OTHER BOOKS AND ARTICLES

Anderson, Peter, *Culloden Moor and the Story of the Battle*, Stirling, 1920.

Annand, A.M., 'Stewart of Appin's Regiment', *The Stewarts*, XI, 1961.

Black, Jeremy (ed), *Britain in the Age of Walpole*, London, 1984.

Black, Jeremy, *Culloden and the '45*, London, 1990.

Black, Ronald, *MacMhaighstir Alasdair: The Ardnamurchan Years*, Isle of Coll, 1986.

Black, Ronald, 'MacMhaighstir Alasdair in Rannoch: A Reconstruction', TGSI, LIX, 1996.

Blackie, J.E.H., 'Duncan VI of Ardsheal', *The Stewarts*, XIV, 1974.

Boardman, Steve, 'The Tale of Leper John and the Campbell Acquisition of Lorne', in Cowan, Edward J. and McDonald, R. Andrew (eds), *Alba: Celtic Scotland in the Middle Ages*, East Linton, 2000.

Browne, James, *A History of the Highlands and of the Highland Clans*, 4 vols, Glasgow, 1832.

Browning, Reed, *The Duke of Newcastle*, London, 1975.

Buchan, John, 'The Country of Kidnapped', *The Academy*, LIII, 1898.

Cadell, Robert, *Sir John Cope and the Rebellion of 1745*, Edinburgh, 1898.

Calder, Jenni, *RLS: A Life Study*, London, 1980.

Cameron, John, 'The Appin Murder: A Summing Up', *Scottish Historical Review*, XXXIII, 1954.

Campbell, Ian M., *Reminiscences of a Vintner*, London, 1950.

Campbell, Marion, *Argyll: The Enduring Heartland*, Grantown-on-Spey, 1995.

Cargill, D.C. and Fairweather, Barbara, *Kinlochlaich and Keil: Memorial Inscriptions*, Edinburgh, 1994.

Carmichael, Ian, *Lismore in Alba*, Perth, 1948.

Carney, Seamus, *The Killing of the Red Fox: An Investigation into the Appin Murder*, Moffat, 1989.

Carswell, Allan L., 'The Most Despicable Enemy that Are', in Woosnam-Savage, Robert C. (ed), *1745: Charles Edward Stuart and the Jacobites*, Glasgow, 1995.

Chambers, Robert, *History of the Rebellion of 1745–46*, Edinburgh, n.d.

Chandler, David (ed), The Oxford History of the British Army, Oxford, 1994.

Charteris, Evan, *William Augustus: Duke of Cumberland*, London, 1913.

Clyde, Robert, *From Rebel to Hero: The Image of the Highlander, 1745–1830*, East Linton, 1995.

Colley, Linda, *Britons: Forging the Nation, 1707–1837*, London, 1992.

Craig, Maggie, *Damn' Rebel Bitches: The Women of the '45*, Edinburgh, 1997.

Cregeen, Eric, 'The Tacksmen and their Successors: A Study of Tenurial Reorganisation in Mull, Morvern and Tiree', *Scottish Studies*, 13, 1969.

Cregeen, Eric, 'The Changing Role of the House of Argyll in the Scottish Highlands', in Phillipson, N.T. and Michison, Rosalind (eds), *Scotland in the Age of Improvement*, Edinburgh, 1970.

Cruickshanks, Eveline and Black, Jeremy (eds), *The Jacobite Challenge*, Edinburgh, 1988.

Cunningham, A.D., *A History of Rannoch*, Rannoch, 1984.

Cunningham, Audrey, *The Loyal Clans*, Edinburgh, 1932.

Daiches, David, *Charles Edward Stuart: The Life and Times of Bonnie Prince Charlie*, London, 1973.

Davison, A.W., *Derby: Its Rise and Progress*, London, 1906.

Devine, Tom, *Clanship to Crofters' War: The Social Transformation of the Scottish Highlands*, Manchester, 1994.

Dickinson, H.T., *Walpole and the Whig Supremacy*, London, 1973.

Dickson, Patricia, *Red John of the Battles: John, 2nd Duke of Argyll*, London, 1973.

Dictionary of National Biography.

Dobson, David, *Directory of Scottish Settlers in North America, 1625–1825*, 7 vols, Baltimore, 1984.

Donaldson, William, *The Jacobite Song: Political Myth and National Identity*, Aberdeen, 1988.

Douglas, Hugh, *Jacobite Spy Wars*, Stroud, 2000.

Dow, F.D., *Cromwellian Scotland*, Edinburgh, 1979.

Duke, Winifred, *Lord George Murray and the Forty-Five*, Aberdeen, 1927.

Edwards, Owen D., *Macaulay*, London, 1988.

Edwards, Owen D., 'The Long Shadows: A View of Ireland and the '45', in Scott-Moncrieff, Lesley (ed), *The '45: To Gather an Image Whole*, Edinburgh, 1988.

Fairweather, Barbara, *Lismore, Duror and Strath of Appin: A Short History*, Glencoe, 1976.

Fay, C.R., *Adam Smith and the Scotland of his Day*, Cambridge, 1956.

Ferguson, William, *Scotland: 1689 to the Present*, Edinburgh, 1968.

Fergusson, James, *Argyll in the Forty-Five*, London, 1951.

Fergusson, James, 'The Appin Murder Case', *Scottish Historical Review*, XXXI, 1952.

Fergusson, James, *The White Hind and Other Discoveries*, London, 1963.

Findlay, J. T., *Wolfe in Scotland*, London, 1928.

Forbes, J. Macbeth, *Jacobite Gleanings from State Manuscripts*, Edinburgh, 1903.

Fraser, A. Campbell, *The Book of Barcaldine*, London, 1936.

Gibson, John S., *Ships of the Forty-Five*, London, 1967.

Gibson, John S., *Lochiel of the Forty-Five*, Edinburgh, 1994.

Gillies, H. Cameron, *The Placenames of Argyll*, London, 1906.

Gillies, William, 'The Causes of the '45', in, Scott-Moncrieff, Lesley (ed), *The '45: To Gather an Image Whole*, Edinburgh, 1988.

Gillies, William, 'Gaelic Songs of the Forty-Five', *Scottish Studies*, XXX, 1991.

Grant, I.F., *Highland Folk Ways*, London, 1961.

Grant, I.F., *Along a Highland Road*, London, 1980.

Grant, I.F., *Everyday Life on an Old Highland Farm*, London, 1981.

Grant, James, *Cassell's Old and New Edinburgh*, 3 vols, Edinburgh, 1883.

Guy, Alan J., *Economy and Discipline: Officership and Administration in the British Army, 1714–63*, Manchester, 1985.

Harrington, Peter, *Culloden*, London, 1991.

Harris, Bob, 'England's Provincial Newspapers and the Jacobite Rebellion of 1745–46', *History*, LXXX, 1995.

Henderson, C. Stewart., 'The Order Book of the Appin Regiment', *The Stewarts*, IX, 1952.

Henderson C. Stewart, 'Bicentenary of the Death of James of the Glen', *The Stewarts*, IX, 1953.

Holmes, Geoffrey and Szechi, Daniel, *The Age of Oligarchy: Pre-Industrial Britain, 1722–1783*, London, 1993.

Hook, Michael and Ross, Walter, *The Forty-Five: The Last Jacobite Rebellion*, Edinburgh, 1995.

Houlding, J.A., *Fit for Service: The Training of the British Army, 1715–1795*, Oxford, 1981.

Jarvis, Robert C., *Collected Papers on the Jacobite Risings*, 2 vols, Manchester, 1971.

Kelly, Douglas F., *Carolina Scots*, Dillon, 1998.

Lang, Andrew, *The Companions of Pickle*, London, 1898.

Lang, Andrew, *Historical Mysteries*, London, 1904.

Lang, Andrew, *Pickle the Spy*, London, 1897.

Langford, Paul, *A Polite and Commercial People: England, 1727–1783*, Oxford, 1999.

Leask, J.C. and McCance, H.M. (eds), *The Regimental Records of the Royal Scots*, Dublin, 1915.

Leneman, Leah, *Living in Atholl: A Social History of the Estates, 1685–1785*, Edinburgh, 1986.

Lenman, Bruce P., *Integration, Enlightenment and Industrialisation: Scotland, 1746–1832*, London, 1981.

Lenman, Bruce P., 'The Scottish Episcopal Church and the Ideology of

Jacobitism', in Cruickshanks, Eveline (ed), *Ideology and Conspiracy: Aspects of Jacobitism, 1689–1759*, Edinburgh, 1982.

Lenman, Bruce P., *The Jacobite Cause*, Glasgow, 1986.

Lenman, Bruce P., *The Jacobite Clans of the Great Glen, 1750–1784*, London, 1984.

Lenman, Bruce P., *The Jacobite Risings in Britain, 1689–1746*, London, 1980.

Lenman, Bruce P. and Gibson, John S. (eds), *The Jacobite Threat: A Source Book*, Edinburgh, 1990.

Lindsay, Ian G. and Cosh, Mary, *Inveraray and the Dukes of Argyll*, Edinburgh, 1973.

Linney, Dorothy S., 'Stewart Burying Places in Appin', *The Stewarts*, VIII, 1950.

Livingston, Alastair, 'The Story of Donald Livingston: A Morvern Hero', *The Stewarts*, XVII, 1984.

Lockhart, John G., *The Life of Sir Walter Scott*, 10 vols, Edinburgh, 1903.

MacArthur, William, 'The Appin Murder', *The Stewarts*, IX, 1956.

MacArthur, William, *The Appin Murder*, London, 1960.

MacDonald, A., *Memorials of the '45*, Inverness, 1930.

MacDonald, Mairi, *The Appin Mystery: Fact and Folklore*, Oban, 1981.

MacDougall, James, *Folk Tales and Fairy Lore*, Edinburgh, 1910.

Macinnes, Allan I., 'Jacobitism', in Wormald, Jenny (ed), *Scotland Revisited*, London, 1991.

Macinnes, Allan I., 'The Aftermath of the '45', in Woosnam-Savage, Robert C. (ed), *1745: Charles Edward Stuart and the Jacobites*, Glasgow, 1995.

Macinnes, Allan I., *Clanship, Commerce and the House of Stuart, 1603–1788*, East Linton, 1996.

MacIvor, Iain, *Fort George*, Edinburgh, 1988.

MacKay, David N., *The Appin Murder: The Historical Basis of* Kidnapped *and* Catriona, Edinburgh, 1911.

MacKenzie, Compton, *Prince Charlie*, London, 1934.

Mackenzie, W.C., *History of the Outer Hebrides*, Edinburgh, 1974.

McKerracher, Archie, *Perthshire in History and Legend*, Edinburgh, 2000.

Mackie, Euan W., *Lismore and Appin: An Archaeological and Historical Guide*, Glasgow, 1993.

Mackintosh, C. Fraser, 'Speech at the Society's Annual Dinner', TGSI, XIX, 1894.

MacLaren, Margaret, *The MacLarens*, Edinburgh, 1984.

McLaren, Moray, *Lord Lovat of the '45*, London, 1957.

Maclean, Alasdair, *A Macdonald for the Prince*, Stornoway, 1982.

Maclean, Alasdair, 'Jacobites at Heart: An Account of the Independent

Companies', in Scott-Moncrieff, Lesley (ed), *The '45: To Gather an Image Whole*, Edinburgh, 1988.

Maclean, Alasdair, 'Highlanders in the Forty-Five', TGSI, LIX, 1996.

McLynn, Frank J., *France and the Jacobite Rising of 1745*, Edinburgh, 1981.

McLynn, Frank J., *Charles Edward Stuart*, London, 1988.

McLynn, Frank J., *The Jacobite Army in England*, Edinburgh, 1998.

MacMillan, Somerled, *Bygone Lochaber*, Glasgow, 1971.

MacPherson, Alan G., 'The Annexed Estate of Ardsheal', *The Stewarts*, X, 1956.

MacPherson, Alan G., *A Day's March to Ruin: The Badenoch Men in the Forty-Five*, Newtonmore, 1996.

MacPherson, Alan G., 'Order Book of the Appin Regiment: Some Discrepancies Corrected', *The Stewarts*, Vol IX, 1953.

Menary, George, *The Life and Letters of Duncan Forbes of Culloden*, London, 1936.

Meyer, Duane, *The Highland Scots of North Carolina*, Chapel Hill, 1961.

Mitchison, Rosalind, 'The Government and the Highlands, 1707–1745', in Phillipson, N.T. and Mitchison, Rosalind (eds), *Scotland in the Age of Improvement*, Edinburgh, 1970.

Morris, David B., *Robert Louis Stevenson and the Scottish Highlanders*, Stirling, 1929.

Mossner, Ernest C., *The Life of David Hume*, Edinburgh, 1954.

Munro, R.W., *Taming the Rough Bounds*, Isle of Coll, 1984.

Murdoch, Alexander, *The People Above: Politics and Administration in Mid-Eighteenth Century Scotland*, Edinburgh, 1980.

Murray, W.H., *Rob Roy MacGregor*, Edinburgh, 1995.

Newton, Norman, *The Life and Times of Inverness*, Edinburgh, 1996.

Norie, W. Drummond, *Loyal Lochaber*, Glasgow, 1898.

Omond, George W.T., *The Lord Advocates of Scotland*, 2 vols, Edinburgh, 1883.

Orr, Willie, *Discovering Argyll, Mull and Iona*, Edinburgh, 1990.

Owen, John B., *The Rise of the Pelhams*, London, 1957.

'P.P', 'Alan Breck Stewart in History: The Story of a Famous Trial', *Scots Magazine*, XXIII, 1899.

Palmer, Roy, *The Rambling Soldier: Life in the Lower Ranks, 1750–1900*, London, 1977.

Pargellis, Stanley M., *Lord Loudoun in North America*, London, 1933.

Petrie, Charles, *The Jacobite Movement*, London, 1959.

Pittock, Murray G.H., *The Myth of the Jacobite Clans*, Edinburgh, 1995.

Pittock, Murray G.H., *Jacobitism*, London, 1998.

Prebble, John, *Culloden*, London, 1967.

Prebble, John, *Mutiny*, London, 1977.

Rendall, Jane, *The Origins of the Scottish Enlightenment*, London, 1978.

Robertson, James I., *The First Highlander: Major-General David Stewart of Garth*, East Linton, 1998.

Rogers, H.C.B., *The British Army of the Eighteenth Century*, London, 1977.

Rogers, Nicholas, 'Popular Disaffection in London during the Forty-Five', *London Journal*, I, 1975.

Royal Commission on Ancient Monuments, *An Inventory of the Ancient Monuments of Argyll: Lorn*, Edinburgh, 1974.

Scott, Walter, *Tales of a Grandfather*, 3 vols, London, 1923.

Scott, Walter, *Waverley*, London, 1972.

Seton, Bruce G., *The House of Seton: A Study of Lost Causes*, 2 vols, Edinburgh, 1939.

Shaw, John S., *The Management of Scottish Society, 1707–1764: Power, Nobles, Lawyers, Edinburgh Agents and English Influence*, Edinburgh, 1983.

Shaw, John S., *The Political History of Scotland*, London, 1999.

Simpson, John, 'The Causes of the '45', in Scott-Moncrieff, Lesley (ed), *The '45: To Gather an Image Whole*, Edinburgh, 1988.

Simpson, L. Eardley, *Derby and the Forty-Five*, London, 1933.

Smith, Annette M., *Jacobite Estates of the Forty-Five*, Edinburgh, 1982.

Speck, W.A., *The Butcher: The Duke of Cumberland and the Suppression of the Forty-Five*, Caernarfon, 1995.

Starforth, Michael, *Clan Stewart of Appin*, Port Appin, 1997.

Stevenson, Robert L., *Kidnapped*, London, 1983.

Stevenson, Robert L., *Catriona*, Edinburgh, 1989.

Stewart, Alexander, *Nether Lochaber*, Edinburgh, 1883.

Stewart, Alexander, 'Murder of Colin Campbell of Glenure', *Celtic Magazine*, IX, 1884.

Stewart, Alexander, *'Twixt Ben Nevis and Glencoe*, Edinburgh, 1885.

Stewart, Angus, 'The Last Chief: Dougal Stewart of Appin', *Scottish Historical Review*, LXXVI, 1997.

Stewart, H.C., 'Correspondence of a Jacobite Exile', *The Stewarts*, IX, 1956.

Stewart, Ian M., 'The Episcopal Church in Appin', *The Stewarts*, XV, 1976.

Stewart, J.K.S., 'The Appin Murder', *The Stewarts*, I, 1903.

Stewart, James, 'Glenbuckie: A Perthshire Tacksman's Estate', *The Stewarts*, XVII, 1986.

Stewart, James, *Settlements of Western Perthshire*, Haddington, 1990.

Stewart, John, 'Stewarts of Glenbucky', *The Stewarts*, VIII, 1950.

Stewart, John, 'The Stewarts of Annat, Ballachallan and Craigtoun', *The Stewarts*, XI, 1962.

Stewart, John, *The Stewarts*, Stirling, 1973.

Stewart, John, *The Camerons: A History of Clan Cameron*, Stirling, 1974.

Stewart, John H.J. and Stewart, Duncan, *The Stewarts of Appin*, Edinburgh, 1880.

Stewart, Robin M., 'Duncan Stewart VI of Ardsheal', *The Stewarts*, XIII, 1970.

Stott, Louis, *Robert Louis Stevenson and the Highlands and Islands*, Stirling, 1992.

Swearingen, Roger G., *The Prose Writings of Robert Louis Stevenson*, London, 1980.

Szechi, Daniel, *The Jacobites: Britain and Europe, 1688–1788*, Manchester, 1994.

Tabraham, Chris and Grove, Doreen, *Fortress Scotland and the Jacobites*, London, 1995.

Tayler, Alistair and Tayler, Henrietta, *Jacobite Letters to Lord Pitsligo*, Aberdeen, 1930.

Tayler, Alistair and Tayler, Henrietta, *A Jacobite Exile*, London, 1937.

Tayler, Alistair and Tayler, Henrietta, *1745 and After*, London, 1938.

Taylor, William, *The Military Roads in Scotland*, Isle of Colonsay, 1996.

Thomson, Derick S., *Gaelic Poetry in the Eighteenth Century*, Aberdeen, 1993.

Thomson, George M., *A Kind of Justice*, London, 1970.

Tomasson, Katherine, *The Jacobite General*, Edinburgh, 1958.

Tomasson, Katherine and Buist, F., *Battles of the '45*, London, 1962.

Trench, Charles C., *George II*, London, 1973.

White, Gavin, *The Scottish Episcopal Church: A New History*, Edinburgh, 1998.

Whitworth, Rex, *William Augustus, Duke of Cumberland*, London, 1992.

Whyte, Ian D., *Scotland's Society and Economy in Transition*, London, 1997.

Young, Ivan, *Appin Cave Guide*, Edinburgh, 1978.

Youngson, A.J., *After the Forty-Five: The Economic Impact on the Scottish Highlands*, Edinburgh, 1973.

Youngson, A.J., *The Making of Classical Edinburgh*, Edinburgh, 1988.

Youngson, A.J., *The Prince and the Pretender: Two Views of the '45*, Edinburgh, 1996.

Index

233